Policing Gangs in America

Policing Gangs in America describes the assumptions, issues, problems, and events that characterize, shape, and define the police response to gangs in America today. The primary focus of the book is on the gang unit officers and the environment in which they work. A discussion of research, statistical facts, theory, and policy with regard to gangs, gang members, and gang activity is used as a backdrop. The book is broadly focused on describing how gang units respond to community gang problems and answers such questions as: Why do police agencies organize their responses to gangs in certain ways? Who are the people who choose to police gangs? How do they make sense of gang members – individuals who spark fear in most citizens? What are their jobs really like? What characterizes their working environment? How do their responses to the gang problem fit with other policing strategies, such as community policing?

Dr. Charles M. Katz received his Ph.D. in Criminal Justice from the University of Nebraska at Omaha. He is currently an Associate Professor of Criminal Justice and Criminology at Arizona State University. Dr. Katz has coauthored or coedited two previous books and has been published in several scholarly journals, including *Criminology*, *Justice Quarterly*, and *Crime and Delinquency*. Dr. Katz has conducted research in more than twenty police agencies across the United States as well as in several state and federal agencies.

Dr. Vincent J. Webb received his Ph.D. in sociology from Iowa State University. He served as chair of the Department of Criminal Justice at the University of Nebraska at Omaha for more than twenty years and as chair of the Department of Criminal Justice and Criminology at Arizona State University for seven years. In 2005 he joined the faculty at Southern Illinois University at Carbondale as Director of the Center for the Study of Crime, Delinquency and Corrections. Dr. Webb has published in a variety of criminology and criminal justice journals, and he is the coauthor and coeditor of three other books on criminal justice topics. He is a former President of the Academy of Criminal Justice Sciences.

CAMBRIDGE STUDIES IN CRIMINOLOGY

Edited by

Alfred Blumstein, *H. John Heinz School of Public Policy and Management, Carnegie Mellon University*

David Farrington, *Institute of Criminology, University of Cambridge*

Other books in the series:

Policing Gangs in America

CHARLES M. KATZ
Arizona State University, Phoenix

VINCENT J. WEBB
Southern Illinois University, Carbondale

CAMBRIDGE UNIVERSITY PRESS
Cambridge, New York, Melbourne, Madrid, Cape Town, Singapore, São Paulo

Cambridge University Press
40 West 20th Street, New York, NY 10011-4211, USA

www.cambridge.org
Information on this title: www.cambridge.org/9780521851107

First published 2006

Printed in the United States of America

A catalog record for this publication is available from the British Library.

Library of Congress Cataloging in Publication Data

Katz, Charles M.
Policing gangs in America / Charles M. Katz, Vincent J. Webb.
   p.   cm. – (Cambridge studies in criminology)
Includes bibliographical references and index.
ISBN-13: 978-0-521-85110-7 (hardcover)
ISBN-10: 0-521-85110-6 (hardcover)
ISBN-13: 978-0-521-61654-6 (pbk.)
ISBN-10: 0-521-61654-9 (pbk.)
1. Police – United States – Gang units.   2. Gangs – United States.
3. Community policing – United States.   I. Webb, Vincent J.   II. Title.
III. Series: Cambridge studies in criminology (Cambridge University Press)
HV8080.G35K38   2006
363.2'3 – dc22   2005015711

ISBN-13   978-0-521-85110-7 hardback
ISBN-10   0-521-85110-6 hardback

ISBN-13   978-0-521-61654-6 paperback
ISBN-10   0-521-61654-9 paperback

Contents

Acknowledgments

Throughout the research project we received help and assistance from numerous people along the way. We would both like to thank the men and women of the Albuquerque, Inglewood, Las Vegas, and Phoenix police departments. They provided us with an invaluable glimpse into their world, and they were always helpful with accommodating our many requests. We would also like to thank Scott Decker and Cheryl Maxson, who provided advice along the way with regard to research methodology and interpretation of findings and who provided valuable feedback after reading various versions of the manuscript. We express gratitude to Robin Haarr for her assistance with data collection in both Inglewood and Las Vegas and to Ken Karpinski, who managed all of the processes associated with the production, copyediting, and typesetting for this book. Additionally, we would like to thank Ed Parsons, our editor, who guided us through the publication process flawlessly.

This research was funded by the National Institute of Justice (grant no. 98-IJ-CX-0078). The opinions expressed in this book are those of the authors alone and are not those of the National Institute of Justice. However, we would like to thank Winnie Reed, our program manager, who provided us with access to technical advisors and to federal task forces that we otherwise would not have had the opportunity to learn from.

Charles Katz would like to thank his colleagues at Arizona State University for creating a supportive work environment. He would especially like to thank Ed Maguire at George Mason University, who first introduced him to organizational theory and who has also generated much enthusiasm toward the field of policing. Likewise, Malcolm Klein, who not only provided much valuable feedback on earlier drafts of the manuscript but whose work has inspired much of what can be found in this book. Additionally, Charles would like to thank Sam Walker, who imprinted the importance of judging the fairness of modern policing strategies and tactics, and Vince Webb, who influenced him on matters related to the understanding of crime control policy. As usual, Charles thanks his parents, Duane and Janet, and his wife, Keri, for all of their love and support over the years.

Vincent Webb would like to thank his former colleagues at Arizona State University as well as those at the University of Nebraska, Omaha, who have made it possible through their support and inspiration to carry out a number of projects assessing crime control policies and practices. Sam Walker and Ineke Marshall, with their penchant for critiquing criminal justice policy, were especially influential in this regard. He is also deeply grateful to Charles Katz for his patience and steadfastness in keeping this research project on track and for sharing his many theoretical insights into the behavior of police organizations. Most importantly, he would like to thank a very special person, his wife Betsy, for all of her love and support.

I

Studying the Police Response to Gangs

That's what they wanted – and that's what they got.
– Former Los Angeles CRASH Unit officer

By the mid-to-late 1980s, Los Angeles, California, had become widely recognized as the epicenter of the nation's growing gang problem. The city had about 280 gangs with 26,000 members who were becoming increasingly involved in violence and narcotics trafficking (Spergel and Curry 1990). Between 1984 and 1992, the number of gang homicides in Los Angeles County skyrocketed from 200 to 800 homicides per year (Maxson 1999). The seriousness of the phenomenon was highlighted in media reporting, both locally and nationally. Local news programs frequently led with gang-related stories in which innocent bystanders had been shot and killed in drive-by shootings. The movie industry was producing popular films such as *Colors* and *American Me*, portraying L.A. gang members as bloodthirsty, minority males who were involved in high-level drug sales (Hagedorn 1998).

As a consequence, a deep fear of gangs gripped parts of the city. The *Los Angeles Times* reported that residents in gang neighborhoods were barring their windows and chaining their doors, sleeping in bathtubs or on the floor, to protect themselves from nighttime drive-by shootings. People avoided wearing clothing in colors associated with gangs to prevent being misidentified by rival gangs (J. Katz 1990). There was talk from the Federal Bureau of Investigation (FBI) that the Crips in Los Angeles were well on their way to bringing together all Crip sects across the nation into "one major organization with a chief executive officer-style leadership structure" to enhance the gang's ability to traffic drugs (Brantley and DiRosa 1994, 3). In fact, the problem in the city became so bad that some FBI officials publicly announced that gangs represented a serious threat to the national sense of security.

In response, then–Police Chief Daryl Gates declared a war on gangs, claiming that he would "obliterate" violent gangs and "take the little terrorists off the street" (Burrell 1990); he urged President Ronald Reagan to do the same (Los Angeles City News Service 1988). As part of his war, Chief Gates allocated additional officers and staff to the police department's antigang unit, the Community Resources Against Street Hoodlums (CRASH). Within five years, the Los Angeles Police Department (LAPD) had about 200 sworn officers assigned to the CRASH unit (Spergel 1995).

Once in full swing, the unit reacted decisively and aggressively, sweeping through gang neighborhoods. Take, for example, Operation Hammer, a series of gang sweeps carried out in the worst neighborhoods in Los Angeles. The sweeps were characterized by the unit moving through neighborhoods, arresting gang members for the slightest infractions, including wearing colors, flashing signs, jaywalking, and curfew violations. In fact, the unit was making so many arrests that year – close to 25,000 – that during one weekend LAPD had to create a mobile booking facility at the Los Angeles Memorial Coliseum to process all of the arrestees (Burrell 1990).

By the late 1990s, LAPD's response to gangs appeared to be working. For example, in the Rampart Area, one of the regions hardest hit, gang crimes dropped from 1,171 in 1991 to 464 in 1999 – a reduction that exceeded the citywide decline for all other violent crime over the same period (Chemerinsky 2000a). As a consequence, Chief Gates and the police department rapidly developed a reputation for being tough on gangs, and the CRASH unit became a national model. Police departments across the country were contacting LAPD for advice on responding to their own gang problems. LAPD began formally training officers from other police departments on LAPD's operational strategies and tactics for policing gangs, gang members, and gang crime.

With the CRASH unit's success, however, came problems. CRASH unit officers in some precincts developed a subculture that embodied the war-on-gangs mentality advocated by their chief. The subculture was characterized by a mindset in which officers saw all young Hispanic and African American males as gang members, believing that any and all efforts to remove them from the community could and should be used. Under the guise of protecting the community, CRASH officers began resisting supervision, flagrantly ignoring policies and procedures that they believed were inhibiting their ability to respond to the gang problem (Chemerinsky 2000b, 1).

This subculture eventually gave rise to the Rampart Corruption Scandal, in which Rampart CRASH unit officers in Los Angeles were found to be engaging in hard-core criminal activity. Officers admitted to attacking known gang members and falsely accusing them of crimes they had not committed. The officers argued that "if the suspect didn't commit this crime, he did another for which he didn't get caught" (Chemerinsky 2000b, 27).

The ensuing investigation revealed that officers were routinely choking and punching gang members for the sole purpose of intimidation. In one case, officers had used a gang member as a human battering ram, forcefully thrusting his face repeatedly against a wall. In several other instances, officers had planted drugs on gang members to make arrests. Corrupt sergeants and lieutenants in the division had promoted these activities, giving awards for misdeeds. One officer had even received an award for what emerged as the shooting of an unarmed, innocent person (CNN.com 2000a). As a consequence, approximately ten years after it had been fully staffed and promoted as the ideal in antigang enforcement, LAPD's gang unit was shut down because of corruption, the use of excessive force, and civil rights violations; and the city had paid out about $70 million to settle lawsuits related to the scandal (Associated Press 2005).

Such happenings were not unique to Los Angeles. Police gang units across the country were coming under close scrutiny for overly aggressive tactics and other police misconduct.

- In Las Vegas, gang unit officers were found guilty of participating in a drive-by shooting. Two officers, one driving and the other hanging outside a van, had driven around a well-known gang neighborhood until they found a group of gang members loitering on a street corner. The officer hanging outside the van shot six times into the crowd, killing a twenty-one-year-old male. The incident sparked an FBI investigation into all unsolved drive-by shootings and gang killings dating back five years, in the belief that some may have been the work of rogue gang unit officers (Hynes 1997).
- In Chicago, gang unit officers were found by federal prosecutors to be working hand-in-hand with four Chicago street gangs to transport

cocaine from Miami to Chicago. The officers were providing gang members with security, pointing out undercover officers, and revealing the names of confidential informants working with the police. Officers were also found to be supplying weapons and mediating disputes between gangs over the street prices that should be charged for drugs (Lightly and Mills 2000).

- In Houston, gang task force officers were discovered to be using unauthorized confidential informants, engaging in warrantless searches and entries, and firing weapons on unarmed and unassaultive citizens. These practices culminated in the death of Pedro Oregon Navarro, who was shot nine times in the back by gang task force officers during a raid, later believed to be guided by misinformation. Subsequent investigations found that such rogue activity in Houston had become common practice (Bardwell 1998; Grazcyk 1998).

The preceding incidents could have occurred in any major U.S. city that had created a specialized police gang unit in response to growing concerns about gangs and gang-related problems. Although questions about how police should respond to gangs, and why they respond in the ways that they do, have been hotly debated in the media and by policy makers and academics (e.g., Burns and Deakin 1989; Huff and McBride 1990; Jackson and McBride 1986; and Weisel and Painter 1997), a number of questions remain unanswered. Why do police agencies organize their responses to gangs in certain ways? Who are the people who choose to police gangs? How do they make sense of gang members – individuals who spark fear in most citizens, and why are they interested in this particular class of offender? What are their jobs really like? What characterizes their working environments? How do their responses to the gang problem fit with other policing strategies, such as community policing?

These questions are especially relevant for police executives who develop and oversee responses to gangs, as well as for academics and policy makers across the country, and they are the focus of this book. Our goal is to provide a detailed description of policing gangs as done by four Southwestern police agencies – Albuquerque, New Mexico; Inglewood, California; Las Vegas, Nevada; and Phoenix, Arizona. Before we turn our attention to these cities, however, we provide an overview of the gang problem and discuss what is currently known about police gang control efforts.

THE CONTEMPORARY GANG PROBLEM

The United States has seen a dramatic resurgence of gangs, gang members, and gang crime over the past twenty years. In the 1970s, one was hard-pressed to find cities with gang problems. In 1976, the National Advisory Committee on Criminal Justice Standards and Goals went so far as to state:

Youth gangs are not now or (sic) should not become a major obstacle (sic) of concern.... Youth gang violence is not a major crime problem in the United States ... what gang violence does exist can fairly readily be diverted into "constructive channels" especially through the provision of services by community agencies. (as cited by Spergel 1995, 9)

Today almost every city in the United States with a population of more than 250,000 reports a gang problem. Gangs are prevalent in many small and medium-sized cities as well. For example, 87 percent of cities with populations between 100,000 and 249,999 and 27 percent of cities with populations of 2,500 to 49,000 report having an active youth gang problem (Office of Juvenile Justice and Delinquency Prevention 2004). Public concern about the nation's gang problem has escalated substantially. Prior to 1985, national polls examining community problems did not register gangs or gang problems as a major concern. However, by 1994, gang violence ranked as the third most important issue facing America – behind education and drugs and before crime in general (Bureau of Justice Statistics 1995, Table 2.3).

Some have argued that public fear has been a consequence of media portrayals of gangs. Between 1983 and 1999, the number of gang stories reported in major newspapers increased from fewer than fifty a year in 1983 to about 900 a year in 1999 (McCorkle and Miethe 2002). Many of the stories reinforced common beliefs about gangs, emphasizing violent behavior associated with gangs and gang members. Television news programs and the front pages of newspapers often showed the outcome of the most recent episode of gang violence, and how it had affected neighborhood residents or resulted in the injury or death of an innocent bystander (Klein 1995a). Media coverage focused on the role of gangs and gang members in the distribution of crack cocaine. News shows broadcast that super gangs such as the Crips and Bloods were migrating to smaller, less urban communities where there was less competition in drug sales and where they could maximize profits in the drug market

(McCorkle and Miethe 2002). Before long, the public began to characterize gang members as violence-prone minority youths – youths who were disinterested in conventional values and morals, and who were willing to kill to protect their drug businesses.

Although many of these images and perceptions were the product of media generalization and sensationalism, most researchers agree that gang behavior had in fact changed over the past two decades, particularly with regard to violence. In the past, gangs had rarely engaged in fights; when they did, the fights hardly ever resulted in serious injury. The use of firearms was an extremely isolated event (Thrasher 1927; Whyte 1943; Miller 1962; Klein 1971). Many academics reported that, prior to the 1970s, the most prevalent offenses committed by gang members involved loitering, theft, truancy, and disturbing the peace (Spergel 1995; Hagedorn 1998).

During the 1980s, however, it became clear to researchers that the level of gang violence was changing for the worse. Gangs were increasingly fighting one another with firearms, and serious injuries were no longer considered isolated events. In Chicago, for example, the number of gang-motivated homicides increased fivefold between 1987 and 1994, from 51 to 240 (*Compiler* 1996). Similarly, from 1984 to 1995, the number of gang-related homicides in Los Angeles County quadrupled, from 212 to 807. The rise in violence was not restricted to large cities, but also affected several smaller communities. In Omaha, Nebraska, for example, between 1986 and 1991, the number of gang-motivated homicides rose from none to twelve (C. Katz 1997).

Over the same time period, researchers began to find consistent evidence that gang members were responsible for a disproportionate amount of crime. Much of this research relied on official data collected by the police. For example, Walter B. Miller (1982) reported that although gang members represented only 6 percent of youths ten to nineteen years old in New York City, Chicago, and Los Angeles, they represented 11 percent of all arrests in those cities, 40 percent of arrests for serious crimes, and almost 25 percent of arrests for juvenile homicides. Similarly, Paul Tracy (1978) found that gang members in Philadelphia were arrested at significantly higher rates than non–gang members. He reported that 63 percent of delinquent gang members were chronic recidivists (i.e., had been arrested five or more times), compared with only 27 percent of delinquent non–gang members.

Charles Katz, Vincent Webb, and David Schaefer (2000) examined how offense patterns differed between documented gang members and delinquent youth with similar characteristics. They found that documented gang members were significantly more likely to have engaged in serious delinquency and were significantly more criminally active than the delinquent comparison group. In particular, they found that documented gang members were about twice as likely to have been arrested for a violent, weapon, drug, or status offense, and they were arrested for these offenses about four times as often as the delinquent youth who were not gang members.

Similar patterns have emerged when comparing self-report data from non–gang members and from gang members in the general population. Much of this research has been conducted through longitudinal studies of delinquent behavior, such as the Seattle Social Development Project and the Rochester Youth Development Study. Both studies gathered self-report data from randomly selected youth in local schools (Battin-Pearson et al. 1998). For example, in Seattle, researchers examined differences among gang members, nongang delinquent peers, and nongang, nondelinquent peers. The data showed that gang members were about twice as likely to self-report both violent and nonviolent offenses, and about ten times more likely to self-report violent and nonviolent offenses, when compared with their nongang, nondelinquent peers.

The Rochester study yielded similar results with a slightly different methodology. The researchers first divided their sample into two groups: gang members and non–gang members. Next, the researchers divided those in the nongang group into four subgroups, based on the extent of their self-reported contact with delinquent peers. Analysis of the data indicated that although increased association with delinquent peers was related to offense rates, "being a member of a gang facilitates delinquency over and above that effect" (Battin-Pearson et al. 1998, 5–6; also see Thornberry et al. 2003).

Similarly, policy makers, media officials, and academics have seen an increase in drug trafficking among gang members, an increase that they argue has fueled violence among gangs. Two explanations have been suggested for increasing gang involvement in drug sales (Fagan 1996). First, in the early 1980s, crack cocaine use escalated dramatically, and a new drug market emerged. Because the new market had not yet stabilized, violence was often used as a regulatory mechanism. Second, at about the same time, the economic infrastructure of many inner cities collapsed. Manufacturing jobs declined, and service and technology jobs, which began to drive the new economy, were being created in suburban communities (Howell and Decker 1999). The economic restructuring of the nation left unqualified and geographically isolated urban minority youth without the means or opportunity for employment. The new crack cocaine market provided opportunities for inner-city youth to make money. It also led to the transition of many youth groups into gangs with the organizational capacity to control local drug markets (Fagan 1996; Howell and Decker 1999).

The extent to which gangs are organized for the purpose of drug trafficking is not clear. On one hand, a number of researchers have argued that gangs are organizationally structured, engaging in operational strategies that enhance their potential for profiting from drug sales. For example, Taylor (1990), Sanchez-Jankowski (1991), and Venkatesh (1997) in their observational studies of gang members in Detroit, Boston, New York City, Los Angeles, and Chicago found that gangs are highly rational and organizationally sophisticated. Similar to any other capitalist enterprise, they have an established leadership hierarchy and formal rules and goals that guide their actions. These authors have maintained that membership in gangs is motivated by a common interest in profiting from criminal activity, and that the corporate-like structure of gangs provides an ideal and highly effective organization for the distribution of drugs.

Jerome Skolnick (1990) examined this issue at length in his study of gang members in California. He found that gang members often were driven to outside drug markets in an effort to enhance profitability in the drug trade, and that this resulted in frequent violent conflicts between gangs over the control of territory. Because of the violent nature of the drug trade, Skolnick argued, gang membership offers advantages to those interested in selling drugs – protection, a controlled drug market, and a stable source of products to sell in the retail market.

An alternative perspective is offered by Malcolm Klein (1995a) and others, who have argued that although gang members are intimately involved in the drug market, they do not have the organizational capacity to control and manage drug trafficking. For example, Fagan (1989) and Decker, Bynum & Weisel (1998), who interviewed gang members in Los Angeles, San Diego, Chicago, and St. Louis, found that although many gang members sold drugs, most did not join a gang expressly for this purpose. Instead, they joined for social interaction and neighborhood identification. Additionally, the researchers reported that gangs in these communities were not well-organized for the distribution of drugs, most members were unable to identify occupational roles in the selling of drugs, and many did not know who supplied drugs. Similar findings were reported by Hagedorn (1988), who interviewed forty-seven gang members in Milwaukee. Of the gang members interviewed, only a few were identified as actual drug dealers. The majority, Hagedorn argued, sold drugs periodically, along with other income-producing activities, simply as a means of survival. Furthermore, he claimed that gang members lacked the needed resources, skills, and commitment to form a corporate-like organization for the purpose of profiting from the drug market. Hagedorn reported that gang members felt that it was "too much of a hassle" to be strongly committed to an organizational goal (1988, 105).

Either way, as gangs, gang members, and gang crime increasingly were perceived as a public safety threat, policy makers and researchers began to call for gang control strategies. Since the early 1990s, a massive mobilization of personnel and resources has been directed at controlling the nation's gang problem. County attorneys' offices have created vertical prosecutorial gang units to increase conviction rates and sentence lengths in cases involving gang members (Johnson et al. 1995); state legislatures have enacted criminal statutes to enhance penalties for gang members who are convicted of gang offenses (McCorkle and Miethe 1998); and city councils have passed antigang loitering laws prohibiting gang members from coming into contact with one another on the streets (Maxson, Hennigan, and Sloane 2003). Some communities have called out the National Guard to patrol streets and to work with police to round up criminally active gang members (Brokaw, Ewing, and Greenburg 1989).

Of all of the responses devised by local communities to control gangs, the establishment of specialized police gang units has become the most common suppression strategy. Although substantial research has examined gangs, gang members, and gang crime, unfortunately, little of it has addressed police gang-control efforts. The paucity of research in this area is surprising, given the central role that police in general, and specialized police gang units in particular, must play in community gang-reduction efforts. In the section that follows, we discuss what is currently known about the police response to gangs. In particular, we discuss the rationale of police gang units, the growth and development of police gang units, and the limitations of prior research that has examined the police response to gangs.

POLICE RESPONSE TO GANGS: THEORETICAL, POLICY, AND ORGANIZATIONAL RATIONALES

Historically, the police response to gangs and gang-related problems has been to assign responsibility for control to existing units such as patrol, juvenile bureaus, community relations, investigations, and crime prevention (Needle and Stapleton 1983; Huff 1993). In the 1980s, however, many police departments began to establish specialized units for gang control, including what is commonly referred to as the *police gang unit*. A police gang unit is a secondary or tertiary functional division within a police organization, with at least one sworn officer whose sole function is to engage in gang control efforts (Katz, Maguire, and Roncek 2002).

In 1999, the Law Enforcement and Management Administrative Statistics (LEMAS) survey reported that among large agencies with 100 or more sworn officers, special gang units existed in 56 percent of all municipal police departments, 50 percent of all sheriff's departments, 43 percent of all county police agencies, and 20 percent of all state law enforcement agencies (Bureau of Justice Statistics 2001, Table C). These findings led to an estimate of approximately 360 police gang units in the country. As see in Figure 1.1 The recency of this phenomenon is illustrated by the fact that more than 85 percent of the specialized gang units were established within the past ten years (Katz, Maguire, and Roncek 2002).

The creation of police gang units has been one part of the national response to the gang problem. In 1988, Irving Spergel and David Curry (1990) surveyed 254 professionals in 45 cities to assess the response at

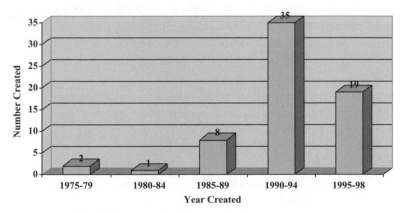

FIGURE 1.1. Establishment of police gang units.

that time. They found that suppression techniques employed by police were the strategy most often cited by respondents. This trend appeared strongest in the newer gang cities, however, where police suppression was relied upon almost exclusively.

With the suppression approach, Klein (1995a) argues, enforcement officials see their primary responsibility as responding to gang street crimes. In other words, officials believe that they are expected to deal with the crimes most likely to come to the public's attention – crimes such as assaults, drive-by shootings, drug sales, and graffiti. Prevention and treatment strategies, on the other hand, are low priorities. In fact, these police officials view gang crime prevention and treatment as completely outside the scope of their responsibility. The underlying assumption of the suppression strategy is based on deterrence theory: that swift, severe, and certain punishment will lead to the reduction of gang-related activity among current gang members, as well as to a reduction in the number of individuals who want to participate in gangs and gang behavior in the future. Accordingly, Klein (1995a, 160) argues that the "assumption of all this is that the targets of suppression, the gang members and potential gang members, will respond 'rationally' to suppression efforts [and] will weigh the consequences of gang activity, redress the balance between cost and benefit, and withdraw from gang activity."

To understand the police response to the gang problem, one must first understand the developments that have shaped and justified the shift toward suppression-oriented strategies. First, policy makers no longer believe that the social intervention approaches of the 1960s and 1970s are successful in dealing with gang problems. Social intervention took many forms, all based on the assumption that gang membership was the by-product of a socially deprived community, and that the values and norms of gang youths could be changed by reorienting the youths' attitudes, values, and expectations toward mainstream society. Social intervention approaches usually relied on a detached case worker who was assigned to work with gangs and gang members, in order to steer the youths away from delinquency and encourage them toward more socially acceptable activities such as athletic teams, club activities, and fundraisers (President's Commission on Law Enforcement and Administration of Justice 1967). Many have argued that this approach did not reduce delinquent activity; instead, it may have led to increased group cohesiveness that, in turn, may have led to increased delinquency. Additionally, some critics claimed that the assignment of a case worker enhanced the local reputation of particular gangs, helping to attract new members and leading to a growing gang problem in areas employing the detached workers (Klein 1971; Spergel 1995).

Second, as discussed in the preceding text, many policy makers and others believe that the scope and nature of the gang problem have changed dramatically. In 1983, only 45 percent of cities with populations of 100,000 or more reported a gang problem (Needle and Stapleton 1983); whereas, by 1992, this figure had risen to over 90 percent (Curry, Ball, and Fox 1994). These studies illustrate that gangs no longer are only a big city problem; they have also become prevalent in many small and medium-sized cities (Office of Juvenile Justice Delinquency Prevention 2003). A number of studies have found that gang members are disproportionately responsible for delinquency, crime, drug use, and drug dealing when compared with non–gang members (Klein 1995a; Spergel 1995; Howell and Decker 1999; Katz, Webb, and Shaefer 2000). As a result, many local officials believe the gang problem will only get worse, and that the way to stop it is to remove gang members from society through the criminal justice system.

The third reason for the shift to suppression-oriented strategies is the combined effect of disenchantment with social intervention strategies and increasing public acknowledgement that the gang problem has grown. Citizen surveys have confirmed that residents are fearful of gangs (J. Katz 1990), and that the public believes that dealing with gang-related problems should be a top police priority (Webb and Katz 1997). State and federal legislators have responded by allocating additional funds for suppression-oriented interventions (Klein 1995b; McCorkle and Miethe 1998). Municipal and state agencies have received additional funding, usually through federal grants, for interagency task forces, information tracking systems, and overtime pay for police to target hard-core gang members. With the implementation of community policing in many agencies, public pressure to address gang problems have forced the departments to prioritize gang control efforts.

Although specialized police gang units represent a relatively new feature in the landscape of American policing, they are embedded in the larger trend toward creating specialized units that address specific law enforcement issues such as repeat offenses, domestic violence, and hate crimes. Such specialized units are said to be created in order to focus departmental resources, energy, and skills on specific community problems. Additionally, the approach is offered as a symbolic act to show the community, potential offenders, and police officers that the police department is taking a particular problem seriously (Meyer 1979; Scott 1995).

For similar reasons, it appears, many police officials and gang scholars have called for consolidation of gang control functions within police departments (e.g., Jackson and McBride 1986; Burns and Deakin 1989; Huff and McBride 1993; Rush 1996). They have argued that assigning primary responsibility for addressing the gang problem to a specialized unit will increase the technical efficiency and effectiveness of the police department's response. They point out that consolidation of gang control functions will permit officers to develop highly technical skills through training and experience, that otherwise would not be possible. They claim that consolidation also allows police organizations to distribute gang-related work rationally, better enabling police departments to develop and coordinate responses to community gang problems.

The creation of a specialized police gang unit also symbolizes police commitment to combating the gang problem, and projects an image of police as leaders in the battle against gangs (Klein 1995a; Spergel 1995). This image is further conveyed through naming protocols. For example, San Bernardino County's interagency task force is called SMASH (San Bernardino County Movement Against Street Hoodlums); the LAPD gang unit was called CRASH; and the Los Angeles County Sheriff Department's gang unit is called GET (Gang Enforcement Team) (Spergel 1995, 192–3). Such acronyms express a Hollywood image of police at war with gangs, and imply that the gang problem can be solved by intensifying our efforts to combat them (Pillsbury 1988).

PRIOR RESEARCH EXAMINING THE POLICE RESPONSE TO GANGS

Much of the research to date that examines the police response to gangs relied upon news media reporting. Media accounts of police responses to gangs have typically involved journalistic depictions of police agencies and their most recent efforts to control gang behavior. Much of the information is obtained from police executives or their spokespersons, commenting on a particular agency's tough stance. Even some of the most recognized pieces of gang scholarship have had to rely on such media accounts as their primary source of information, due to a lack of academic scholarship on this topic (Klein, Maxson, and Miller 1995; Spergel 1995).

The few studies that have examined the police response to gangs are typically focused at the macrolevel. This research relies on mail surveys of police leaders, asking whether their communities had a gang problem. If so, respondents were asked to identify their department's particular strategies for dealing with gangs. Such studies reported that departments claiming to have a gang problem were significantly more likely to have established a specialized gang unit (Needle and Stapleton 1983; Curry et al. 1992). Based on this data, a number of researchers have made inferences and assumptions about why police had responded to gangs in the ways that they had. In particular, many researchers have claimed that the relatively rapid development and growth of police gang units seemed more or less natural, given the spread of gangs and gang members across America's communities (Jackson and McBride 1986; Burns and Deakin 1989; Huff and McBride 1993). They point out that according to surveys of police, almost every major city and most medium-sized cities have gang problems (Curry, Ball, and Decker 1996). As Huff explains (1993, 401), "Gangs pose a significant challenge to law enforcement agencies as well as to citizens, schools, and the quality of life in our communities."

Within this body of research, others have specifically argued that special police gang units were created as a consequence of the growing amount of gang crime, including drug trafficking, that accompanied the rise in the numbers of gangs and gang members (Jackson and McBride 1986; Burns and Deakin 1989). For example, some academics have pointed to the fact that nationally, gang crime incidents reported by the police increased eight- to twelve-fold just between 1991 and 1993 (Curry, Ball, and Decker 1996).

Most of the preceding arguments have been based on supposition, however. Weisel and Painter (1997) examined this issue directly in their study of the police response to gangs in five cities. Although the authors relied primarily on data from police leaders, they also conducted brief interviews with police gang control specialists in each city to gain a deeper understanding of each community's response to gangs. The interview data revealed that most police agencies had responded to gang problems because of well-publicized gang homicides and fights. They reported that the police departments in their study typically had responded by establishing specialized units that emphasized suppression. Many police officials, policy makers, and researchers maintain that the emergence of specialized gang units is a rational police response (a gang unit) to an environmental contingency (a community gang problem). They explain that specialized police gang units have been created as a result of *rational considerations* on the part of police agencies, that their organizations are faced with *real* gang problems, and that through specialization, they can more effectively and efficiently control gang-related crime.

A few researchers examining the police response to gangs have proposed an alternative perspective, arguing that establishment of specialized police gang units has been a response to a moral panic, not to environmental contingencies. For example, Marjorie Zatz (1987) examined the police response to gangs in Phoenix, Arizona, using a variety of data obtained from community members, media reports, and court records. She reported that there was no serious gang problem in Phoenix at the time that the gang unit was established, but that police officials constructed the gang problem in an effort to campaign for federal resources. She argued that the police department, along with news media, constructed an image of gang members as dangerous, crime-prone Chicano youth – an image that fit with the Anglo notion of gang members. At the same time, police officials were claiming that if they were not given resources to combat it, the gang problem was sure to escalate. She found that official court data and interviews with social service agents indicated that gang members did not pose a significant threat to the community, and that the police department claims of a serious gang problem were exaggerated.

McCorkle and Miethe (1998) examined legislative records, media reports, and official crime data in Las Vegas, Nevada, to assess whether that city's response to gangs was the consequence of a moral panic. Examining the objective threat posed by gangs, the authors reported that gang members accounted for a relatively small proportion of arrests for violent crimes and an even smaller proportion of drug arrests in the city. When describing factors that led to the moral panic, the authors reported that at the time that the specialized police gang unit was established, the police department had a tarnished public image, and was in desperate need of additional resources. Accordingly, McCorkle and Miethe suggested that police officials in the Las Vegas Police Department linked national reports of a growing gang problem to local concerns about escalating crime in order to divert public attention away from problems within the local department and to justify an infusion of financial resources.

Archbold and Meyer (1999) extended the research mentioned in the preceding text by including data obtained from police officials. In particular, their study of a specialized police gang unit in Cedar Springs included data obtained from observations of gang unit officers, in-depth interviews with police officials, and official documents and newspapers.

Their analysis suggested that a series of homicides committed by local youths, coupled with the emergence of a gang problem in nearby large cities, had resulted in a heightened public fear of gangs. Archbold and Meyer further explained that in response to the community's fears, the police department began to document minority youth in the community as gang members. As the number of documented gang members rose, so did media reports and the community's fears about gangs. The authors reported that the perceived problem eventually spun out of control, resulting in community panic, even though there was no actual evidence of any gang-related activity in the city. The authors reported that within about eight months, the gang unit was no longer active due to the lack of gang-related action in the city.

To date, most academics examining this issue have argued that the police response to gangs in communities across the country is the result of police officials becoming actively involved in the social construction of gang problems at the local level. Zatz (1987) and McCorkle and Miethe (1998) reasoned that in order for local agencies to have access to some forms of federal or local money, they had to demonstrate a gang problem within their communities. These researchers, along with Archbold and Meyer (1999), found that construction of the problem was accomplished by the police creating a public image of minority and other marginalized youth as gang members – an image that the researchers argued is consistent with Anglo society's perception of those who are dangerous and violent, and who pose a social threat.

Charles Katz's (2001) fieldwork in Junction City is one of the few exceptions. He argued that much of the previous research examining the police response to gangs failed to consider the perspective of the police and their constituencies, as well as the general environment within which the police work. In the police department studied, he found that the gang unit was created under pressure from influential community stakeholders. Creation of the gang unit was the department's attempt to maintain its organizational legitimacy and to communicate to its institutional environment that it was responding to the local gang problem. He further found that once created, the gang unit was required to incorporate often competing ideas and beliefs into its organizational structure and operational strategy, in order to project an image of operational effectiveness, even when it was otherwise unable to demonstrate success. Katz concluded that an institutional perspective of policing, rather than the social constructionist perspective, might be the more appropriate theoretical framework for understanding the police response to gangs.

Katz, Maguire, and Roncek (2002) attempted to examine the factors that influenced the creation of specialized police gang units in about 300 large cities in the United States. In particular, they examined the impact of the number of gangs, gang members, and gang crime on the creation process, along with other factors related to crime (violence, property, drug, weapons, assault arrests), social threat (percent African American, percent Hispanic), resource dependencies (external funding to support the police response to gangs), organizational characteristics (agency size, vertical and functional differentiation), and environment (population size and region). The authors found no relationship between the size of a community gang or crime problem and the creation of a gang unit. Instead, they found that specialized gang units were most likely to be created in communities that had larger Hispanic populations. They reasoned that police organizations might be creating gang units when the community feels threatened by a minority group – particularly Hispanics. They also found that police departments that had received funding for gang control efforts were significantly more likely to have established a specialized police gang unit than agencies that had not received funding. They noted that there might be a number of explanations for this finding. However, they posited that some gang units might have been created prior to receiving external funding for the purpose of justifying the need for more resources, as found by Zatz (1987) and McCorkle and Miethe (1998).

All of this demonstrates that although a discussion of the police response to gangs has begun to emerge, several deficits in our understanding remain. First, the body of literature has been methodologically limited. Policy makers and academics have used anecdotal evidence to understand the police response to gangs, or alternatively, they have conducted single-shot, qualitative case studies, limiting the generalizations that can be drawn from their research.

Similarly, most research to date has failed to include information from the police organization and from stakeholders in the organization's environment. When attempting to understand how and why a police organization responds to a gang problem, it would seem important to consider how the organization and those in the organization make sense of their reality. Similarly, it would seem important to consider how sovereigns, that is, powerful actors who have the capacity to influence policies, decisions, and financial resources to the organization, might affect the police response to gangs (DiMaggio and Powell 1991; Scott 1995). Sovereigns for police agencies might include such actors as the mayor, city council members, police unions, special interest groups, citizens, and other criminal justice agencies. As noted in the preceding text, research that does not consider the institutional environment will fail to fully capture how an organization conceptualizes, comprehends, and makes sense of the social system in which it operates (Weick and Roberts 1993; Weick 1995).

A second limitation to this body of literature is its narrow focus on factors that affect the establishment of police gang units. Researchers as yet have failed to examine what gang unit officers actually do, and how such factors as gang unit culture, training, and the impact of organizational mandates affect the day-to-day activities of gang unit officers. Research that examines the organizational structure and administrative oversight of gang units, and their effect on gang unit officer behavior is also missing from the literature. Incidents in Los Angeles, Chicago, Las Vegas, and Houston suggest that such factors may well have important consequences for the administration of police gang units.

Last, little research has examined the role of community-oriented policing in the control of gang behavior. Community policing has altered how police and policy makers think about how police work should be organized and performed. The dialog about the response to the gang problem thus far has been focused on the core function of police work – patrol – and has rarely attended to how broader organizational changes in policing may have affected other specialized police functions, such as gang control efforts.

THE PRESENT STUDY

This book is concerned with advancing our understanding of how police gang units respond to community gang problems. To date, little research has examined the realities and experiences of those working day-to-day within a police gang unit. The research reported in this book describes assumptions, issues, problems, and events that have characterized, shaped, and defined the police response to the gang problem. In particular, this research had five major objectives:

1. To identify and examine the factors that have led to the creation of specialized police gang units, and to examine how those factors have influenced the units' responses to the gang problems in their communities.
2. To examine alternative ways in which police agencies have organized resources to respond to their local gang problems.

3. To examine the relevant beliefs of gang unit officers, and how their beliefs might have affected the police response to gangs.
4. To identify the activities that gang unit officers have been engaging in, and to clarify conceptually the roles of specialized police gang units within their departments.
5. To assess the goodness of fit of the police response to gangs with the community-oriented policing paradigm.

Reasons for Establishing Gang Units

Achieving the first objective will help to understand the reasons for which police gang units are established. Research to date has neglected this question, shedding little light on why the police have been responding to the gang problem as they have over the past fifteen years (cf. Zatz 1987; McCorkle and Miethe 1998; C. Katz 2001; Katz, Maguire, and Roncek 2002). The research reported here systematically examined factors, situations, and events that have given rise to police gang units. For each community that we studied, this included 1) examining the nature and extent of the gang problem prior to the establishment of a gang unit, 2) identifying significant events that preceded the decision to establish a gang unit, and 3) identifying internal and external pressures placed on the police department that might have influenced the decision-making process.

We also considered how these factors might have influenced the gang units' responses to the community gang problems. Although limited research has examined influential factors in the creation of gang units and how these factors affected established units' organizational structures and operational strategies, little additional research has been conducted to confirm earlier findings. Our intent was to examine how the gang units' responses might be affected by the same factors that led to the units' creation in the first place. Pinpointing factors that motivate the establishment of gang units will lead to a better understanding of why gang units respond to community gang problems in the way that they do.

Alternative Organizational Forms

The second objective of our research was to deepen our understanding of the different ways in which police agencies organize resources for responding to the local gang problem. A variety of organizational configurations are in use, yet little attention has been paid to the implications of differing configurations for shaping specific responses. In some agencies, the gang unit is a subunit of the investigations bureau; in others, it is a subunit within a larger organized crime unit. A stand-alone gang unit is another frequently occurring configuration.

The specific configuration and location of a unit within its parent organization might affect the organizational perception of the nature of the problem, and may also shape the specific programs and practices of the unit. For example, a unit located within an investigation bureau may be more likely to support and engage in incident-driven investigations than a unit located within an organized crime bureau. It may be more likely to view gangs as groups of individuals engaging in occasional, nonsystematic criminal behavior. Specific responses might include investigating gang-related offenses using traditional investigative techniques or assisting other units with investigations of gang-related incidents. On the other hand, a gang unit located in an organized crime bureau probably would perceive gangs as groups of individuals who organize to engage in systematic criminal activity. Such a unit might pattern its responses after those used to address non-gang-related organized crime. The research reported in this book provides detailed information on alternative gang unit configurations, as well as insight into how different configurations pattern gang unit responses.

Gang Unit Officers

The third objective of this study was to examine how the beliefs of gang unit officers influenced their responses to the gang problem. Several previous studies have examined police culture and its effect on the police response to special populations,[1] but little research has specifically addressed the belief systems of gang unit officers. Accordingly, we examined such issues as what officers in gang units considered to be the realities of their work situation, what the unit officers believed they must do to perform effectively, and the officers' perceptions of gang members in their community. Similarly, we examined such issues as the construction of officers' attitudes and beliefs, including how training had shaped those attitudes and beliefs.

---

[1] For example, persons on skid-row (Bittner 1967), domestic violence (Sherman 1992), and minorities (Bayley and Mendelsohn 1969; Westley 1970; Skolnick 1994).

We also focused on the impact of the larger organizational culture in which the gang unit officers worked on the response to gangs. Anecdotal evidence has suggested that a police department's organizational culture might significantly influence the types of activities engaged in by gang unit officers (Freed 1995; Klein 1995a). Accordingly, we were interested in examining informal organizational expectations that may have influenced the gang units' responses to their community gang problems.

Gang unit officers often act as primary claim makers, educating the public about the scope and nature of community gang problems. Therefore, we wanted to examine the officers' perceptions of the problem, and we collected data specifically related to these perceptions. We were interested in the officers' perspectives on the typical gang member, the primary activities in which gang members engage, and changes in gang-related crime over time. Related to this, we examined how officers cognitively constructed their images of community gang problems. We compared the officers' perceptions to official data retrieved from the police department, in an effort to assess how closely those perceptions matched departmental data.

Gang Unit Functions and Activities

The fourth objective was to understand exactly how specialized police gang units responded to community gang problems. Despite the importance of documenting the activities of gang unit officers for the purposes of planning and performance measurement, little attention has been given to understanding what gang unit officers actually do. Accordingly, this study examined such issues as how officers spend time, the types of problems that gang unit officers face on the job, and the types of actions that gang unit officers take while interacting with citizens and other criminal justice officials.

We also focused on how the gang unit's formal organizational properties influenced gang unit officers' responses to the gang problem. In particular, we were interested in understanding how the officers were officially directed to conduct themselves. We examined how formal documents such as departmental and unit Standard Operating Procedures (SOP) and other official documents influenced the units' responses to gangs.

The study also examined how the social system or environment in which the gang units operated influenced their responses to the gang problem. Researchers to date have focused primarily on how gang members and their activities influence the police response (Rush 1996; Weisel and Painter 1997); few have identified other powerful factors within the gang units' environments that might also shape that response. Accordingly, this study examined how the gang units' operational activities were influenced by those in their institutional environments, including, but not necessarily limited to, key community stakeholders, citizens, criminal justice officials, and gang members.

Compatibility of Gang Units with Community-Oriented Policing

The fifth objective of this study was to examine the compatibility of the police response to gangs with community-oriented policing. The growth of police gang units paralleled the development of community-oriented policing, yet there has been an absence of attention paid by scholars and policy makers to the role of the gang unit in furthering community-oriented policing goals and objectives.

Several important questions remain unanswered. For example, do suppression-oriented gang-unit activities facilitate or hinder the police-community coproduction of public safety? Does a strong emphasis on community-oriented policing facilitate gang unit performance by improving intelligence-gathering capacity through improved community relations? How do gang unit officers perceive community-oriented policing and their role within it? This study attempted to answer these and related questions about the compatibility of the police response to gangs with community-oriented policing, by examining the views of police managers, gang unit officers, and gang unit stakeholders. In addition, we assessed the characteristics and features of the four gang units selected for our study against the backdrop of the principal features of community-oriented policing that have been previously identified by police scholars.

After reviewing the literature on the emergence and functioning of gang units as a principal police response to community gang problems, we identified what we considered to be critical gaps in the research to date, and set an ambitious agenda for answering some of the more compelling questions. In the next chapter we describe our research methodology for answering these questions.

2

Setting and Methods

Ultimately, my sense of the report is that the Board of Inquiry was created by the management of the Los Angeles Police Department to study the Rampart Scandal and it is the management account: it minimizes the problem and spares management of criticism. What is desperately needed is external investigations and accounts to learn the full magnitude of the problems and to propose the needed comprehensive reforms to ensure that this never happens again.
> – Erwin Chemerinsky, Independent Auditor of the Los Angeles Police Department Board of Inquiry Report on the Rampart Scandal 2000b, 11.

This chapter describes the methodological strategies used in our study of police gang units. In particular, we describe the settings in which the study took place, explain the characteristics of the police departments and the gang units that were examined, and discuss the approaches that were used to collect data.

STUDY SETTING

Data for the study were gathered in four cities located in the Southwestern region of the United States: Albuquerque, New Mexico; Inglewood, California; Las Vegas, Nevada; and Phoenix, Arizona. We selected these cities for our study for two major reasons.[1] First, although

---

[1] In addition, there were practical reasons for selecting these cities. They were geographically proximate to the researchers' home institution, simplifying the logistics and minimizing the costs of the field work.

police departments across the country claim to have gang problems, researchers have found that police departments in the Southwestern United States have been significantly more likely than others to respond to the problem by establishing specialized police gang units (Curry et al. 1992, 65). Selecting these cities allowed us to focus our efforts where specialized gang units were most likely to be the police response to gang problems.

Second, the gang units in these four cities presented a variety of organizational configurations. The Phoenix Police Department's gang unit was located in the Organized Crime Bureau, the Inglewood Police Department's gang unit was located in the Criminal Investigation Bureau, the Las Vegas Metropolitan Police Department's gang unit was located in the Special Operations Division, and the Albuquerque Police Department's gang unit was located in the Special Enforcement Bureau. These sites allowed us to examine how gang units fit organizationally into police departments, and how differing organizational configurations might influence the police response to gangs.

Table 2.1 shows the characteristics of each city, all four of which are located in the largest metropolitan areas of their states. Phoenix is by far the largest, with a population well over one million residents. Las Vegas and Albuquerque are each moderately sized cities with about half a million residents. Inglewood is the smallest, with about 100,000 residents, although it is the most urban and ethnically diverse of the cities. Located in the heart of the Los Angeles metropolitan area, Inglewood is twelve miles southwest of downtown Los Angeles and one mile from the Los Angeles Airport. Inglewood's population is about 47 percent black and 46 percent Hispanic. Inglewood is also more economically stressed than the other cities. In comparison, it has higher levels of unemployment, more female-headed families with children, lower levels of home ownership, and lower incomes. This is in part due to the faltering local economy, which supports few major employers. Among the largest employers are Hollywood Park Race and Casino, two local hospitals, and two retail stores – The Price Club and Home Base.

In contrast, the other three are fairly typical of Southwestern cities. All three are comprised predominately of white residents, but have substantial Hispanic communities. Each of the three cities has experienced a massive increase in population over the past ten years. Between 1990 and 2000, Albuquerque grew by 18.9 percent, Las Vegas grew by 73.9 percent, and Phoenix grew by 17.5 percent. All three have enjoyed strong economies, and are characterized by relatively low rates

TABLE 2.1. *Study Site Characteristics*[a]

	Albuquerque	Inglewood	Las Vegas	Phoenix
Population	448,607	112,580	478,434	1,321,945
Race or ethnicity (%)				
White	71.59	19.10	69.85	71.02
Black	3.08	47.13	10.36	5.09
American Indian	3.88	0.68	0.74	2.01
Asian	2.24	1.13	4.78	2.00
Hawaiian	0.10	0.36	0.44	0.13
Other	14.77	27.37	9.74	16.38
Mixed	4.30	4.20	4.05	3.72
Hispanic (all races –%)	39.90	46.00	23.60	34.10
Unemployed (%)	3.10	7.40	4.10	2.90
Homeowners (%)	60.40	36.30	59.10	60.70
Female-headed families with children (%)	9.09	18.16	8.53	9.37
Per capita income (%)	$20,884	$14,776	$22,060	$19,833
Individuals below poverty level (%)	13.5	22.5	11.9	12.4
2000 crime rate (per 1,000 population)				
TOTAL	101.4	52.1	52.7	82.5
Violent	11.7	11.9	6.2	7.5
Property	78.5	28.7	40.5	67.7
Size of police department (sworn officers)	851	210	2,244	2,617
Size of gang unit (sworn officers)	9	4	41	36
Organizational location of the gang unit	Special Enforcement Bureau	Criminal Investigations Bureau	Organized Crime Division	Organized Crime Bureau

[a] U.S. Bureau of the Census 2000; Census of Population and Housing.

25

of unemployment, fewer female-headed households with children, and relatively high levels of homeownership and income. The strength of their economies can be attributed in large part to new and booming industries. The economies of Albuquerque and Phoenix are grounded in such sectors as computers, electronics, and communications, all of which have provided an increasing number of job opportunities for residents. Similarly, Las Vegas, whose economy is based on hotels, gaming, and recreation, benefited from the strong national economy over the past twenty years, which led to a massive increase in tourism and the construction of several billion-dollar casinos, providing tens of thousands of jobs for residents and migrants.

The magnitude and character of the crime-related problems faced by each city vary considerably. Albuquerque has the highest total crime rate, and Inglewood has the lowest. Both Las Vegas and Phoenix had violent crime rates about about 40 to 60 percent lower than Inglewood and Albuquerque. There were, however, substantial differences in property crime rates. Albuquerque had the highest rate with about 79 property crimes reported per 1,000 population, followed by Phoenix (68 per 1,000), Las Vegas (41 per 1,000), and Inglewood (29 per 1,000).

Police Departments Studied

The police agencies in the four cities varied in size, enabling us to study large, medium-sized, and small departments. Two of the agencies at the time of our study could be characterized as large municipal police departments. The Phoenix Police Department employed about 3,300 persons, of whom 2,617 were sworn police officers. This made Phoenix the tenth largest police agency in the United States. Similarly, the Las Vegas Metropolitan Police Department employed 3,150 persons, including 2244 sworn police officers. The agency was responsible for policing the city of Las Vegas and all unincorporated areas within Clark County. The Las Vegas Metropolitan Police Department was the twelfth largest local police department in the country. One of the agencies included in the study was moderately sized. The APD employed 1,222 persons, of whom 851 were sworn police officers. Last, one small agency was included in the study. The Inglewood Police Department employed approximately 210 sworn police officers.

Community policing was fairly well developed in both Phoenix and Las Vegas. Both of the departments stressed the importance of maintaining a strong relationship with their community. For example, each engaged in community outreach whether it was through the use of school programming (i.e., Drug Abuse Resistance Education [DARE], Gang Resistance Education and Training [GREAT], school resource officers), citizen police academies, or the establishment of neighborhood block watch groups. Likewise, managers in each of the departments regularly met with residents to identify and target neighborhood crime and disorder problems and police executives regularly met with key community stakeholders to address issues facing various segments of the community.

Organizational changes were also made in both departments in an effort to facilitate community policing and problem solving. For instance, Las Vegas and Phoenix Police Departments decentralized operations to the precinct level for the purpose of increasing geographic responsibility and to increase responsiveness to the community. Precinct commanders also had primary responsibility for assuring quality of life within precincts, and were given additional resources to combat identified problems. In Las Vegas, for instance, each precinct was staffed with several community policing and problem-solving squads to facilitate the identification of problems and to coordinate responses to those problems. In Phoenix, each precinct was staffed with a community action team, which was responsible for community capacity building and bringing departmental resources to bear on crime problems identified by the community. Each precinct was also staffed with a neighborhood response team, which was responsible for identifying and responding to neighborhood problems within its assigned precinct. Phoenix precincts had lieutenants serving as area unit managers to narrow down the geographical scope of operations and to promote accountability and beat integrity. Precinct commanders and area managers worked closely with neighborhood associations, and in some precincts, commanders were in frequent contact about local problems and police operations with the elected city council representatives whose districts were within precinct boundaries.

Community policing was less well developed in Albuquerque and Inglewood. In Albuquerque, the implementation of community policing was primarily restricted to police executives and managers. The chief of police was hired from an outside agency based on his reputation for promoting community policing. Upon his arrival in 1998 he encouraged police supervisors and administrators to frequently meet with community members and key community stakeholders, and made a number of organizational changes in an effort to facilitate community policing among line-level officers. For example, he had all personnel in the department trained in problem solving and restructured academy training and promotion requirements to include a heavy emphasis on community policing (Wood and Davis 2002). The chief also decentralized almost all of the department's investigative units. This organizational change was intended to empower precinct commanders to identify and respond to neighborhood problems and to enhance geographic accountability among investigators. However, most of the changes implemented by the chief were met with substantial resistance from line-level officers and supervisors. For example, problem solving was almost never used by officers in Albuquerque, even after training; and officers and their supervisors rarely, if ever, engaged in organized interaction with the community. In the words of one local researcher "... with APD five years into community policing, implementation [had] failed" (Wood and Davis 2002: 5)

Inglewood Police Department's approach to community policing could best be described as in transition. Two years prior to our study, the department had one division, Inglewood Community Oriented Policing and Problem Solving (I-COPPS), which was dedicated to the implementation of community policing. I-COPPS was staffed with a sergeant, thirteen officers, and two civilians. These personnel were responsible for supporting the department's community outreach programs such as DARE and GREAT (i.e., Gang Resistance Education and Training) as well as grant activities related to community and problem-oriented policing. However, in 1997 and 1998 the department lost these positions and the division, due to the conclusion of the grants and as a consequence of budget cutbacks. At the time of this study, the implementation of community policing was largely restricted to outreach programs such as neighborhood watch, a police activities league, and a citizen police academy. Problem solving, formalized and integrated partnerships with the community, and organizational change to achieve community policing were nearly nonexistent in the department.

Gang Units Studied

Both Phoenix and Las Vegas had sizable gang units – about four times larger than the average gang unit in the United States (Curry et al. 1992).[2] In Phoenix, the gang unit was staffed with about thirty-eight

---

[2] Curry et al. (1992) reported that the median size gang unit in the United States was ten personnel. They further reported that only approximately 20 percent of established gang units have twenty or more personnel.

gang unit officers. Officers were assigned to one of five gang squads located within the police department's Organized Crime Bureau. The unit was staffed with one intelligence analyst and one police assistant. Similarly, in Las Vegas the gang unit was staffed with forty-nine officers and eleven civilians. The gang unit was located in the police department's special operations division with in the Organized Crime Bureau. The Albuquerque gang unit was comprised of nine police officers and one part-time civilian volunteer. The unit was located in the department's Special Enforcement Bureau. The Inglewood gang unit, located in the police department's Criminal Investigation Bureau, was staffed with four officers.

A MULTIMETHODOLOGICAL RESEARCH DESIGN

The research design for this project was constructed to gain a comprehensive view of how and why police responded to the gang problem. The present study brings together multiple sources of data (e.g., field observations, in-depth interviews, and documents) to focus on a single point and to help explain, clarify, and corroborate issues of question (Lincon and Guba 1985; Merriam 1988).

Field Observations

Altogether at the four sites, we spent approximately 470 hours in the field accompanying gang unit officers, between May 1999 and August 2000. (See table 2.2 pg. 31) We were interested in such issues as the beliefs of gang unit officers, how gang unit officers spent their time, and the types of persons with whom the gang unit officers had contact. Therefore, we spent the majority of our time with gang unit officers, rather than with gang unit managers or civilian personnel.

The observation period at each site was initially determined by the number of officers in the gang unit, the shifts that the gang unit operated, and the patterns in which officers were assigned to squads within the gang unit. The relatively small size of the Albuquerque and Inglewood gang units and the large size of the Phoenix and Las Vegas gang units led us to plan for eighty hours of observation at each of the two smaller sites and 160 hours of observation at each of the two larger sites. In principle, however, we were guided by a type of nonprobability judgmental sampling known as *maximum variation sampling*. This technique is guided by the idea of "sampling as widely as possible within the specified sociocultural [gang unit] context until exhaustion or redundancy is reached" (Snow and Anderson 1993, 22). Thus, we planned to spend as much

time as possible with each unit and its officers, until we believed that
what we were observing had become redundant and that we had developed a full understanding of that unit's operation. If we did not achieve
these two objectives within the time originally set aside, we expected to
extend our time in the field. However, this did not occur, and in the end,
eighty hours of field observation were spent each in Albuquerque and
Inglewood, 150 hours of field observation were spent in Phoenix, and
160 hours of field observation were spent in Las Vegas.

We also developed a ride-along sampling plan, seeking to cover all
shifts in which at least one gang unit officer was assigned and to observe
all of the squads (or persons) within the gang unit. Our goal was to
obtain a representative sample, by time, of the various subpopulations
(e.g., squads that worked different areas of the city, squads that worked
different shifts) and behaviors (e.g., squads that were responsible for
different functions or activities) that existed within a gang unit. For
example, if 10 percent of the sworn officers assigned to the unit were
scheduled to work graffiti detail during the day shift, approximately
10 percent of field observation time was spent with that detail. In contrast to many previous police observational studies, ours was designed
not to oversample busy days, active locations, or hectic time periods.
Rather, we were interested in obtaining a sample of ride-alongs that
closely approximated the distribution of officers by shift and squad, to
provide an unbiased view of the gang unit and its activities.

In Inglewood and Albuquerque, the gang units were too small for
the assignment of officers to squads, and all officers worked the same
shift. At these sites, the field observer's time was divided equally among
the officers in the unit. For example, in Inglewood, three officers were
working within the gang unit at the time of the study, one of whom
declined to participate in the ride-along portion of the study. As a result,
forty consecutive field observation hours were spent with one officer,
followed by forty consecutive hours with the second officer. A similar
strategy was used in Albuquerque where the gang unit was staffed with
three officers during the period when field observation data were being
collected.[3]

In Las Vegas and Phoenix, after the sampling plan was developed and
approved by gang unit supervisors, the field observer selected a squad

---

[3] As will be discussed in subsequent chapters, Albuquerque was later staffed with an additional six officers, bringing the total number of officers assigned to the unit to nine. As
a consequence, field observation in Albuquerque involved three officers, while we interviewed nine officers.

TABLE 2.2. *Data Collection: Data Types, Sources, and Dates*

Data Type	Albuquerque		Inglewood		Las Vegas		Phoenix		Totals
	No.	Date	No.	Date	No.	Date	No.	Date	
Field observation (hours)									
Gang units	80	Aug. 1999	80	May 1999	160	June–July 1999	150	June–Aug. 2000	470
Interviews									
Police managers	3	Aug.–Dec. 1999	4	May-June 1999	6	July-Aug. 1999	7	Sept.–Oct. 2000	20
Gang unit officers	3(9)	Aug.–Dec. 1999	3	May-June 1999	31	July-Aug. 1999	22	Sept.–Oct. 2000	59(65)
Stakeholders	21	Aug.–Dec. 1999	14	May-June 1999	19	July-Aug. 1999	15	May-Aug. 2000	69
Documents									
Official documents	36	June–Aug. 1999	40	May-June 1999	51	July-Aug. 1999	48	June–Oct. 2000	175
Newspaper articles	42	April 1999	30	April 1999	112	April 1999	101	June 2000	285

for observation, based on convenience. The squad sergeant was notified, and he assigned the field observer to a particular set of officers who worked together, after which time the field observer asked permission to ride along with another set of officers in the same squad, until the allotted time for observation in that particular squad was completed. Often in the larger squads, only one day's worth of data was collected with a particular set of officers. Thus, the sampling of officers in a particular squad was based on the convenience of the field observer and the officer, not on random selection.

The vast majority of our field research was conducted in the summer. This undoubtedly had an impact on the data. As has been shown in past research, in general, youth are more likely to hang out on the streets, engage in unsupervised activity, and engage in criminal activity during the summer months. Researchers have found that during the summer, gangs and gang members are more active, and gang crime is much more pronounced. As a consequence, the interaction between our population (the gang unit) and the season probably resulted in data that are biased toward the activities most likely to take place during the busy season for gang unit officers.

Using an ethnographic research method, we accompanied officers during their regular shifts, which averaged eight to ten hours in length. A notebook and pencil were used to record field notes, consisting of descriptive and reflective data. During data collection, a time diary was also kept to record all activities that took place during a ride-along. The time diary was constructed at the level of the episode, so that at minimum, the primary activity (what was happening), temporal location (the time the episode began and ended), secondary activity (other activities happening at the same time as the primary activity), location of the activity (where the activity was taking place), and contacts (who was present during the activity) were recorded (Harvey 1999, 19). In the case of a ride-along with partners, the driver was designated as the primary subject of the observation.

At the same time, other descriptive data were recorded. This included observations and discussions that took place on the job, the roles played by gang unit officers in the field, informal relationships that developed between the gang unit officers and those in their internal and external environments, and decisions made by gang unit officers. Close attention was also given to conversations between the gang unit officers and those with whom they had contact. This listening typically took two forms. The first was listening and interviewing, by comment. If a conversation was taking place, and the field researcher was in a position to question those in the conversation about a particular comment or phenomenon, the researcher would do so. The second method of listening was eavesdropping. This often took place in the office or field when officers were discussing such issues as a case they were working, department politics, or their opinions about a particular person or departmental policy.

Much of the field data came as a consequence of gang unit officers acting as teachers. They were at times unclear about the field researcher's prior knowledge and experience with policing and gangs, and often went to great lengths to teach the researcher the ropes. They offered descriptions of the gang unit and its role within the community, and shared their knowledge about local gangs and gang activity.

The longer that the field researcher spent with each of the gang units, the more the researcher participated in what was viewed as gang unit work. This included detaining suspects, searching vehicles and houses, documenting gang members in gang intelligence systems, collecting witness information, and filling the role of lookout. All of this information and experience played a major role in interpreting and understanding the police response to gangs in each site.

Reflective data were recorded throughout the researcher's time in the field. These notes included "personal thoughts, speculations, feelings, problems, ideas, hunches, impressions, and prejudices" (Bogdan and Biklen 1992, 121). In a sense, these notes served as potential hypotheses to be tested. Reflective as well as descriptive data were continually analyzed as the study progressed. This constant comparative method allowed for adjustment and modification of our observational focus over the course of the study for the purpose of checking and testing emerging ideas (Lofland and Lofland 1995).

Interviews with Gang Unit Officers

In-depth interviews with gang unit officers gave us insight into the officers' daily lives and furthered our understanding of the gang problem from their perspectives.[4] In particular, interviews were used to elicit the officers' subjective views of the realities of their work situations, what they must do to effectively perform their jobs, and what they actually did on the job. The interview schedule was structured to ensure that the interviewer asked the same questions, in the same way, of each gang unit officer, while keeping the questions open-ended to allow for discovery.

[4] Dr. Robin Haarr was instrumental in conducting many of the gang unit officer interviews in Las Vegas, Inglewood, and Albuquerque. We thank her for her assistance.

We also encouraged the officers to introduce outside information not explicitly called for by the interview schedule.

In each police department, interviews were conducted with gang unit officers during normal working hours. The interviews focused on five major areas: officer characteristics and background, goals and objectives of the gang unit, primary activities performed by gang unit officers, officer perceptions of the gang problem, and community-oriented and problem-oriented policing practiced within the police department and gang unit. We also conducted interviews with individuals in the chain of command: the chief of police or designate, bureau commanders, lieutenants in charge of the gang unit, and sergeants who supervised gang unit officers. These interviews focused on organizational constructs, such as the background of the gang unit, decisions regarding personnel selection, measures of success, and budgetary issues.

Interviews took approximately two hours to complete. Each session was recorded, then transcribed and entered into a computer software program. If an officer did not want the interview session documented with a tape recorder, we were prepared to use paper and pencil; this occurred only once. The interviews complemented our field observations, allowing us to gather data on matters that had not necessarily been discussed in the field.

Ninety gang unit officers in total were officially assigned to the four gang units that we studied. Of these, seventy-six were available for interview. Ten of the officers who were not available were from the Phoenix Police Department: three were on administrative leave due to injuries, one was gone for a family emergency, and one had been temporarily assigned to another agency. The remaining five officers who were unavailable for interviews in Phoenix were all assigned to an FBI gang task force. Although the Phoenix Police Department gave permission to interview these officers, the FBI declined our request. In addition to the Phoenix officers, three officers in Las Vegas and one in Inglewood were unavailable for interviews. The officer from Inglewood was on disability leave, and the three officers in Las Vegas had either been transferred to another unit or were on temporary assignment to another local police department.

Of the seventy-six gang unit officers who were available to be interviewed, sixty-five participated, for an 85 percent participation rate. Three Las Vegas officers refused to be interviewed, and eight officers could not be reached to schedule interviews (four in Phoenix and four in Las Vegas). Of the sixty-five officers that were interviewed, nine were from Albuquerque, three were from Inglewood, twenty-two were from Phoenix, and thirty-one were from Las Vegas.

As mentioned previously, we also interviewed supervisors in the gang unit and police managers in the unit's chain of command. In all, we interviewed twenty police managers and supervisors. We interviewed four police managers in Albuquerque – the sergeant and lieutenant in charge of the gang unit, the division commander, and the chief of police. In Inglewood we interviewed four officers in the chain of command, specifically, the sergeant who supervised the gang unit (although he was physically assigned to the robbery unit), a lieutenant in charge of the Criminal Investigations Division, a captain in charge of the Detective Bureau, and the chief of police. In Las Vegas we interviewed six police managers: the bureau commander, two section supervisors, and three sergeants who supervised gang unit officers. Two supervisors in the Las Vegas gang unit could not be reached for interviews. In Phoenix, we interviewed all six gang unit sergeants and the lieutenant in charge of the gang unit.

Document Reviews

Official Documents. More than 175 official documents produced by the police departments and the gang units were used for the present study. These included the gang unit's SOP, annual reports, intelligence, training and task force bulletins and updates, interoffice communications, statistics kept by the gang units, grants obtained by the gang units, booklets produced by the gang units, and arrest statistics obtained from the police departments.

These documents served as both primary and secondary research materials. They served as primary research materials in that they documented how officers in the gang units had been directed to conduct themselves. In other words, the official documents produced by the gang units or the police departments were expressive of the gang units' organizational arrangements, and they provided historical context. For example, examination of a gang unit's SOP from one year to the next served as a source of data communicating the gang unit's official mandate, and also showed how that mandate had changed over time.

Official documents such as sign-in sheets and bulletins distributed by the gang unit and police department served as secondary research materials. Documents such as gang informational bulletins helped define not

only the community with which the gang unit was trying to communicate, but also those to whom the unit looked for assistance. These
documents shed light on the common practices and beliefs of the gang
unit, and illustrated how the unit had changed over time. Statistics kept
by the gang unit revealed the current scope of the local gang problem
and assisted in constructing the realities of the community's gang problem or at least realities as documented by the police department. Accordingly, these documents provided a rich source of support for the findings derived from our observations and interviews (Jorgensen 1989;
Marshall and Rossman 1995).

Newspaper Articles. We used 285 articles obtained from local newspapers. These dated back to 1995 in Albuquerque, 1981 in Inglewood,
1984 in Las Vegas, and 1978 in Phoenix. The articles provided an
historical account of gangs and gang control in each community, and
gave researchers insight into the various external forces that may have
affected the gang units' responses to community gang problems. A newspaper serves as a forum for the community to speak about its concerns.
As such, newspaper articles often are a rich source of data on how the
community feels about and expects from the police department that
serves it. We counted on the newspaper articles for the public perspective on the community's gang problem, and a variety of opinions about
how the problem should be approached and how each gang unit should
respond to its local gang problem.

Two methods were used to locate articles related to the gang units.
First, we conducted a computer search using the Lexus newspaper indexing system with the key terms "gang," "unit," and "police." Although
these search terms brought up several hundred articles for each site,
many of which provided only vague references to the gang unit, only
those articles that provided insight into the police response to gangs
were extracted. The second method was simply to read the local newspaper during our time in the field, clipping articles that offered insight
into the police response to gangs in the community.

Interviews with Non–Gang Unit Personnel and Stakeholders

We interviewed non–gang unit personnel and stakeholders because
many were direct beneficiaries of the gang unit's work. At the same
time, they potentially served as important members of the gang unit

environment who could help legitimize the gang unit's existence. We were interested in understanding their perceptions of the local gang problems, their gang units, and the ways in which their own activities might be influenced by their gang unit. We believed that these individuals could offer yet another view of the gang problem, and different opinions about how the gang unit should respond to the city's gang problem. Finally, we were interested in obtaining stakeholder assessments of the effectiveness of their respective gang units.

The stakeholder interview schedule contained about twenty questions focusing on five major issues: 1) their perceptions of the local gang problem, 2) the nature of the relationship between the respondent's unit or agency and the gang unit, 3) the influence of the gang unit on the respondent's unit or agency, 4) advantages of the working relationship with the gang unit experienced by the respondent's agency or unit, and 5) problems that the agency or unit may have had with the gang unit. The interview schedule was designed to obtain subjective reactions, positive and negative, from those who had contact with the gang unit. Each interview lasted approximately one hour.

Two methods were used to determine which internal stakeholders (i.e., colleagues within the gang unit's parent police department who interact with gang unit officers) would be interviewed. First, over the course of our field time with the gang unit, we kept a log of individuals with whom the gang unit had professional contact. Second, during interviews we asked gang unit officers for the names of individuals whom they thought we should contact in order to learn more about the unit.

Interviews were also conducted with external stakeholders, individuals outside the police department who worked in some capacity or were interdependent with gang unit officers. These included both criminal justice and non-criminal justice agency personnel. With respect to criminal justice officials, individuals such as county attorneys, probation and parole officers, and jail and corrections personnel were interviewed. Non-criminal justice personnel such as nonprofit administrators and leaders of various special interest groups were also interviewed. This sample was comprised of individuals who had either been identified by gang unit officers as persons who had frequent contact with the gang unit, or who were seen or heard of as having had contact with or influence on the gang unit during the observational portion of the study. The sample included individuals and organizations that were viewed favorably and unfavorably by gang unit officers.

We interviewed a total of sixty-nine individuals stakeholders, twenty-one in Albuquerque, fourteen in Inglewood, nineteen in Las Vegas, and fifteen in Phoenix. In each of the study communities, about one-third of those interviewed were external stakeholders and the other two-thirds internal stakeholders. Most stakeholders interviewed were employed in some capacity within the local criminal justice system. Every stakeholder who was asked to participate in the study volunteered and was interviewed.

Data Analysis

Data analysis was based on field notes, the time diary, primary informant interviews (gang unit officers), secondary informant interviews (stakeholders), and official and unofficial documents (e.g., gang unit SOPs, newspaper articles). These data were subjected to both qualitative and quantitative data analysis. For the quantitative analysis, time diary data were entered into Statistical Package for the Social Sciences (SPSS). We used this data to examine such issues as how gang unit officers allocated time, the number and length of contacts made by gang unit officers, and how gang unit officers were mobilized.

For the qualitative analysis, we relied on strategies outlined by Schatzman and Straus (1973). From the inception of the study, data were continually reviewed and organized, both chronologically and categorically. This "analytic cycle" allowed us to continuously test emerging ideas, as well as to identify patterns, relationships, and processes. Additionally, the constant comparative method was used to analyze the data after the completion of data collection. This process involved "unitizing" and "categorizing" information units (Glaser and Strauss 1967). We identified and coded these categories and units of meaning after carefully reading the field notes, interviews, and documents collected during the study. To assist in the process, all data (except documents obtained from the police department) were entered into a computer using the Non-numerical Unstructured Data Indexing Searching and Theory-building (NUD*IST) program. The NUD*IST software allowed us to code data so that "chunks of data" could be selected and organized into meaningful categories and patterns.

Verification

A number of prior studies have found that the police subculture is beset with secrecy and fear of outsiders (Westley 1970; Skolnick 1994). As a result, Mastrofski and Parks (1990) argue that data obtained through direct observation of police may be contaminated. First, they argue that observed officers may alter their behavior out of fear of being misinterpreted by the observer. In particular, police may feel that the observer might not understand the true nature of police work and will not consider the many hidden complexities that police must take into consideration when making a decision. Second, the authors argue that because observers are viewed as outsiders by the police, information presented by the police to the observer – usually in the form of conversations, interviews, or debriefings – may not be reliable or valid. The authors claim that the officers' desire to conform or appear competent, as well as the officers' mistrust of how the observer will understand and use a truthful response, may have a significant impact on the information that is presented to the observer.

Qualitative researchers have not reached consensus on the matter of how to address these issues, but several techniques are generally accepted for ensuring the accuracy of observer interpretations. Following the advice of Merriam (1988), we used three strategies to ensure reliability and validity in the present study. First, we brought together multiple sources of data (observations, interviews, and documents) and focused them on a single point. This process was used to help explain, clarify, and corroborate issues of question. Second, we repeatedly observed gang unit personnel over an extended period of time. Specifically, gang unit officers were observed for a minimum of eighty hours at each site. Third, gang unit officers were included in many phases of the research project, and were frequently used to verify and interpret research findings.

NARRATIVE

Similar to the findings in prior ethnographic research, for the most part, ours are presented in words rather than numbers. We rely on thick and rich descriptions to present our research findings, including the use of short and long text-embedded quotations that display the data for the reader (Creswell 1994). Our purpose is to communicate a deeper understanding of *how* the police responded to gangs, and *why* they responded to gangs in the ways that they did.

In the past, some academics have criticized ethnographers, as well as those who practice more traditional research methods, for reliance on single data sources and methods. Critics have called for researchers in general, and ethnographers in particular, to use multiple data sources and methods in an effort to include the perspectives of a variety of actors who exist within a particular social setting (Snow and Anderson 1993, 34). This multiperspectival strategy is an attempt to gain a more holistic, multidimensional perspective of a social phenomenon.

Therefore, we have tried to include in our study a number of actors who have stakes in responding to the local gang problems. But we have also included the perspectives of gang unit officers themselves through field observations and semistructured interviews; it is their world, after all, that we are trying to understand. This is not to say that all participants' voices are heard equally. Some informants are more articulate, more outspoken, and more participative than others. As Snow and Anderson suggest, we did try to present a cross-section of voices representative of all of those with whom we came into contact.

The interviews with the gang unit officers, police managers, and internal and external stakeholders were conducted with a tape recorder.[5] The audiotapes were later transcribed by a professional transcriptionist; quotations from interviews are the actual words used by our subjects. In the field, it was not possible to record conversations with a tape recorder or other electronic device; we used paper and pencil to record these conversations. The researchers made their best effort to manually record the words of those observed completely and accurately. In some situations, it was either not possible or not appropriate to document conversations in real time. In this case, the field researcher documented the conversation and his comment following the shift. Consequently, some quotations from the field are the researcher's reconstruction of conversations and comments.

We believe that what we have presented here is accurate in all essential ways. Snow and Anderson (1993) point out that ethnography is not subject to the whims of the researcher, but is constrained by the data collected and methodological strategies employed in the study. We let the data speak for itself with regard to how the officers spent their time, their career histories, the number and types of contacts they had in the field, or their actions or conversations. We have not altered the statements of the subjects, even when they were not as articulate as we would have liked or when they were particularly profane.

With this said, we did use editorial discretion when to maintain confidentiality. When necessary to use names, they are pseudonyms. Also,

---

[5] A small number of internal and external stakeholders who were law enforcement personnel did not want their interviews recorded.

very few women participated in the study, so to maintain their confidentiality, the generic pronoun *he* is consistently used throughout the text. In those cases where a particular characteristic of a subject would identify a subject, we either omitted the characteristic or altered it in a way that maintained the confidentiality of the subject.

3

Historical Analysis of Gangs and Gang Control

Youth gangs are not now or should not become a major object of concern.... Youth gang violence is not a major crime problem in the United States...what gang violence does exist can fairly readily be diverted into "constructive" channels especially through the provisions of services by community agencies.

– National Advisory Committee on Criminal Justice Standards and Goals, 1976

The four cities we studied – Albuquerque, Inglewood, Las Vegas, and Phoenix – are located in the Southwestern United States, where gangs have been predominately comprised of Mexican Americans and Mexican Nationals. This differentiates our research from that conducted in communities where the character of the gang problem has been substantially African American (New York, Chicago) or Asian (San Francisco, Seattle). In this chapter, we describe the context of gangs and their activity, identify characteristics of area gangs and gang members, and explain the historical police response to the gang problem, in each of the four cities.

We examined gang behavior within an historical context in order to determine how communities and police have perceived it over time. In describing how police have responded to gangs historically, we focused on the organizational and environmental factors that influenced their responses, and the conditions that ultimately gave rise to each department's gang unit.

INGLEWOOD, CALIFORNIA

Of our four sites, Inglewood was the first to have developed a gang problem. Most Inglewood police managers, gang unit officers, and stakeholders with whom we talked recalled gangs having begun to emerge as a public concern in the mid-1960s to the early 1970s. However, a few older Hispanic police officers argued that the gang problem started much earlier. These officers shared stories told by their parents and grandparents, suggesting that gangs in Inglewood could be traced back to the Zoot Suit Riots in June 1943, or perhaps even earlier.

Historical accounts of gangs in Southern California supported their claims. Bogardus (1926) studied gangs in Los Angeles in the early twentieth century, and Rubel (1965) reported that gangs had been part of barrio life in the Southwest since the 1890s. Research indicates that most Mexican American gangs of this time were comprised of young people from families working as agricultural laborers. Historians claim that the public had considered gangs at their worst as "aggressive youth" who had become involved in fights; at their best, gangs had been considered respectable, participating in neighborhood athletic clubs and aligning themselves closely with local churches (Moore 1985, 5). Of special interest to us, this body of research noted that the police had not concerned themselves with gangs or gang-related activity during this early period.

In the 1920s, the number of Mexicans immigrating to the Southwest substantially increased. Vigil (1988) notes that during this period, between 1.5 and 2 million Mexican immigrants relocated to the United States, almost all of them to the Southwest, doubling the population of Mexican Americans. Over the following twenty years, according to Vigil, a cultural shift took place within the Mexican American community, driven by severe economic stress, conflicting cultural values, and class immobility. Second-generation Mexican American youth who were seeking identities, support, and excitement joined the gangs affiliated with their barrios. Others joined gangs because they felt pressured to do so.

By the early 1940s, gangs in the Los Angeles area had become embedded in barrio life, where a strong gang subculture had developed. Rules and norms guided members' beliefs and actions, and they began to differentiate themselves by their style of dress. Gang members frequently wore "zoot suits," characterized by baggy pants and a broad-shouldered jacket, typically accompanied by a wide-brimmed hat. Zoot suits not only differentiated gang youth from others in the Mexican community, but they also symbolized ethnic and barrio pride for Mexican youth. Although zoot suiters were known to drink and use drugs such as marijuana and heroin, neither the public nor the police viewed them as dangerous or a threat to the community (Vigil 1990).

By 1943, however, the Anglo community, the police, and the media began to view zoot suiters as deviant. Rumors started that zoot suiters were bloodthirsty savages, a trait inherited from their Aztec ancestors (Moore 1985). Others accused zoot suiters of being responsible for local homicides and of attacking vulnerable white women. Military personnel started to harass them for wasting cloth needed for the war effort (Covey, Menard, and Franzese 1997). Resentments boiled over in June 1943, during a five-day period known as the Zoot Suit Riots. During the riots, service members, citizen mobs, and police officers chased and beat anyone wearing a zoot suit (Vigil 1992). Most gang researchers today regard the Zoot Suit Riots as the turning point for Hispanic gangs. They argue that the riots led to further social isolation of the Mexican community, reinforced notions that Mexican youth gangs were a serious problem, and crystallized Mexican youth groups into gangs for the purposes of protection and support (Moore 1978).

Response to Gangs: Late 1960s Through 1980

Most of the interviewed officers told us that the gangs in their communities had started in the 1960s and 1970s. These officers explained that gang activity in the 1960s and 1970s had centered on neighborhood clashes and turf issues. Most believed that gang violence then had been moderate compared with today. Two police managers who had been with the department for well over twenty years spoke to this point:

That was the beginning of the gangs . . . it was black gangs. It was Bloods, primarily Inglewood Family, up in the North end. They were punks, they were not challenging the police. The guns that they had back then, they were stolen, they were just pieces of junk. It was more warring around with themselves, intimidating the neighborhood kind of a thing. [Interviewer: What fueled the gangs in the '70s?] You know, that is a very good question, because gangs in Southern California had been around for a long time. I was born in Compton, raised in Wilmington, known as Willimas, down in the harbor area, and I was around gang members, Latino gang members, because that was part of life. The vatos, the vachutos, we used to call them, the old-timers. I had an uncle who had tattoos and stuff and had done time in prison . . . [Interviewer: The old time barrio gang, but without the violence?] Yes, although they were violent. I mean, we were well aware that there had been murders and certainly major assaults and this kind of thing, but it was always, you didn't see it that much. It occurred at night, or it occurred in the bad businesses, or the bad parts of town kind of thing. You didn't mess with these guys because you knew they were trouble....

In 1980, the Inglewood Police Department established a gang unit. However, the institutional memory about factors that had led to the creation of the unit was fuzzy, at best. Some officers focused on the growing magnitude of Inglewood's gang problem. They pointed out that the police department, prior to the gang unit, had had few resources to respond to gang-related problems. They said that there had been little understanding of gangs in the city, or nationally for that matter, and that specialized knowledge had been necessary in order to coordinate the police department's responses to gangs. A senior officer who was with the department when the gang unit was created explained:

Well, I think here in Inglewood it was the just absolutely rapid quadrupling and tripling, just growth of gangs that seemed to explode in the late 70s and early 80s, and we just realized all of a sudden that not only did we have hundreds, we had thousands of gang members in the city, and probably hundreds of different gangs, and so it was born out of the necessity to understand the gangs, identify the gangs, identify the gang leaders, and stuff like that. It was specifically an intelligence gathering as opposed to an enforcement unit, and remains an intelligence gathering unit today.

However, not everyone interviewed believed that the gang problem had been the impetus for the creation of the gang unit.

One internal stakeholder officer explained that the police department had established the gang unit only after the hiring of a new chief from Compton, California. The new chief, this officer stated, had been appalled that Inglewood did not have a gang unit, and had believed that such a unit was essential for the department's crime control efforts. Still another internal stakeholder, one of those responsible for establishing the original gang unit, argued that the media had played a large role in its creation:

The media had a lot to do with starting the gang unit. We were always in the media with gang problems, and this led to politicians [pressuring us so] that we had to do something about it. The media has caused problems for the PD and forced the PD to focus on gangs. Gang problems affect local economy. No business, no shoppers – you have to do something. Gang unit has been aggressive, but behind the scenes. They give intelligence to other units.

When the gang unit was created in 1980, it was placed in the Office of Special Enforcement and staffed with two officers, one of whom remains with the unit today. From our interviews, we gathered that the chief had not given the gang unit a strict mandate or mission. Instead, unit officers had determined their own responsibilities. However, the two officers were known to have been involved already in the collection, processing, and dissemination of gang intelligence. Over time, they had been compiling files and pictures of local gang members. The assignment of these two officers in the new unit formalized a process already in place, and allowed the officers to pursue this work full-time.

Both police managers and officers explained that Inglewood's response had been limited to two officers because of the small size of their police department. They explained that in the 1980s, although more than 4,000 gang members had been active in the city, only a few more than 200 police officers had been available to respond to all law enforcement needs. Therefore, the department simply had not had enough resources to assign more gang unit officers.

Response to Gangs: 1981 Through 1989

Beginning in the 1980s, Inglewood's gang problem began to change. In particular, the number of gangs, gang members, and gang crime had rapidly escalated, according to police officers. Some officers thought it was this time when they started seeing younger people joining the same gangs that their parents had. According to senior officers, during the 1980s, gang violence had increased because of gang involvement in street-level drug distribution.

Despite the general perception that the nature of the gang problem was changing in the 1980s, little evidence suggested that the response to gangs changed with the problem. For example, officers were unable to pinpoint any major organizational changes that had taken place at this time, and newspaper articles reflected little activity on the part of the gang unit. Asked about the apparent absence of discussion about the police response to gangs, most police officials attributed it to the nature of the gang unit – the unit worked in the background and was rarely on the front lines of the war on gangs. Instead, gang unit officers were said to have quietly and diligently collected data, making it available for use by other units within the police department.

From its inception, the Inglewood gang unit did not engage in enforcement. Officers, both within and outside the gang unit, believed that there was a natural incompatibility between intelligence and enforcement functions. One detective who was a former gang unit officer explained that gang members saw enforcers as "blue suiters" (cops), and were unwilling to share information with them. He then described his own experience working in the gang unit:

> If we found someone doing serious crime, we would make an arrest. Often times we passed over the less serious crime. So we'd sit and talk and listen; gangsters will tell you something. And then we'd drive away, and we'd get a black and white to do the enforcement. We were cool [to the gang members because] we didn't [make] arrest[s]. We shot the shit with them instead.

Accordingly, it was the shared belief among those in the police department that if gang unit officers engaged in suppression activity and arrested gang members, it would be more difficult for them to gather future intelligence. Instead, it was widely understood that when gang unit officers had intelligence about criminal activity, whether it was a one-time event or an ongoing conspiracy, they would turned the intelligence over to other units for action.

The gang unit at this time also participated in formal partnerships and task forces – activities that earned them little recognition. Their participation in such activities might have been driven by the few resources available to the gang unit. By participating in formal organizational arrangements, with both criminal and noncriminal justice agencies, they were able to use and acquire resources that otherwise would not have been obtainable. For example, in 1985, the gang unit had participated in Operation Valentine, a task force comprised of members from the Inglewood Police Department, the LAPD, the sheriff's department, the district attorney's office, the county probation department, and the California Youth Authority. The task force focused on gang members who trafficked drugs in the south Los Angeles area (United Press International 1985). This effort brought the unit into partnership with much larger and better-resourced agencies, and provided a mechanism for Inglewood to access and bring resources to bear on their own gang problem.

In late 1988, Inglewood's city council unanimously approved a Serious Habitual Offender Program, sponsored by the State of California. The program was designed to identify repeat offenders and to inform the district attorney's office, so that attorneys could follow targeted youths' cases in order to seek the maximum penalty if the youth was convicted (Martin 1988). The Repeat Offender Program (ROP) unit, placed in the Inglewood Police Department, was responsible for coordinating activities among the department and other police agencies to encourage aggressive prosecution of repeat offenders. The Serious Habitual Offender Program was another attempt to control gang crime. Four nongang criteria were used to identify repeat offenders: 1) a record of five arrests, with three of the arrests occurring within the last year, including three arrests on felony charges; 2) ten arrests, with three occurring within the last year, including two arrests on felony charges; 3) ten arrests with three within the last year, including eight on charges of petty theft, misdemeanor assault, or narcotics use; and 4) ten arrests within the last year, including one on multiple felony charges (Martin 1988). Approximately 71 percent of those certified as Serious Habitual Offenders had been involved in gangs (Easley 1995).

A year later, in 1989, the Gang Intelligence Unit began to collect data on gang-related crime. The collection of data resulted from the work of a committee comprised of chiefs of police within Los Angeles County who had advocated for a county-wide gang reporting system. The committee of chiefs determined that a designated number of gang-related crimes (primarily crimes against persons) would be tracked and reported to the Los Angeles County Sheriff's Department, which would then be responsible for compiling and disseminating the data (Easley 1996).

Despite all of the Inglewood Police Department's efforts to combat gangs in the late 1980s, 1989 was still one of the most violent years on record. According to the department, gang violence and drug dealing were related to the 50 percent increase in homicide that year, making it the second most deadly twelve months in the city's history. Of forty-six homicides, about half were attributed to gangs and drugs. In the same year, the number of officer-involved shootings increased, from three in 1988 to eleven in 1989. Inglewood ranked third in the county in the number of officer-involved shootings, just below the Los Angeles Police and Sheriff's Departments, both of which had substantially larger jurisdictions and departments than Inglewood (Lacey 1990a).

Response to Gangs: Late 1980s Through 1999

To respond to increasing violence in the 1990s, the Inglewood Police Department began to take a more suppression-oriented approach toward gang control. It is interesting to note that in strengthening its response to gangs, the department decided to create new specialized units rather than to expand the existing gang unit. In January 1990, for example, the police department established the Anti-Crime Team (ACT). This unit was funded by a voter-approved property tax assessment, with the proceeds to be used to hire twenty officers to combat gangs and drugs. ACT was staffed with seventeen officers, two sergeants, and one lieutenant. This was a substantial allocation of resources for one unit, given that the size of the entire agency at the time was only 187 officers; the new officers represented more than a 10 percent increase in the size of the department (Rotella 1989).

ACT's mission was to perform directed patrols in known gang areas, and to work in concert with the gang unit to target hard-core gang members. However, the unit also focused on a number of other problems, such as chronic prostitution, drug dealing, robberies, shakedowns, violence, and vandalism. Although ACT was created for the specific purpose of suppressing gangs, gang members, and gang activity, it devoted a large proportion of its time to providing directed patrols in nongang areas that were also identified as having substantial and chronic problems (Easley 1993).

In late 1990, community members became emotionally charged about the city's gang problem – a rare event in a city with little community cohesion. Much of the concern might have resulted from a renewed surge in local gang-related activity. In 1990, the city tied its own record for the highest number of homicides in a single year. Of the fifty-five homicides, thirty-three were gang-related (60 percent). Inglewood experienced more gang homicides, felony assaults, rapes, robberies, and burglaries in 1990 than in any other year between 1989 and 1998 (Table 4.2).

The community's concern about the gang problem peaked following the 1990 killing of three high school students in an off-campus shooting, and a robbery of several cafeteria workers at a junior high school. School board members and members of the Inglewood High School Parent-Teacher Association (PTA) met to express their concerns and to debate potential responses. The president of the PTA asked the school board, "How would you feel if you had to fight gang members to get to your office? How would you feel if when you left at 5:30 in the evening, you had to fight gang members up and down the street? This is what our children have to deal with on a daily basis." By the end of the emotion-charged meeting, the school board and PTA members had agreed to revive an antigang task force comprised of community members. They had also organized a march to protest recent violence in the city (Lacey 1990b).

Gangs in Inglewood continued to be especially violent through 1994. During this period, an intense feud broke out between two rival gangs. Drive-by shootings became commonplace, and students had to rely on alternative methods, including rides from teachers, counselors, and parents, to get home from school. Gang members were so emboldened that they carried out many slayings in daylight, in front of witnesses. On a few occasions, shooters told witnesses their street names, confident that the witnesses were terrified enough not to testify against them.

In 1993, another gang war started between an Inglewood gang and a gang from the Crenshaw district of Los Angeles. Violence between the two gangs peaked in January 1994, after two days of shooting left eleven people gunned down and five, including a two-year-old girl and a fourteen-year-old cheerleader, dead. At the following week's city council meeting, 150 citizens protested, demanding a solution. They did not feel safe going out at night, no matter the reason. Many complained that they could no longer walk home from work, but had to find rides with others. Some people complained that even their choice of clothing was limited by the gang war. They feared that wearing blue or red might cause them to be mistaken for gang members and shot.

Interestingly, police officials addressing the public at this time did not seem to be trying to calm their fears. Instead, police were blunt in their commentary on the nature of the problem. For example, one sergeant told the crowd attending the council meeting that in most cases, gang members were not the victims of gang violence; victims, he explained, were frequently ordinary citizens. He stated, "Gang members seem to be satisfied if they shoot anybody in the enemy's territory. It's just random. We aren't dealing with brain surgeons here." Similarly, in an announcement made a week before the meeting, the chief stated that it would be "appropriate for Inglewood residents to remain at home after dark to avoid violence" (Richardson and Dillow 1994).

As the gangs were becoming increasingly violent, police were attempting to initiate a number of suppression strategies. First, in the summer of 1991, the police department announced that it would perform regular gang sweeps in known gang hot spots for the purpose of "discouraging criminal gang activity through high-profile enforcement" (Ford 1991). On the first night of the sweeps, fifty officers from the

Inglewood Police Department, the county probation department, and the California Youth Authority patrolled one neighborhood, resulting in twenty-six arrests for probation violations, ten impounded vehicles, and fifty-five traffic tickets (*Los Angeles Times* 1991).

Then in 1992, the Gang Intelligence Unit was relocated organizationally from the Office of Criminal Investigations to the Office of Special Enforcement. The ACT and the Transit Safety Team (TST), both of which focused on gangs, were already located there. This move brought all three units dealing with gangs and gang activity together under one administrative umbrella. The rationale for the change was to help the unit better coordinate with other street enforcement units on its gang control efforts. Even with this change, however, the gang unit's function continued to center on collecting gang and gang activity data. The unit still did not engage in enforcement activity, which was left to ACT and the TST.

In 1992, the Inglewood gang unit received funding for computer equipment needed in order to access the Los Angeles County Sheriff Department's Gang Reporting Evaluation and Tracking (GREAT) system.[1] The GREAT system enhanced the unit's ability to collect and disseminate intelligence more systematically on Inglewood gangs, gang members, and gang crime (Easley 1993).

In the same year, the police department began to use the Street Terrorism Enforcement and Prevention (STEP) Act to suppress gang activity. The STEP Act, a statute enacted by the California legislature in 1988, permitted longer sentences for any convicted individual who had been documented as a member of a criminal street gang. The TST, whose mandate was to address safety issues related to public transportation, coordinated the STEP program. The TST was responsible for collaborating with the gang and ROP units to gather evidence on street gangs engaged in continuing criminal enterprises. An officer would then present the evidence to a judge, who would issue a judicial order if the gang met the criteria spelled out in the STEP Act. The unit could then

[1] Within the "gang officers world" the acronym GREAT can be used to describe two different concepts. One is the Gang Reporting Evaluation And Tracking (GREAT) system. This is a special software program that is used by police agencies to organize and distribute intelligence on gang related matters. The other is the Gang Resistance Education And Training (GREAT) program. This educational program is taught to middle school students and introduces them to conflict resolutions skills, cultural diversity, and the problems associated with gangs and gang-related behavior. The software and education programs are unrelated to one another.

notify members of the criminal street gang in writing that the provisions of the act would be applied if any member was convicted of a gang crime (Easley 1993). It is unclear, however, how well this strategy was received by those in the police department or the courts.

Maxson and Allen (1997), in a qualitative study of the Inglewood Police Department, argued that by 1994, the Los Angeles County District Attorney's office was no longer encouraging police agencies to make use of the statute, and was discouraging agencies from certifying new gangs under the STEP Act. In particular, they reported that the county attorney's office believed that certifying STEP gangs simply required too much paperwork, and that the "three strikes" law of 1994 minimized the STEP Act's usefulness. Consequently, the researchers reported, after 1994, gangs in Inglewood were "STEPped" only when there was no other option. The gang unit's own data, however, suggested that although gang members were rarely arrested on charges related to the STEP Act from 1989 through 1998, the number of gang members who were STEPped began to increase in 1994. The reason for this increase was unclear.

In March 1994, following a gang-related killing spree that had taken the lives of a number of children and innocent bystanders, renewed community complaints resulted in the creation of a city curfew ordinance. The police chief explained that after these killings, citizens had wanted to know why so many young people were on the streets at night, and whether something could be done. As part of the police department's commitment to community policing, he had worked with the city council to create the new curfew ordinance, requiring juveniles to be accompanied by parents or to have a specific destination after 10 p.m. Sunday through Thursday nights, and after 11 p.m. Friday and Saturday nights. The ordinance had been considered one of the toughest in the country, implemented with the help of a cadre of officers, reservists, and civilians. On Friday and Saturday nights police officers and community members participated in curfew sweeps. Police officers and police reservists used large vans to pick up juveniles, and community volunteers assisted officers with paperwork and fingerprinting.

Some community members believed that the curfew program was successful. They cited the fact that during the first three weekends, more than forty-eight juveniles had been rounded up; a little more than half of them turned out to be suspected gang members (*Los Angeles Times* 1994). Some young people argued that the program would have little, if any, effect on gang violence. They pointed out that many gang members were not juveniles, that most juvenile gang members would not be deterred by the new ordinance, and that gang violence does not occur only at night. The local paper supported some of their points, noting that five of eleven weekend shootings had occurred between 7 and 8:30 p.m.

Also in 1994, the police department increased the number of officers allocated to the gang unit. The original two officers were joined by one sergeant, three investigators, and one "on-loan" patrol officer. By this time, the role of the unit had begun to crystallize within the police department. The gang unit was given three functions: 1) collecting and maintaining intelligence on gangs, gang members, and gang crime in the city; 2) disseminating gang-related intelligence to investigators within the department; and 3) disseminating intelligence to officers and staff in other area police departments.

The gang unit was also engaging in prevention and intervention activities. Officers had started a midnight basketball league in an effort to provide gang members with a prosocial activity and to bring members of various gangs together to get to know one another. Gang unit officers personally contacted gang members throughout the city to participate, and along with patrol officers, they monitored games to assure that there would be no problems. Additionally, gang unit officers worked with the Employment Development Department to provide job opportunities for gang members. In spring of 1994, gang unit officers passed out fifty job applications to gang members; ten gang members were placed in jobs over the summer (Easley 1995).

In 1995, the Inglewood Police Department received about $790,000 from the Office of Community Oriented Policing Services (COPS), allocated for responding to youth firearms violence. The Inglewood Youth Firearms Violence Initiative (IYFVI) lasted eighteen months, focusing on reducing firearms violence among gang members in the Darby-Dixon neighborhood, identified as one of the worst neighborhoods in the city. According to an evaluation report by Maxson and Allen (1997), the program had three components: 1) A civil court injunction to enjoin targeted gang members from engaging in specified nuisance activities; 2) a six-officer task force to support development and enforcement of the injunction, and to monitor target locations, and 3) a probation officer to increase arrests of repeat offenders. Two evaluations examining the effectiveness of the initiative, however, showed mixed results (Maxson and Allen 1997; Bynum 1998).

In October 1997, the Inglewood gang unit was relocated once again, this time, from the Office of Special Enforcement back to the Criminal

Investigations Bureau, where it had been in 1991 and remained at the time of the study. The unit was staffed with four investigators, who were remotely supervised by a sergeant located in the homicide unit. Officers indicated that the unit was moved back to the investigations bureau in order to work more closely with other investigative units. It provided those units with substantial intelligence for use in investigating robberies, homicides, assaults, and property crimes. That same year, the Inglewood police department disbanded the ROP unit (Easley 1998).

ALBUQUERQUE, NEW MEXICO

From interviews with police officers and stakeholders and our review of departmental documents, it appeared that the gang problem in Albuquerque had begun in the mid-1970s. Police documents suggested that prior to this time, members of what were called "neighborhood groups" had been involved in drug use and property crime. The neighborhood groups had existed in Albuquerque barrios as far back as people could remember, having been established originally for the purpose of protecting their neighborhoods. The groups were territorial and received family support. Many police officers commented that it had not been uncommon for families to have had a long tradition of involvement in a group, going back generations, and some officers described their own participation in such groups.

Although the neighborhood groups had rarely engaged in violence, some police officers began considering them a potential threat. Veteran police officers mentioned that the department started monitoring the groups in the 1960s, assigning two officers from the intelligence unit to identify group members. This response had been developed in consultation with the Los Angeles police and sheriff's departments. As one officer explained:

Originally it was two officers that went to the chief of police.... They went to him, and they had attended a conference out in California and they saw what was going on out there. Our chief at that time did not want to admit that we had a gang problem or gang issue, so he wouldn't even let them call themselves a gang unit. They were called a street group information team, and it started out of this division because this is where the intelligence division was. The idea was to gain information. And the two detectives went out and basically spent a lot of time on the streets in areas that were known for gang activity and documented a lot of that activity, and then they grew from there.

Then we got into the '70s and '80s, we got more sophisticated about it. We got some people trained; went out to Los Angeles and did a lot of cooperative training with them, and established a very proactive gang unit. But the nexus was actually just intelligence gathering. You know, find out the scope of the problem, and then when they found it out, they were like, wow! This turned into a nightmare.

In the mid-to-late 1970s, Albuquerque police officers had observed that California gang members were beginning to migrate to the city, especially members of the California-based gangs, Happy Homes and 18th Street. Established neighborhood groups saw the migrating gangs as a threat. This eventually led to conflict, which in turn led the California gang members to move to the west side of the city. Police officials claimed that conflict with California gangs had motivated various neighborhood groups to begin calling themselves gangs, and they began to develop identifying symbols such as hand signs, styles of clothing, and turf-defining graffiti (Albuquerque Police Department 1999).

The first known police report documenting the nature and extent of a gang problem in Albuquerque was compiled by a school squad officer in 1979. He reported that in the summer of 1978, gang activity had begun to increase in the South Valley and Westgate areas of the city. According to his report, gang members were getting involved in activities ranging from petty misdemeanors to violent felonies. The officer did not provide data on the numbers of gangs, gang members, or gang crimes, but he concluded that Albuquerque's gang problem at the time was not as serious as the problem in Los Angeles. However, he argued, if the city chose not to respond, it risked having a more substantial gang problem in the future:

In Los Angeles these gangs are more organized and hard-core compared to the gangs we are now seeing in Albuquerque. Gangs in Los Angeles are holding up people in the street, breaking into homes and shops, extorting money from businessmen for "protection," shooting people from moving automobiles, torturing victims before killing them, and terrorizing entire neighborhoods and schools. This is far more frightening and threatening than youth gang activity in Albuquerque, but it can happen! If we continue to overlook this problem, all schools and neighborhoods will eventually see more and more of this type of activity.

(Montano 1979, 1)

Response to Gangs: 1980 Through 1997

In the 1980s, Albuquerque police officials began noticing that black street gang members were immigrating from California. They associated the incoming gang members with one of two gangs: the Bloods or the Crips. Memoranda from that period indicated that gang members were not as turf oriented as they had been in the past, but rather, membership was revolving around the sale of drugs. In particular, the police believed that the Bloods and Crips were coming to Albuquerque to sell crack cocaine. Our review of police documents suggested that the drug market in Albuquerque had not been well-organized at that time. The new gangs from California had both the skills and the desire to operate from Albuquerque, where they could make greater profits than in Los Angeles. Police reports also suggested that competition for greater profits had caused an increase in violence, as each gang tried to capture territory and market share from the others.

Police officials claimed that from 1985 through 1990, Albuquerque gangs had been deeply involved in drug trafficking, so much so that the department's research analysts and planners had written to the federal government, pleading for resources to assist in their gang and drug control efforts. They wrote that Albuquerque gangs were consolidating into "illicit conglomerates" for the purpose of distributing crack cocaine. The analysts indicated that the gangs had international connections with the capacity to traffic large quantities of drugs, and that they were equipped with sophisticated automatic weapons.

In March 1989, the APD created a specialized gang unit. Staffed with five officers, the unit operated from a substation under the direction of a field commander, and its officers assumed responsibility for gang intelligence-related activities. Within six months, other field commanders were clamoring for the unit's assistance and for their own gang units. In response, the chief allocated another three officers to the unit and placed it in the Field Services Bureau, making the unit more accessible to patrol managers and officers. About this same time, the police department purchased the GREAT software information system to facilitate collection, processing, and dissemination of gang intelligence. The chief later expanded the functions of the gang unit, adding primary responsibility for conducting gang-related investigations to the unit's intelligence function.

Gang unit officers told us that by 1991, Albuquerque was experiencing increased gang activity, and the gang unit quickly became overburdened with investigations. The unit was assigned another four officers, bringing the total to eight. As the gang unit continued performing intelligence and investigative functions, officers also worked to raise public awareness of the gang problem. That year, gang unit officers made more than seventy-five presentations to civic groups, neighborhood associations, and city, county, state, and federal law enforcement officers. The expanded unit was also able to conduct directed patrols in known gang hot spots and to organize neighborhoods to suppress gang activity (Albuquerque Police Department 1992).

That same year, the United Way of Greater Albuquerque created the New Mexico Gang Strategies Coalition in order to sponsor a gang prevention and intervention proposal for a grant offered by the New Mexico Youth Authority. The coalition included thirty task force members representing youth service agencies such as schools, police, corrections, and social services. They met monthly to discuss antiviolence initiatives and other city agency activities directed toward juveniles. However, much of their time was eventually devoted to a gun buyback program in which individuals received gift certificates and other items in exchange for their handguns (Youth Resource and Analysis Center 1994).

By 1992, the public had begun to recognize the seriousness of Albuquerque's gang problem. The City of Albuquerque Planning Department surveyed 1,000 adults living in the metropolitan area to examine citizen perceptions of quality of life and satisfaction with city services. When residents were asked what they least liked about living in Albuquerque, problems with gangs and youth ranked second, just behind traffic congestion. Asked what they thought was the biggest issue or problem facing Albuquerque residents, they responded that gang and youth problems were the biggest issue (22 percent), followed distantly by high crime rates (14 percent) and a poor educational system (13 percent). Not surprisingly, Hispanics were much more likely than members of other ethnic groups to perceive a serious gang problem in the city. Twenty-eight percent of Hispanics stated that the gang or youth problem was the most serious issue faced by the city, compared with 19 percent of Anglos (Research & Polling, Inc. 1992).

The scope and nature of the gang problem in Albuquerque was not systematically examined until 1994, when the mayor established a special council. The Mayor's Council on Gangs was mandated to "mobilize, coordinate, and focus the major institutions of the community on preventing youths from engaging in violence and gang involvement, on intervening to divert current gang members to productive alternatives, and on suppressing the spread of criminal activities and violence involving youth by effective law enforcement" (Youth Resource and Analysis Center 1994). The council was comprised of thirty members who represented agencies responsible for administering prevention, intervention, and suppression programs throughout the city. As one of the council's

TABLE 3.1. *Albuquerque Street Gangs (1990 and 1993)*

	1990	1993
Street gangs (#)	111	155
Gang members (#)	–	3,253
Gang ethnicity (%)		
Hispanic	55.0	56.1
Black	27.9	23.9
White	17.1	13.0
Asian	0.0	0.6
Multi	0.0	6.4

Data from the Mayor's Council on Gangs, no date.

first actions, it commissioned an ad hoc study to examine Albuquerque's gang problem.

Much of the council's final report consisted of data obtained from the city's gang unit. According to that report, as of 1993, the police and sheriff's departments had documented 3,253 gang members living within city limits. However, the council also reported that the police department's own gang unit was estimating that there were actually 6,000 to 7,000 gang members living in the area. As seen in Table 3.1, the council reported 111 active street gangs had been documented by the police in Albuquerque in 1990, of which 61 were Hispanic, 31 were black, and 19 were white. By 1993, the number had grown to 155 gangs, of which 87 were Hispanic, 37 were black, 20 were white, and 10 had members of mixed or other racial backgrounds (Mayor's Council on Gangs).

Analysis conducted by the Mayor's Council on Gangs found that the scope and nature of the gang problem geographically varied within the city (Table 3.2). Gang membership was the most concentrated in the southwestern part of the city where members primarily belonged to turf-oriented gangs. Gang members in southeastern Albuquerque, an

TABLE 3.2. *Numbers of Gangs and Gang Members in Albuquerque (1994)*

	Northeast		Northwest		Southeast		Southwest		Unknown	
Type	Gangs	Members	Gangs	Members	Gangs	Members	Gangs	Members	Gangs	Members
Drug	4	47	3	11	21	327	6	170	2	20
Turf	4	33	13	492	3	10	33	1,889	10	103
Tagger	10	92	0	0	6	32	0	0	1	6
Total	18	172	16	503	30	369	39	2,059	13	129

area with a moderate number of documented gang members, were most likely to be associated with gangs focusing on drug trafficking. The northeastern part of the city had the fewest number of documented gang members, who were predominately associated with tagger groups.

The work of the Mayor's Council on Gangs led to a number of public safety policy recommendations, all requiring increased spending. The mayor and the council called for a 0.25-cent increase in property taxes that would raise an additional $21 million a year. The money would be used to put 150 new officers on the street, to create several gang prevention programs, and to build a forty-eight-bed juvenile boot camp (McCutcheon 1995). Albuquerque's business leaders were among the strongest advocates for the property tax increase. They argued that the gang problem had become serious enough to discourage new businesses from moving to the city. The police union, however, opposed the tax. Union leaders believed that too little of the money was being earmarked for increasing the number of officers, and too much was being dedicated to intervention and prevention initiatives (Crowder and Heild 1995).

Shortly after the mayor's call to increase taxes to fund strategies for combating gangs, a series of articles in the local paper began documenting the nature of crime in the city. One article proclaimed that Albuquerque had one of the worst violent crime problems in the country, ranking fourteenth just behind two western cities (Heild 1995). Another article reported that in 1995, as the rest of the country was experiencing the biggest decline in thirty-five years in homicide rates, Albuquerque's homicide problem was the worst that it had ever been. Many of these homicides, journalists wrote, were the consequence of increasing gang and drug activity (Juarez 1995). One front-page article reported the grip that gangs had on the city, describing the migration of California gangs to New Mexico and the role of gang members in crack cocaine sales; it claimed that gang members were responsible for more than 200 drive-by shootings a year. It described the lives of barrio youth, and how difficult it was to escape the gang lifestyle (Crowder, Heild, and Roybal 1995).

Not long afterward, a drive-by shooting resulted in the death of a seventeen-year-old youth in one of the city's worst neighborhoods (Domrzalski 1996a). In response, the police chief announced a thirty-day "in your face" antigang action plan. The plan called for twenty-five to fifty officers to patrol the neighborhood where the shooting took place around the clock, using horses, bikes, motorcycles, and gang, canine, and patrol units. He called upon the fire department to watch over neighborhood schools. At a news conference unveiling the plan, the chief also announced that he would expand the department's gang unit (Domrzalski 1996a). When it ended, the action was proclaimed to have been a success. Police announced that they had made 444 stops, resulting in 290 traffic tickets, seventeen felony and forty-four misdemeanor arrests, the confiscation of two guns, and the recovery of three stolen vehicles. They reported that no drive-by shootings had occurred in the neighborhood during the thirty-day period, and that neighborhood residents were experiencing a decline in their fear of crime and an increase in their quality of life (Domrzalski 1996b). The police chief followed through on his pledge to expand the gang unit, increasing the total number of officers to twenty.

Explanations for why the department responded the way that it did toward gangs was somewhat mixed. Many internal stakeholders argued that politics, the media and, to a certain extent, the public, played a major role in the development of that department's response to gangs. In their view, the department's response, and the increased amount of resources directed toward the gang unit were primarily political reactions to the publicity surrounding outbreaks of violence. For example, one area commander explained:

Primarily the publicity.... One of the reasons why the gang unit grew to the extent that it did was a series of gang-related homicides that occurred down in [another command] area. So our response to the gangs basically was how much bad publicity we are going to get in terms of the number of homicides and ... the number of gang-related crimes that are being committed out there.

One sergeant from a violent crimes unit described the development of the gang unit at this time in terms of "the squeaky wheel [getting] the oil." He went on to identify the squeaky wheel as "media, politics, the mayor's office, and neighborhoods," and he explained:

[Internal Stakeholder] But you get a high-profile gang case ... and it's been that way with administrations since I've been a cop. When the caca hits the fan, every resource this place has goes to it. [Interviewer] Could those resources have been used to prevent it? [Internal Stakeholder] Maybe, maybe not, but they're never put there. It's always a reactive situation. That is my problem, my complaint. And it's not this department, it's all departments. Nothing gets done unless something bad happens, and that's just the way this thing goes.

Some stakeholders, however, indicated that the rationale for the development of the gang unit was to respond to the increase in violent crime. They saw the development of the unit as a natural response to the crime problem and made no mention of media, political, or public influence.

Regardless of the reason, with the expansion of the gang unit came a broader mission. Now, along with its intelligence, investigation, and public awareness functions, the unit was directed to engage in street enforcement. About fourteen officers worked nights, conducting directed patrols in areas with known gang problems; the other six officers worked during the day handling investigations and community presentations. The captain in charge of the unit expected it to be aggressive on the streets. In the words of one officer assigned to the unit at the time, the captain wanted his officers to "smash heads and have zero tolerance for gang members."

Although street enforcement had become an important function of the gang unit, officers continued to be held responsible for collecting and disseminating gang intelligence. The officers countered that the gang unit's enforcement mandate made it too difficult for them to gather intelligence. They explained that enforcement resulted in a lack of rapport with gang members that prohibited the kind of relationships that could facilitate open communication between police and youth on the street. They tried to explain this to the command staff and other officers in the department, but the message was ignored. Eventually, the gang unit officers had become frustrated and stopped trying to gather intelligence altogether; instead, they explained, they spent their time stopping cars and writing tickets.

Response to Gangs: 1998 Through 1999

In February 1998, the mayor and an acting police chief were searching for ways to free time for patrol officers to engage in community policing. They were reviewing the allocation of officers in the police department in an effort to place more officers on the street. They determined that far too many specialized units existed, and they asked the special unit supervisors whether they could manage with fewer officers. When the supervisor of the gang unit responded positively, the chief reallocated six of the twenty gang unit officers to patrol (Contreras 1998).

A few months later, a major gang war broke out in one of Albuquerque's worst gang neighborhoods. Over a two-week period, drive-by shootings occurred nightly, leaving one person dead. Neighbors were terrified to leave home after dark. In response to the shootings, neighborhood organizations, local businesses, and individuals collaborated to organize a Stop the Violence campaign, a series of antigang rallies protesting the gang war. During a three-week period, five rallies were held (Kruger 1998). A week later, Albuquerque's new police chief instituted a number of organizational changes.

The reorganization was publicly linked to the movement to implement community policing, and to the effort to decentralize and generalize the organizational structure of the department. A few in the department have argued, however, that some of the changes under this umbrella were designed more to respond to escalating gang violence than to implement community policing. In the process, the new chief disassembled several specialized units, reallocating officers to patrol districts. For example, officers who had been assigned to centralized units that investigated crimes against persons and property were reallocated to district commanders, who then assigned the officers as they saw fit. The only units left untouched by the reorganization were homicide, narcotics, and vice.

As part of this change, the gang and Special Weapons and Tactics (SWAT) units were merged into one Metro unit, comprised of twenty SWAT-trained officers. The Metro officers were divided into five teams, four responsible for street enforcement and one composed of former gang unit officers responsible for gang intelligence. The chief placed the Metro unit within the Patrol Division, ensuring its accessibility to patrol commanders. Metro officers were required to wear uniforms and to drive marked vehicles.

As it turned out, the Metro unit was short-lived, disbanded by the summer of 1999. A number of reasons have been proposed for the unit's apparent failure. Many officers in the department believed that the Metro unit was simply not productive; its officers were not perceived to be hardworking or to be generating the amount of activity expected of a proactive, hard-charging unit. One officer stated, "They would not do shit. They would come in in the morning and would never be seen again." Sergeants assigned to the Metro unit were said to either lack experience or to be near retirement; either way, they were seen as lacking focus and energy. Interestingly, Metro unit officers were scheduled to work from 6 a.m. to 2 p.m., not ordinarily hours during which street enforcement is most needed.

As the city's gang problem escalated, the department was dealing internally with its *gang unit* problem. One police manager explained to us, however, that he believed that the disruptions and the ultimate failure of the Metro unit were caused by factors much more complex than a group of officers with a poor work ethic. He maintained that the new chief had modeled the Metro unit after the LAPD CRASH unit, with SWAT officers performing street-level enforcement in their down time, and gang unit officers working with SWAT officers to gather and disseminate gang intelligence. Contrary to the chief's vision, Metro's direct chain of command (i.e., captain, lieutenant, and sergeant in charge) believed that SWAT officers should not engage in street enforcement or gang control functions, and they had directly prohibited their officers from carrying out those kinds of actions. The new chief had aimed to expand the unit to a total of fifty officers, but whenever he assigned officers to the unit, the Metro command staff would require them to undergo enhanced physical training tests that few could pass. The command staff believed that only the most elite officers should be allowed into "their SWAT unit."

According to this police manager, Metro's command staff had not believed that the new chief's idea was sound, and so they had ignored and defied his orders. Under their command, unit officers had performed only SWAT-related duties. In the unit's final six months of existence, the twenty Metro officers made only one felony arrest. According to gang unit officers and department managers, the chief would rather have reassigned poor performers to another unit, but departmental politics had prevented this option. Finally, the chief elected to disband the Metro unit entirely. Then shortly afterward, he recreated a gang unit with new officers and a more trustworthy chain of command.

In August 1999, the reformed gang unit began operating with four officers; a few months later, another five were added. The unit adopted an operational strategy that emphasized intelligence gathering and dissemination. To facilitate this function, the unit was divided into two teams, each with four officers. One team was assigned to each of the two districts with the worst gang problems. The teams served as liaisons with district patrol officers, attending daily briefings and presenting gang intelligence, and they scanned for gang-related problems in their assigned districts. Once a problem was identified, the entire unit responded.

The reformed unit was no longer required to investigate gang-related crimes, as its predecessor had been. The captain of the Special Enforcement Bureau believed that conducting investigations would overburden the unit and cause less intelligence to be gathered. He wanted the unit to serve as an auxiliary support team for other units conducting gang-related investigations, enabling gang intelligence to be used without forcing gang unit officers to assume specific case responsibilities.

For a short period, the gang unit did not report to any bureau or division. Officers as well as department managers were unclear exactly where the unit belonged organizationally. Most managers were very reluctant to take responsibility for the unit. Eventually, however, the gang unit was placed in the Special Investigations Division with the narcotics and repeat offender units. A lieutenant advocating for the unit was also a friend of the new gang unit sergeant; he believed that gang members were often involved with narcotics and were typically repeat offenders. As such, he thought that the gang unit would complement the other units in Special Investigations. With this change, gang unit officers could again drive unmarked vehicles and wear street clothing.

LAS VEGAS, NEVADA

Police first identified a gang problem in Las Vegas in the late 1960s or early 1970s. The problem was concentrated on the west and east sides of the city in neighborhoods with public housing and inexpensive apartment complexes. African American gang members resided primarily on the west side, while Hispanics resided primarily on the east side of the city.

Initially, the emergence of local neighborhood gangs attracted little attention. Some of the officers with whom we spoke attributed this to the fact that, in the 1970s, Las Vegas had experienced a rapid increase in population. New job opportunities were resulting from the expanding casino industry, jobs that required little education and few skills. As a result, minority adults, mostly black and Hispanic, had moved to Las Vegas to work in the service industry, bringing with them children who were already members of Los Angeles gangs. Although no gang data were collected by the Las Vegas Police Department during this period, police officers recalled that immigrating gang members had become involved in criminal activity, and that most violence between gangs had involved issues of turf and respect.

Response to Gangs: 1980 Through 1986

By all accounts, the gang problem began to escalate in the 1980s. The first two documented gang homicides had been recorded in 1980 (Flanagan 1997a), and then in 1983, two other gang homicide cases captured the attention of both police and the public. The first involved a fifteen-year-old African American male who shot and killed a rival gang member in front of 200 other partygoers in the north part of the city. By Las Vegas standards, this was an almost unimaginable crime. It had been committed in plain view of innumerable witnesses, and yet none were willing to testify (*Las Vegas Sun* 1984, July 3). In the second case, an altercation in the street at a party occurred between two rival Hispanic gang members. The victim, unarmed and attempting to flee, was stabbed repeatedly and then was run over by a car (McCorkle and Miethe 2002, 126).

Several reports from that period suggested that the gang problem had begun to escalate rapidly. For example, in 1984, police estimated that only fifty to seventy gang members were in the area, with fewer than twenty characterized as hard-core (Cornett 1983). A year later, in 1985, police recorded fifteen gangs and approximately 1,000 gang members (Shetterly 1985a). Police officials also stated that during this period, an increasing number of African American gang members were migrating to the city, and concurrently, police were witnessing an increase in the number of gang fights for control of territory. Some officers thought that the increasing violence had been related to gang members' attempts to control drug territories; others believed that the gangs had been fighting over broader turf issues.

The police department created a temporary two-officer detail to address gang problems in 1980, after the first two gang homicides had occurred. However, this detail was active only intermittently, its existence at any given time "depend[ed] on [the] immediacy of problems, school sessions and even the weather" (Shetterly 1985b). In January 1985, as gang activity escalated the chief resurrected this detail permanently, renaming it the Gang Diversion Unit. Staffed with two uniformed officers, the unit was given a prevention-oriented mission: It was responsible for preventing youth from joining gangs and for talking youth already in gangs into getting out. The unit was also responsible for giving prevention-oriented presentations to school officials, social workers, and church leaders.

News reports from the mid-1980s indicated that officers in the gang unit had made a point of emphasizing that they did not respond to calls for service, nor did they engage in any other enforcement activity. Instead, the officers spent time with gang members learning about gang culture, gang signs, and other gang lifestyle issues. They also worked with gang members who wanted legitimate employment opportunities. In the first four months of the unit's existence, the two officers boasted, they had found four gang members jobs through police ties with local employers (Shetterly 1985b).

The Las Vegas Police Department, however, had begun to attract criticism for the prevention-oriented gang strategy. A Los Angeles lieutenant

in charge of gang control publicly condemned Las Vegas's strategy for
not being more aggressive. In a local paper, the *Las Vegas Sun*, the L.A.
lieutenant was quoted as having said:

If that's what they're doing [to control gangs], in my opinion, they're making a
big mistake. Our posture is an aggressive one. We have 160 guys out there in their
face continuously. We initially took the same approach as the Las Vegas Police
Department: We watched them, monitored them, kept files and didn't try to stamp
them out. But don't go out there...with two guys, go out there and get heavy
with them. (Shetterly 1985b)

Las Vegas police officials countered that local gang members were
a different breed than those in Los Angeles. Police spokespersons explained that gang activity in Las Vegas was primarily the consequence of
boredom, trying to impress other youth, lack of job opportunities, and
the desire to belong (Shetterly 1985a). They also pointed out that the
police were unaware of any gangs in Las Vegas being involved in the
drug supply market (Shetterly 1985b).

Even with the creation of the Gang Diversion Unit, however, the
gang problem in Las Vegas continued to grow. For example, in the
first four months of 1986, between fifteen and twenty gang-related
shootings, assaults, and attempted murders occurred, most of which
occurred between black gangs in black neighborhoods (Beall 1986a).
Police officials explained that gangs at this time were ethnically homoge-
nous. Of the twenty or twenty-one gangs in the city, twelve were comprised primarily of black gang members, six were comprised primarily
of Hispanic gang members, and two or three were comprised of white
gang members. Hispanic gangs were neighborhood-oriented and limited their activity to minor burglaries and vandalism within their turf.
White gangs, police noted, were of less interest because technically, they
were not formal gangs, and they were engaging in few troubling activities other than satanic rituals. Black gangs were a much more serious
problem. They operated outside their own neighborhoods, and they
were becoming involved in narcotics trafficking and violent assaults. As
a result, the police explained, they were spending most of their time
monitoring and focusing on black gangs.

As the gang problems persisted, local African American stakeholders began to mobilize community members. More than 300 Westside
residents joined together to urge the police to do something about
gang violence in their neighborhoods. A meeting took place about
two weeks after a drive-by shooting had wounded six bystanders and

caused the death of a local paperboy. Residents told police that they felt like hostages in their own neighborhoods; they wanted the police to crack down on gangs and gang behavior. In turn, gang unit officers explained that they were using diversionary tactics to get gang youth back into schools and churches, and they urged the citizens to call the police whenever gang activity occurred in their neighborhoods (Joyce 1985).

A few months later, in early 1986, a citizen action group calling themselves Citizens Interested in Today's Youth (CITY) began meeting weekly to discuss the youth gang problem in the metropolitan area and to brainstorm about alternative prevention tactics. Within a month, the group was sponsoring a conference for sixty representatives from public agencies and private corporations. At the conference, members of CITY talked about current gang-related problems and facilitated discussions about strategies that might help to control gang crime. Police and juvenile court officers argued strongly that in order to prevent youth from engaging in gang crime, jobs and recreation programs were needed. They pointed out that most youth were joining gangs because they lacked jobs and educational opportunities, and that to succeed, gang-reduction efforts would need to increase the youths' self-esteem and make them feel that they "belonged" (Shetterly 1986).

Several other community-driven gang control intervention efforts were initiated around this time. For example, in neighborhoods that were complaining about gang members selling drugs, police-trained residents participated in the Crime Watch program (Beall 1986b). The Juvenile Court Services Division created a program to divert youth from gang membership. Juvenile offenders listed as gang members were being required to participate in a probation program meant to "rehabilitate a gang member by working through his family, returning him to school, getting him a job and beginning to show him that his gang association will take him only to a jail" (Beall 1986c).

Response to Gangs: 1987 Through 1990

In 1987, the gang problem shifted in nature. The kinds of activities engaged in by local, homegrown gangs were giving way to the more serious disruptions of the immigrating Los Angeles gangs. Local law enforcement officials were quoted in a newspaper article as saying that "gang activity [was] mushroom[ing] as Los Angeles street gang members ... flooded into the Las Vegas Valley, bringing with them a seemingly boundless supply of narcotics and an unscrupulous brand of 'machismo'" (Bates 1987). The officials went on to suggest that Las Vegas was virgin territory for Los Angeles gang members, who were seeking new places to market cocaine. Law enforcement officers from both Las Vegas and Los Angeles pointed out that the same rock of crack cocaine that sold for ten dollars in Los Angeles would sell for twenty dollars in Las Vegas. Los Angeles gang members were migrating in droves to Las Vegas for the purpose of increasing the profitability of their street-level drug sales (Bates 1987). Although law enforcement officials were unable to estimate precisely the number of Los Angeles gang members in Las Vegas at the time, officials believed that in April 1986, about 900 known gang members were in the city; within eighteen months, that number had risen to 4,000 (Bates 1987). Although some officers argued that gang migration in pursuit of drug profits accounted for much of the rise, others believed that the increase indicated that a greater number of local youth were joining gangs.

The police department responded to the increase in documented gang members by increasing the number of officers assigned to the Gang Diversion Unit. The unit doubled in size, increasing from two to four officers, who were given greater latitude with regard to policies and procedures. For example, officers wore plain clothes to help in building rapport with gang members. They had explicit permission to work anywhere in the county to gather intelligence. The Gang Diversion Unit's focus remained on gathering intelligence and on prevention-oriented activities (Bates 1987).

Despite these efforts to control it, the gang problem continued to escalate. Most troubling to Las Vegas police was that intergang violence was often occurring in public areas frequented by children. On one occasion, six West Coast Bloods attempted to kill members of the rival Gerson Park Kingsmen, firing a gun into a roller skating rink filled with more 300 children and parents. No gang members were injured, but during the panic that ensued, three nongang teenagers were shot and another was injured from trampling. The shooting, police later discovered, was an act of revenge for an earlier drive-by shooting (Hyman 1988).

Another incident occurred in a parking lot across the street from a local high school during a school-sponsored dance. Police believed that initially, a fight had broken out between two gangs. The fight resulted in six to eleven shots being fired, four students being injured (one with multiple fractures and another who was hit in the face with a baseball bat), and five windows and several cars being damaged (Schumacher 1988b).

Three weeks later, another fight broke out between two gangs at a baseball field. A group of gang members on one side of the ball field began shooting across the field at members of a rival gang on the other side, and the rival gang returned their fire. It did not seem to matter to either gang that between them, a Little League baseball game was underway. Witnesses stated that the seven- and eight-year-old youngsters had dropped to the ground to avoid being shot, many crying uncontrollably. Those in attendance stated that it had been one of the most brutal things that they had ever seen. Their anger was exacerbated by the fact that police had failed to respond to their calls for help until more than a half hour later. Parents held a press conference at the field to make their feelings about the situation clear (Schumacher 1988a).

Gang violence continued to increase, and city officials raced to respond. Government officials held public meetings to define the nature and scope of the city's gang problem and to discuss potential solutions. In October 1988, when a county commissioner organized a meeting of twenty-four public officials to discuss the county's gang problem, more than seventy citizens crowded into the small meeting room. Both public officials and citizens voiced concerns about gang violence running rampant throughout the city, exemplified by the gunfight during the Little League game. By the end of the meeting, both groups had agreed that they needed "more police, more state and local funding to fight gangs and drugs, and more parents taking responsibility for the illegal acts of their children" (McCabe 1988).

A few weeks later, the mayor organized a series of town hall meetings, one in each ward, to discuss public safety and community concerns about gangs (Koch 1988). At the meeting in Ward 3, comprised primarily of African Americans and the area where gang problems were said to be most serious, a police undersheriff told the audience that "youth gangs have created the most serious problem we have faced in the last two to three decades." He also told the crowd that the gang problem was the department's number one priority, and he discussed several of the efforts that the department was making to control the gangs (Koch 1988). In 1988, on two occasions the sheriff had substantially increased the resources available to the gang unit. In March 1988, the sheriff had expanded the unit from four to eighteen officers, and officers had been assigned to both day and night shifts. The unit's mission had also changed at this time, from a concentration on prevention and intelligence to enforcement. In particular, the unit had become responsible for directed patrols in known gang areas.

A police spokesperson stated that "the Metro gang unit will roam all of Clark County and give gang members an ultimatum from the sheriff. It is to cease their activities, leave town, or go to the penitentiary" (*Las Vegas Sun* 1988a). After its first five weeks, the unit was considered a smashing success. The local paper reported that more than 300 gang members had already been arrested, and the unit had confiscated $10,000 worth of crack cocaine and twenty-five handguns (*Las Vegas Sun* 1988b).

The sheriff had continued increasing the number of officers assigned to the gang unit, and it reached a total of thirty-six officers by December 1988. Police officials said that the rationale for expanding the unit was to prevent the number of gang killings from increasing further. With the added gang unit officers came diversification in gender and ethnicity. The unit had always been comprised of white males. Now the department was assigning female and black officers, in response to criticisms from black community leaders who complained that white male officers were making themselves up with black faces to go on sting operations – tactics that were offensive and unnecessary, according to the community, given that the department had black officers within its ranks. Females were assigned to the unit to interact with female gang members who were selling drugs. The department believed that female gang unit officers would help with investigations and other suppression-oriented activities (Tobin 1988).

The concern demonstrated by political officials and the police department matched public opinion on the issue. A telephone survey conducted by the University of Nevada at Las Vegas examined the perceptions and attitudes of 1,214 randomly selected Nevadans in late 1988. Seventy-seven percent of respondents expressed concern about gangs, compared with 67 percent in 1986 (Pappa 1989). Eighty-nine percent of those surveyed believed that the gang problem was worsening or might be out of control (McCorkle and Miethe 2002, 131).

The next several years were marked by strategic realignments in gang control strategies employed by the city and state. Criminal justice policy makers began to shift resources from prevention and intervention-oriented strategies to suppression-oriented strategies. The state legislature enacted a new statute aimed at curbing gang violence. A Nevada statute addressing juvenile court waivers was revised, restricting the court's jurisdiction in homicide cases. The legislature also enacted a drive-by shooting law, making it easier for police to arrest suspects, and lengthening sentences. Prison terms were doubled for anyone convicted of using a juvenile to sell illegal drugs, making it easier for public housing authorities to evict residents who engaged in unlawful activities, and penalties were increased for bringing weapons to school. Possibly the most dramatic legislative act was a statute subjecting documented gang members to stiffer penalties upon conviction of a gang-motivated crime (McCorkle and Miethe 2002).

As the legislature was considering various gang-related legislation, the police department was campaigning for more resources to combat gangs. First, the sheriff asked the state legislature for $1.2 million to hire another two sergeants and sixteen officers for the gang unit (Wingard 1989). He then requested $250,000 from the federal government to pay officers overtime to patrol the Gerson Park Housing Project area, turf of the worst gang in the city (Koch 1988).

Police began employing several suppression-oriented gang-reduction strategies. They began sweeping gang neighborhoods in an effort to take gang members off the street. In a practice known as jamming, gang unit officers identified and stopped gang members on the street or in cars, hoping to find drugs, weapons, or a warrant outstanding. One well-publicized crackdown took place at the Nevada State Fair, where officers identified forty-five gang members and arrested them all as a "preventive measure." Police noted that "several gangs were congregating to fight each other and other fairgoers.... All were wearing gang colors, but were apprehended before any fights or disturbances..." (*Las Vegas Sun* 1989). The gang unit reported that between December 1988 and August 1990, its thirty-six officers had made 1,200 gang-related arrests, recovered 200 handguns, and executed 130 search warrants (Burbank 1990).

With the crackdowns, however, came renewed criticism from the African American community. Residents were concerned about the impact that gangs were having on their neighborhoods, but they were equally concerned about the excessive force used by officers, and at a public meeting, they asked the undersheriff what he intended to do about it. He responded that such behavior was unacceptable, and assured the crowd that the Internal Affairs Bureau would look into all allegations (Koch 1988).

Less than a month later, twenty-five African American community leaders assembled at a church to complain that police harassment had occurred during the recent Martin Luther King Day parade.

Community leaders believed that gang unit officers had harshly treated juveniles attending the parade, and that several non–gang members had been detained without reason for questioning. Gang unit managers explained that officers had attended the event to identify gang members and to prevent gang crime. Officers had observed two underage youths drinking alcohol; searching them, the officers had discovered that they were carrying handguns. Concerned about a potential gang fight, they had then stopped and searched other possible gang members. Over the course of the entire day, a sergeant noted, the officers may well have stopped some youths who were not gang members. But he warned, "Sometimes we don't know if people are in gangs until we stop and talk to them... but what if we weren't there and someone was shot?" (Austin 1989).

Response to Gangs: 1990 Through 1999

By 1991, most of the public in Nevada and across the country recognized that Las Vegas had a major gang problem. In October, the *New York Times* featured Las Vegas as one of a select number of western cities with a major gang problem. In the first nine months of the year, gang homicides and 135 shootings had marked a new high in local violent gang crime. The commander of the gang unit at that time commented that the gang problem was unmanageable. In 1991, the unit had documented 5,000 local gang members, compared with only 1,500 in 1988. He voiced his concern that the gang problem might spread to The Strip, where it would affect the tourism industry (Cohen 1991).

Gang unit data showed that the gang problem in Las Vegas had continued to worsen through the mid-1990s. For example, between 1994 and 1996, the number of documented gang members increased by 45 percent, and the number of gang homicides increased from twelve to thirty-nine. Many police officials attributed the growth to government housing developments having been torn down and residents having been relocated to homes and apartments across the city (a move that police had advocated for years). This, police officials argued, led to the spread of gangs into neighborhoods that had not previously had a gang problem. It also led to the creation of new gangs, an outcome that police had not anticipated. They contended that the relocation of gangs resulted in a "hybridization" process, where newly relocated gang members from different gangs intermingled with each other and in some instances formed new or "hybrid" gangs.

City leaders blamed one another for not controlling the ever-increasing gang problem. Some blamed lack of parental supervision; others argued that school busing was the cause; still others criticized the way police were trying to handle the situation (*Las Vegas Review-Journal* 1997c). An FBI agent and several Los Angeles police officials pointed the finger at the continuing migration of Los Angeles gang members to Las Vegas. The FBI estimated that after 1994, following passage of California's three strikes law, at least 5,000 gang members had moved from Los Angeles to Las Vegas. A Las Vegas police crime analyst noted that casino robberies were being committed by gang members from Los Angeles. Over one two-year period, seven casino robberies had taken place, and Los Angeles gang members were suspects in five of them (Cogan 1998.)

Not everyone in the 1990s was convinced that Las Vegas had a substantial gang problem, however. Richard McCorkle and Terance Miethe (1998), researchers at the University of Nevada at Las Vegas, examined legislative records, media accounts, and official city crime data. They concluded that the police department had been grossly exaggerating the local gang problem to fuel an effort to acquire more resources and to repair a poor image. According to their findings, while police officials were publicizing the growing gang problem, the department was suffering considerable financial pressure exerted by community growth, and it was under public scrutiny following the filing of several police misconduct charges. Accordingly, the authors argued, police officials had decided to link national reports of a growing gang problem to public concerns about increasing crime rates in Las Vegas, all in an attempt to justify requests for additional resources and to divert attention away from internal problems.

However, McCorkle and Miethe's explanation for the police response to gangs may have been overstated. Las Vegas internal stakeholders, like their counterparts in the other police departments we studied, saw their department's response, in part, stemming from media and public pressure in addition to an objective gang problem. One lieutenant said, "... media, public pressure – drive-bys are not good for tourism." Another Las Vegas lieutenant also attributed the development of the gang unit to public pressure, and the political response that it produced:

Public pressure. They closed down housing projects, and gang members have moved all over. Now they are all spread out. We had a big drive-by problem in one area ... so political figures in the area criticized the police department for allowing it to happen. People got upset. The public wanted something to happen, so the police department got a lot of resources as a result.

Public pressure to respond to the city's gang problem was further evidenced by the political campaign run by a new sheriff who was elected to office in 1995. In response to growing concern among the citizenry about the gang problem the sheriff had run on a platform that placed combating the gang problem among his highest priorities. Immediately after election, he reorganized the police department's gang unit, reconfiguring it and changing its name to the Gang Investigations Section (GIS). The GIS included four units: intelligence, investigations, enforcement, and a task force. The task force was staffed with GIS officers who were assigned to work with the Drug Enforcement Administration (DEA) and the FBI to investigate high-level narcotics gangs.

In early 1997, just a few years after the creation of the GIS, Las Vegas gang control efforts encountered a major stumbling block. Two gang unit officers committed a drive-by shooting, and the FBI conducted an investigation. As a result, the National Association for the Advancement of Colored People (NAACP) and other local black organizations asked the FBI to look into all drive-by shootings that had occurred in the past five years. A local African American church leader said that for years, gang members had been claiming that they were being blamed for shootings committed by the police (Hynes 1997). The FBI concluded that the shooting had been an isolated incident, taking place late at night after another officer's birthday party. The two police officers had left the party drunk, with the intent of harassing gang members and drug dealers. Their "playful harassment" had become violent when one of the officers opened the side door of their van and shot six times into a crowd of young people on a street corner, killing one gang member. The officer driving the van turned himself in twenty-four hours after the shooting (Hynes 1997). The officer that shot and killed the youth turned himself in thirty-six hours later.

Following this shooting, the African American community became even more vocal in their criticism of the police, claiming that officers were routinely abusing African American residents. African American community leaders were outraged when they learned that the driver of the van would not be charged for his part in the crime, especially because the sheriff had previously stated that typically, everyone in any vehicle used for a drive-by shooting would be charged (*Las Vegas*

Review-Journal 1997a). The anger sparked by this incident was not limited to the African American community. Police officers had become frustrated with the overall situation, and were angry with the public for its concern for the dead gang member. One officer anonymously sent this message to the newspaper:

Lately you wrote an article concerning Metro and the 18th Street gang member who was shot. I really don't think that you have any idea of the nature of the gang he represented, and personally I thought your comments are not based on true justice and equality.

Before you read anymore, I am not in position to reveal my name. It is not that I am cowardly, it is just that I am connected with this whole thing and my supervisors would not think highly of me to expose an "implied" conflict-of-interest regarding theories brought about by exposing my own personal opinion.

As for the poor, stupid, innocent gang member, that has spread hatred, vandalism, crime, and murderous-intent-through-profit-motive-legacy of his organization, all that I can say is what goes around comes around...and THE only good gang member is a dead gang member.

(Smith 1997)

The officer who shot the youth was sentenced to life in prison without parole. The officer driving the van was never charged, although during federal grand jury proceedings, several department officers testified that they had overheard the driver discussing the idea of doing a drive-by shooting at least six times (*Las Vegas Journal-Review* 1998).

Afterward, the gang unit kept a low profile for several months, although the gang problem continued to be considered serious by the public as well as by criminal justice policy makers. In a statewide survey, residents were asked about their current priorities for legislative spending. About 80 percent of those polled favored additional funding for combating juvenile gang crime, ranking the issue among Nevada's top public priorities (Chereb 1999).

PHOENIX, ARIZONA

Phoenix police records indicated that the gang problem in that city dated back to the early 1900s. At that time, only a few gang members had been positively identified, and they were rarely involved in activities requiring police attention. From the 1940s through the 1960s, the number of gangs increased, primarily in small, exclusively Hispanic neighborhoods. These gangs adopted a street culture represented by unique styles of dress and graffiti. They were not responsible for a disproportionate amount of crime; therefore, police did not focus on gang members as a crime control effort. They believed at the time that gangs were restricted to the Hispanic community and did not exist among other ethnic groups (McCort 1994b).

Response to Gangs: 1970 Through 1983

By the mid-1970s, gang activity had increased in Phoenix. Gang unit officials argued that the Los Angeles gang problem had found its way into the public's awareness, which in turn influenced Phoenix's barrio culture and gang activity. The police also believed that a series of movies recently produced had glorified the gang lifestyle, aggravating the local gang problem.

Gang unit documents from this period indicated that a number of Phoenix gangs were emerging, taking "names that gave them their own identity such as Wedgewood Chicanos, Westside Chicanos, Mini Park, Sherman Park, Southside and Happy Homes" (Phoenix Police Department 1998). Although police officials claimed that the Hispanic gangs were not accounting for a significant amount of crime, the gangs were becoming more frequently involved in thefts, burglaries, disturbing the peace, assaults, and some drug trafficking, primarily marijuana and heroin. Police emphasized, however, that Hispanic gangs placed greater value on territory and neighborhood than on making profits, and that much of their activity in the mid-1970s was still confined to Hispanic neighborhoods located in the central and southern parts of the city (McCort 1994b).

Then in the late 1970s, several Phoenix neighborhoods were redeveloped in order to expand Sky Harbor International Airport. Hispanic gang members were among those relocated to other areas of the city. A former gang unit commander noted that the relocation had had a long-term impact, as the gang culture became diffused, resulting in more gangs and gang members locating throughout Phoenix. Gangs and gang crime until then had been concentrated within a few neighborhoods; redistribution of the gang population caused new gangs to emerge in other parts of the city. As many relocated gang members were forced to move into other gangs' territories, turf disputes and violence increased substantially. The problems were concentrated on the west side in an area known as Maryvale, a middle-class, suburban community. The increase in gang-related problems attracted media attention.

In 1978, the police department created a juvenile prevention squad, funded by a federal Law Enforcement Assistance Administration grant. The squad was placed within the Community Relations Bureau. Eight officers were assigned to it, including one sergeant. The squad was responsible for responding to community relations issues involving gangs and for collecting gang intelligence (McCort 1994a). Officers who were in the unit at the time explained to us that they had attended gang parties, had gotten to know gang members, and generally had worked with them in a friendly way in order to collect intelligence. The officers wore plain clothes, did not wear vests, and rarely made arrests. At the time that the squad was created, the department estimated that thirty-four gangs were active in the city, of which twenty-three were Hispanic and nine were black (McCort 1994a).

A year later, the Phoenix police chief began a public awareness campaign highlighting the city's gang problem. He asked Hispanic community leaders to become involved, arguing that the problem was essentially restricted to Mexican American neighborhoods, and that gang members were hard-core criminals whose parents were Mexican immigrants. He stated that the police department had recorded fifty to seventy-five gangs and ten gang-related homicides in 1979. The chief's presentations often included vivid descriptions of his perceptions of gangs. Following are some of his comments:

Youth gangs move into a neighborhood and take over the neighborhood, robbing homes, terrorizing other young people, declaring wars on other gangs.

Youth gang arsenals routinely include sawed-off shotguns and pistols.

The typical gang member is 16 years old and dropped out of school as a freshman or at the beginning of his sophomore year. The Hispanic mother has little help in keeping her kid in school.

(*Arizona Republic* 1980; 1981)

Perhaps in part because the chief was Mexican American and he had strong connections with the Mexican American community, his presentations were taken seriously by the public.

Others in the department disagreed that the gang problem was serious at that time. A sergeant in the gang unit insisted that Phoenix did not have gangs and gang members until the late 1980s, and that earlier, there probably had been little reason to create a unit that focused on gangs. He told us that gang unit officers had spent most of their time monitoring car clubs.

Marjorie Zatz (1987), a local professor at Arizona State University, examined the police response to gangs in Phoenix, reviewing data obtained from social workers, media reports, and court records from 1981 through May 1983. According to Zatz, these data indicated that gang members were not actually posing a significant threat to the community, and that the police department's claims of a serious gang problem were being grossly exaggerated for the purpose of obtaining additional organizational resources.

Response to Gangs: 1984 Through 1990

In 1984, Phoenix police officers began to notice black gang members migrating from southern California. Police documents state that they were migrating from Los Angeles for the purpose of distributing crack cocaine. Police noted that gang members were being sent to the city to explore the demand for the drug and to assess the potential for profitability. After it had been determined that Phoenix was ripe for the distribution of crack cocaine, the gangs had sent part of their "nationwide syndicate" to establish control over the Phoenix drug market (McCort 1994b). As other black gangs became aware that the city was open, they also began to migrate to Phoenix, expecting to make money from drug dealing, property crime, prostitution, and gambling. Many of the immigrant gangs influenced the formation of local Crip and Blood sets, even "taking the names of confirmed gangs in the Los Angeles area such as 74 Hoovers, Corner Pocket Crips, ... Bounty Hunter Bloods, and Blood Stone Villains ... " (Phoenix Police Department 1998, 8).

Police documents showed that the rise in gangs and gang members had resulted in a street culture in which gang members were free to sell drugs on the street, establish crack houses, and engage in high-level drug trafficking. Likewise, the police found that levels of violence associated with the street-level drug trafficking and associated turf disputes increased.

Police estimated that in 1987 and 1988, thirty gang homicides had taken place, most of them tied to the drug trade (Rossmiller 1989a). In the summer of 1988, at least one drive-by shooting occurred each week in Phoenix for twelve consecutive weeks. In April 1989, a pair of drive-by shootings by Crip gang members killed one teenage girl and injured five other people. A series of news articles appeared, updating the condition of those wounded and discussing more broadly the nature of the gang problem. As part of the public discussion, the police estimated that approximately 3,000 Hispanic and 500 black gang members were then living in the city (Winter and Walsh 1989). Although the Hispanic gangs had more members, police were now most concerned about black gangs, because of their greater involvement in violence and drug trafficking (Rossmiller 1989a).

During the first three months of 1989, the trend toward greater gang violence continued with six gang homicides, fourteen drive-by shootings, and nine aggravated assaults. At the same time, the city was experiencing a dramatic increase in non-gang-related violence (Schultz 1989). Some police managers told us that the gang problem in the city had gotten serious enough for the police chief in Los Angeles to warn Phoenix's police chief that he had better stop denying the problem and start responding. One police manager explained:

Prior to this time, we were in great denial, we were denying a gang problem, and that was the biggest fault that we had, is that we were denying it....Rumor has it that the chief was told, our chief, which was Rueben Ortega at the time, by a California chief at the time, and I think it was Gates, and I am not sure, says, "Hey, you got a problem, and admit you have a problem, and get on it." He goes, "We did the same thing you guys are doing. We were denying we got a problem, but we [had] a problem, and then when we finally accepted the problem, it was too big to handle, where you guys got a chance to jump on it and curtail it, handle it, whatever, if you jump on it now." And I think that's what happened. He did, and he says, "Hey, we have a street gang problem that's mostly involving black gangs involved in crack cocaine distribution," and he formed, officially, formed two night-time gang squads.

Over the next eighteen months, there was a flurry of official activity. The Speaker of the State House of Representatives created a committee to examine the scope and nature of Arizona's gang problem. A Guardian Angels chapter was established in the city and began to patrol city streets (Flannery 1989). At about the same time, the police chief initiated several departmental responses. First, he requested additional funding from the city council to dedicate $48,500 a month to overtime pay in order to place another twenty-four officers on patrol in the South and Maryvale precincts, the areas with the most gang and nongang crime. Before the chief's request was presented to the council, the mayor made a friendly amendment, asked that funding be approved to hire twenty-three new officers for assignment to those areas (Schultz

1989). Within less than a week, the city council had approved the request (Harold 1989).

Second, the chief created a second gang squad staffed with one sergeant and five officers, assigning both squads to the Organized Crime Bureau. The change in organizational structure meant a shift in the operational strategy of the two gang squads, now totaling two sergeants and twelve officers. Although the squads were still responsible for collecting gang intelligence, they were no longer to conduct community relations activities. Instead, the squads focused on directed enforcement, including the investigation of violent gang offenses in the South and Maryvale precincts.

Third, the Organized Crime Bureau reassigned one of the unit's sergeants and two of its detectives to a federal task force. The task force was responsible for suppressing gang activity in the Phoenix Metropolitan area, and it was mandated to identify gangs and gang members involved in the most sophisticated criminal enterprises, targeting them for intensive investigations. A departmental spokesperson noted at the time that although all gangs would be monitored, the task force would concentrate its attention on black gangs involved in high-level drug trafficking. In addition to the assigned officers, the task force included agents from the FBI, Immigration and Naturalization Services (INS), and the Alcohol, Tobacco, and Firearms Bureau (ATF).

Fourth and last, in 1990, the chief established the Operation Safe Streets program, which assigned school officers to the gang unit seasonally, during the summer months. The school officers carried out directed patrols in known gang hot spots during the summer, when police believed that gang activity was greatest.

Response to Gangs: 1990 Through 1999

The Phoenix Police Department initiated a number of gang control efforts in 1989 and 1990; still, gang violence increased (Phoenix Police Department 1998). Between 1990 and 1994, the number of documented gangs and gang members doubled, and the number of gang homicides increased from three to twenty-seven. Police officials noted that in 1992, gang-related violence surpassed domestic violence as the leading cause of homicide in the city, and the federal Office of Juvenile Justice and Delinquency Prevention included Phoenix in its list of the top ten cities with gang problems (Winton 1993). Meanwhile, the escalating gang problem in Phoenix had eroded the public's confidence in the police and other public institutions.

Early in 1990, in the middle of the day, gunshots were heard outside an elementary school. For their protection, students were locked in their classrooms for over an hour. The following day, 150 parents came to the school to protest conditions in their neighborhood. They complained that their children no longer wanted to come to school for fear of being threatened, harassed, and assaulted by gang members. Some parents threatened to withdraw their children until problems were solved. They felt entitled to additional police protection in the South Phoenix neighborhood, but they found police reluctant to provide more service in this poor section of the community. At the meeting, one parent's comments received an outburst of applause when he stated, "If this happened on the north side, you would have had the SWAT team, the National Guard... " (Kwok 1990).

Responding to the increasing gang activity and the consequent increasing pressure on local government, the city council passed two ordinances in 1993. The first prohibited juveniles from possessing firearms without written permission from a parent. Next, the juvenile curfew ordinance was revised to facilitate arrests of juveniles who were on the streets past curfew. To assist with processing truancy arrests, police worked with the parks and recreation department to establish three juvenile disposition centers, located at three recreation department facilities, staffed by police along with parks and recreation personnel. The disposition centers allowed officers to make arrests more quickly, reducing the paperwork required at county booking facilities. The curfew program had its critics. Some public officials from the recreation department stated that this program, initiated to take gang members off the streets, had cost about $600,000 a year to run; yet in its first two months, only 519 youths had been detained and just a few of them had been gang members (Rossmiller 1993).

In 1993, the mayor proposed a 0.1 percent sales tax increase to put still more officers on the street. The mayor's plan, dubbed Zero Tolerance for Gangs, called for the hiring of 200 new officers, ten of whom would be allocated to a new gang squad. The proposal was estimated to cost about $2 million (Kwok 1993). The public voted to approve the tax increase, and within two months the city council had ordered the creation of another gang squad, staffed with one sergeant and nine officers. This brought the total number of squads to three, with one lieutenant, three sergeants, and twenty-two officers.

With the addition of the new officers, the unit was reconfigured with four squads: 1) daytime investigations, staffed with one sergeant and four detectives, responsible for taking case dispositions on all gang-related violent crime; 2) intelligence, staffed with one detective, one civilian analyst, and one administrative assistant; and 3) two night squads, each staffed with one sergeant and nine officers, responsible for gang enforcement.

Although there was little public disagreement about the scope and nature of the city's gang problem at this time, a report from an Arizona Department of Juvenile Corrections official asserted that the focus on gangs was primarily the consequence of politicians, police, and media capitalizing on public fear of gangs. The authors of the report had been careful not to explicitly state that the city had no gang problem, but they did argue that politicians were using the issue for election purposes, and that media and police frequently reported inaccurate information, claiming with little or no evidence that incidents were gang related. Their report concluded that Phoenix gangs were being scapegoated, mainly because they were largely comprised of minority youth (Veloz and Spivak 1993).

However, contrary to these assertions Phoenix internal stakeholders tended to attribute the police response to gangs to objective conditions – an increase in gang members and gang crime. One homicide detective explained:

There was an increase in violence that...peaked in the mid-'90s...the amount of shootings and drive-bys, homicides, and it was the influx of the black street gangs that really changed and dictated how we were going to have to deal with the problem, and from that point forward, it was different than how we'd dealt when it was only the Spanish-speaking gang, and fights in the park with knifes and chains. With the Crips and the Bloods came semi-automatic handguns, fully automatic weapons, a proliferation of fire-power that we had never seen before, as a city or a police department. All that came over with the Crips and the Bloods in the late '80s and early '90s and dictated our response, and we had no choice to respond to it but by beefing up the gang unit squad, and taking them and training them in unique ways that our previous gang detectives and officers had not received.

This was not to say that internal stakeholders believed that the media did not play an important role in the police department's response to gangs. Stakeholders repeatedly commented that the media had helped bring attention to the city's gang problem and that they forced politicians to give the police department more resources, which was used to expand their gang unit. According to a homicide sergeant, once it became impossible to deny the existence of the gang problem, the political machine helped secure funding for additional gang unit positions and equipment, which in his view was something "the police would not have been able to do on its own."

After 1994, the violence among gang members began to deescalate. Instead, police officials stated, the police themselves became the target. In early 1995, gang members were reported to have shot at officers more than twenty times, injuring three officers, in an attempt to control six Phoenix neighborhoods. One commander told a local reporter, "We've seen a startling increase in officers being shot at.... We've seen an increase in gangs trying to set up ambushes against officers. They have had plans of action to draw an officer in to kill him. They haven't succeeded yet, but we are afraid it's just a matter of time" (Hermann 1995). Two weeks later, another officer was shot and wounded during an ambush by gang members. Afterward, the police confiscated three Molotov cocktails from individuals in the area (Villa 1995).

The mayor proclaimed that he was willing to take any and all action necessary to curb the gang activity. He supported the chief's decision to assign 100 officers to patrol the two-square-mile south central neighborhood nightly (Pitzl and Villa 1995). Police officials claimed that this crackdown was aimed at the forty to sixty members of the Westside Crips who were responsible for the ambushes (Moeser et al. 1995). In less than twenty-four hours, the police had made eighty-three arrests in the area, mostly for weapons, drug charges, and for outstanding warrants, and many of those arrested were identified as gang members. The crackdown lasted for a little over two weeks (Steckner 1995).

In spite of its success, the police action was subject to criticism. Many in the community believed that the attacks on the police had been in retaliation for the deaths of two black men who had been shot by police. One of the deceased youths, a twenty-two-year-old Westside Crip member, had become a neighborhood martyr after being shot by thirteen officers firing eighty-nine rounds, thirty of which struck him. Residents claimed that the boy had not been carrying a gun at the time that he was shot; police claimed that the youth had pointed a handgun at them (Wagner and Moeser 1995a; 1995b). Other residents, community leaders, and politicians had pointed out that the police shootings were the natural consequence of years of police harassment (Steckner and Moeser

1995). In particular, they had argued, police had been routinely stopping residents in the area for no apparent reasons. For example, they said area bicyclists were routinely stopped for trivial violations such as not having reflectors (Casey 1995). Many of the residents made statements in the newspaper similar to the following comment from a twenty-year-old black male from the area:

They don't like nobody. You can walk across the street and they'll try to stop you just for that. It's like you don't count. I think just because they're pushing everybody, people are getting sick of it. You can be at the ice cream truck and they'll flash their lights on and take a look at you. Then they'll laugh about it – like they don't have any rules just because they have a badge. They suck.

(Wagner and Moeser 1995a)

Six months after the two-week crackdown, residents in the area were continuing to complain about police tactics. In particular, they complained to the city's Human Relations Commission, a civil rights advisory group, about police use of discriminatory practices. Citizens argued that police were stereotyping all residents living in the area, treating them as criminals and gang members. The discussion prior to and during the meeting was so heated that one commissioner refused to attend, and another walked out during the meeting. The committee chair noted that the gulf between the police and the community was widening (Kwok 1995).

As residents in the south central neighborhood continued to complain about their treatment in the name of gang control, the police department moved forward with a number of gang control initiatives. In 1995, the police department and county prosecutor's office collaborated to create a repeat offender program to identify juvenile and adult gang members who were involved in frequent and serious crime. Upon arrest, individuals on the repeat offender list were handled by a special team of gang unit officers and were prosecuted by the ROP/Gang prosecutorial unit (Kossan 1995). In mid-1996, the police department received a $1 million grant from COPS to support gang control efforts in the city. The program allowed each precinct to develop its own gang reduction strategy using the Scanning, Analysis, Response, Assessment (SARA) problem-solving model (Fernandez 1997).

Even with these efforts, however, Phoenix residents continued to demand that more resources be expended on the gang problem. In May 1996, the city conducted a community survey, randomly selecting and interviewing 703 residents. Respondents were asked to indicate whether they would or would not be willing to pay more to improve particular services. Programs to counter gang activities were found to be the highest public priority; 80 percent of the residents surveyed supported spending more for gang control efforts. Residents were also asked to rate (on a scale of 1 to 10, 10 being the highest) the city's performance with regard to providing programs to counter gang activities. About 25 percent of the respondents rated the city at 1 to 4 (low), and 28 percent gave ratings of 5 or 6 (moderate). Only 7 percent of those surveyed gave ratings of 9 or 10 (very high). The mean average rating, 5.4, was only slightly higher than the 5.2 rating that the city had received in 1993 (Behavior Research Center Inc. 1996).

In 1998, the police chief added another squad to the unit, for night enforcement in the northern part of the city. While gang unit officers and crime analysts stated that the gang problem in north Phoenix was minimal, community activists in north Phoenix lobbied for a squad of their own. They argued that they were not receiving the police protection that was needed to deter gang crime. As a consequence, while north Phoenix was not facing a serious gang problem at that time, a squad was established to address the demands of key stakeholders in that part of the community. One officer who joined the squad at that time explained:

I know when my squad came on that it was the citizens [who] were pushing for us ... to work ... the north zone ... because ... the other 2 or 3 squads that were on at the time were so busy with the other 3 precincts [in] the south zone ... that they rarely had [the] opportunity to go north to locate and find and document where these guys were living and whatever, to the point that they would go up there if there was ... a shooting or a car load of gangbangers were stopped and they needed to get documented, otherwise they never crossed north of Thomas.

[Interviewer: Do you know who the major players were in arguing that another squad needed to be working up north?] I think it was the neighborhood associations. I don't know exactly which one, but it was the neighborhood associations. In the past 3 to 6 years, the community-based policing with the city of Phoenix, has really taken a hold, and it's given the citizens [a voice] ... I think that the police department says, well, you know, we need to start going that direction. If that's what the citizens want, then that's what we're going to do.

SUMMARY

The histories of the police response to gangs in the cities that we studied were enormously complex. Single-factor explanations obscure that complexity, overlooking the broader contexts within which the police responses to gangs developed. Our historical review and analysis revealed a variety of factors, that shaped the police response to gangs in these cities. Each factor in the following text was, to some degree, at work in all four sites, producing a gang response life cycle.

First, local gangs were an historical artifact that preceded the rise of the nationwide gang problem that took root in the 1980s and 1990s. All of the cities had had gang problems dating back at least to the 1960s; some had documented gangs dating back to the early 1900s. Before 1970, gangs in these communities were neighborhood oriented, with no affiliation with or attachment to other cities. It was generally acknowledged that gang behavior at this time was focused on issues of cultural and neighborhood identity. Although gang members occasionally engaged in violence, it typically remained inside the barrio, rarely involved anyone outside the gangs, and related to protecting turf and reaffirming group or individual status. As such, there was little police focus on gangs, and when there was, the focus was limited to the collection of gang intelligence.

In the 1970s and 1980s, all four cities had experienced an increase in gangs, gang members, and gang activity. With the exception of Inglewood, which bordered Los Angeles, police attributed the increases to the immigration of Los Angeles gang members into their cities. Generally, two explanations were given for the gang migrations. First, families from across the nation, including Los Angeles, were moving in ever-larger numbers to cities such as Albuquerque, Phoenix, and Las Vegas that offered employment and a better quality of life; along with local population increases came increases in the number of gang members and in gang activity. A second explanation posited that gang members migrated expressly for the purpose of selling drugs in these cities; gang members had engaged in market research and had learned that they could make greater profits away from Los Angeles. Supporters of both explanations agreed that gang violence had increased in each city along with increases in the numbers of gangs and gang members.

In response, all of the police departments that we studied had consolidated gang control efforts and created small gang units. Although some agencies had already assigned staff to gang control, the creation of the designated gang units was intended to consolidate and focus resources and personnel on gangs, gang members, and gang crime. Each unit was mandated to carry out a "soft response." The gang units were all made responsible for gang prevention efforts and/or for the collection of gang intelligence, but not (initially) for gang suppression activities.

Even after the creation of police gang units, however, the gang problem in each city had continued to escalate, and gang violence had increased at a rapid pace. Additionally, each city had experienced a defining gang incident, crystallizing in the public mind the nature and magnitude of the gang problem. For example, in two of the cities, drive-by shootings left at least one innocent juvenile bystander dead and many others injured. In another city, a series of gang shootings occurred in a public setting, resulting in the deaths of several juvenile gang members.

In all cases, the public responded with outrage and protests. Citizens, particularly from the minority community (typically the hardest hit by gang problems), gathered in public places to protest the violence. They met in public forums to voice their outrage to public officials, and they demanded that police respond to the gang problem with more resources, emphasizing suppression activities. They characterized inadequate responses as racist; some minorities claimed that if similar gang activity had been concentrated in white neighborhoods, the police would already have acted. More often than not, the public addressed their demands to elected officials, who in turn shaped the police response through the provision of resources. In three of the cities, public officials and citizens joined together to advocate for tax increases to fund gang control efforts.

Police and city government officials also sponsored meetings with community leaders from businesses, churches, criminal justice agencies, and minority organizations to discuss the nature and scope of the problem. In a number of cities, local government leaders appointed groups that were commissioned to investigate the seriousness of the problem and to recommend responses. Media played a major role in defining the nature and scope of the cities' gang problems. Journalists highlighted critical gang incidents, performed in-depth analyses of the cities' gang problems, and commented on the responses of criminal justice officials. As such, the media was pivotal in fostering dialogue about local gang problems and the official responses to those problems.

Pressure placed on the police by citizens, public officials, and the media caused them to intensify their focus on gangs. All of the police departments studied had allocated more officers and funds to their gang units as gang problems had mounted. Increases in gang unit personnel were accompanied by changes in organizational strategy. In Phoenix,

Albuquerque, and Las Vegas, the officers' responsibilities were expanded to include gang suppression activities. In Inglewood, as the unit maintained its focus on intelligence, other units throughout the department were called upon to perform gang-related enforcement activities. Additionally, all of the agencies began to participate in multijurisdictional task forces, in one form or another, that focused on gangs.

In three of the cities, the new emphasis on police suppression of gangs eventually gave rise to citizen claims that police were using excessive force. Residents made clear that although they wanted increased police protection, they did not want their children subjected to harsh physical treatment, and they did not want to be unreasonably stopped and searched. However, as they were complaining about police harassment, the public continued to respond to signs of growing gang violence with demands that the police to do more to control the communities' gang problems.

A subsequent wave of gang violence and public outcry in each community had led lawmakers and police to respond to gangs still more severely. All of the police departments reacted with zero-tolerance law enforcement for gang members, and by initiating gang sweeps and saturating gang neighborhoods. City councils and state legislatures enacted ordinances and statutes addressing gang members and gang violence, establishing juvenile curfews, prohibiting recruitment of gang members, and enacting more severe punishments for those convicted of gang crimes.

We found that police agencies in these cities rarely used their own intelligence to help guide their agencies' response to gangs. As a consequence, organizational responses to gangs in these cities were heavily influenced by external stakeholders (i.e., citizens, public officials, media) and operational strategies were based on officer beliefs (as will be discussed in the next few chapters) rather than through strategic-planning initiatives or by data-driven decision-making processes.

Another commonality among the sites was that as the gang problem had escalated in each community, police and lawmakers had responded more and more aggressively. Alternative or nontraditional approaches were rarely considered or implemented. In fact, the more serious the problem became, the more the police responded with intense, traditional crime-fighting tactics. Interestingly, the police were not necessarily the primary advocates for suppression-oriented strategies; rather, the police department's institutional environment demanded such tactics.

We also observed that the LAPD had had a profound effect on the police response to gangs in each city. Los Angeles police officials had publicly ridiculed some of the agencies for not being aggressive in responding to the gang problem. Los Angeles officials told local police leaders that they were making a mistake they would regret if they did not employ suppression-oriented tactics. Local police acknowledged that they were strongly influenced by the equipment, crime analysis techniques, strategies, and tactics that the LAPD used to respond to gangs.

In each of the cities, the gang problem had worsened dramatically after gang members had been geographically displaced from their former neighborhoods. For example, in Las Vegas the gang problem spread after the gang unit successfully advocated for a public housing development to be demolished. Families deeply entrenched in the gang lifestyle were relocated all across Las Vegas, in effect distributing gangs and gang activity throughout the city. In Phoenix, a similar phenomenon occurred after the city reclaimed land from several adjacent neighborhoods in order to build an airport. Many families were displaced, and along with them, the neighborhoods' gang members relocated across the city. Gang problems spread and intensified accordingly.

Last, we found that as the gang problem escalated in each city, the public had consistently requested allocation of more funding for managing the problem. Citizens and public officials successfully lobbied for tax propositions and bills for the select purpose of increasing the capacity to combat gangs, which in turn led to the creation of new and expanded police gang unit squads. In some communities, public officials successfully ran for office on the promise that they would respond to the gang problem with additional resources. Much of the increased funding for gang control efforts had come from local communities. Police departments received federal assistance only after they had committed considerable state and local money and personnel to the problem.

In summary, we found that the police response to gangs was much more complex than each of the police department's creating a specialized gang unit in response to a growing gang problem. Instead, we found that each police department's institutional environment played a major role in the response to gangs. The data illustrated that the media, the public, politicians, *and* increasing gang crime within each city had all been influential in the police response to gangs. Our findings describe a spiraling process that starts with an emerging gang problem and associated violence, which then gets the attention of the media and the general public. The public, armed with personnel experiences or with media accounts of growing gang violence, then demands action from elected officials who, in turn, place responsibility for responding to the problem on the shoulders of the police.

Historically, then, we found that the four cities that we studied had traveled similar paths in the development of their gang problems, and had responded similarly in their initial attempts to control their problems. As we turn our attention to the current situation, we continue to observe similarities, but as the next chapter shows, we also found a number of differences.

4

Scope and Nature of the Current Gang Problem

> There is nothing more insidious than these gangs. They are worse than the Mafia. Show me a year in New York where the Mafia indiscriminately killed 300 people. You can't.
> – Police Chief William Bratton, Los Angeles Police Department (*Arizona Republic* 2002)

We examined the gang problems of the four study sites by analyzing official police gang data collected by the police departments. In particular, we focus on recent trends in the numbers of gangs, gang members, and gang crimes in each city. This data serves as a common reference point to which we can observe the current or objective gang problem. When we refer to the "current" or "objective" gang problem in each city, our understanding of that is based on and limited by information provided to us. Although we attempted to gather official police data from each department dating back ten years or more for an examination of recent trends in gangs, gang members, and gang crime, many agencies had not collected this data or had not retained it. Some of the agencies were able to provide information for all ten years, but others were able to provide only one year's worth of data, and still others could provide official data only on some issues and for intermittent periods.

We also augment the official data with interview data obtained from gang unit officers as well as each unit's internal and external stakeholders. As noted in Chapter 2, internal stakeholders are those individuals, or groups of individuals, who are part of the larger police organization in which the gang unit operates, and external stakeholders are affiliated with organizations outside of the police department, but who have some special significance for the gang unit. Together, the ideas and beliefs held by these individuals, or groups of individuals, comprise the institutional environment in which the gang units operate. Clearly, the stakeholders whom we interviewed were but a small fraction of each organization's population of potential stakeholders, and they were unlikely to have constituted a representative sample. Nevertheless, these particular stakeholders were viewed as holding some special insight into the gang unit and their community's gang problem.

The interview data were intended to provide context for the official police data and to help examine whether the gang unit officers' and stakeholders perceptions of their local gang problem are congruent with the objective threat posed by gangs, as represented by the department's own data. Furthermore, we were interested in gauging the extent to which stakeholders shared a common perspective on the nature and scope of the local gang problem. By triangulating the four data sources (i.e., official police data, gang unit officer interview data, and internal and external stakeholder data), we were interested in understanding how perceptions on the magnitude and nature of the gang problem in each city converge or diverge. Understanding the convergence and divergence of perceptions on the magnitude and nature of each community's gang problem might further reveal why the police have responded to their gang problem in the way that they have.

INGLEWOOD

Inglewood Police Department's gang information system indicated that in 1999, 7,191 gang members and thirty-one "permanent" gangs were located in the city (Table 4.1). As such, about 6.4 percent of the city's residents were documented as gang members. Data obtained from CALGANG, California's gang information system, indicated that most gang members in Inglewood belonged to one of the city's eight major gangs (Table 4.2).

Inglewood gangs were geographically dispersed; almost all neighborhoods were claimed by at least one gang. A gang unit officer explained, "We have so many bad areas, whoever complains the most gets the treatment. The squeaky wheel gets the grease." In general, Blood gangs such as Black P Stone, Crenshaw Mafia Gangsters, and Inglewood

TABLE 4.1. Annual Statistics: Gang-Related Crimes in Inglewood (1989–1998)

Crime	1989	1990	1991	1992	1993	1994	1995	1996	1997	1998
Homicide										
Gang-related incidents	23	32	27	31	25	32	22	16	13	20
Total incidents	45	55	48	37	44	46	41	28	24	35
Gang related (%)	51.1	60.0	56.3	83.8	56.8	69.6	53.7	57.1	54.2	57.1
Felony assault										
Gang-related incidents	259	329	377	339	275	253	232	249	216	166
Total incidents	903	917	1,063	1,122	858	832	814	902	810	738
Gang related (%)	28.7	35.9	35.5	30.2	32.1	30.4	28.5	27.6	26.7	22.5
Rape or attempted rape										
Gang-related incidents	11	33	28	23	17	13	23	19	11	18
Total incidents	69	103	69	65	68	47	60	61	61	33
Gang related (%)	15.9	32.0	40.6	35.4	25.0	27.7	38.3	31.1	18.0	54.5
Robbery										
Gang-related incidents	210	485	601	444	244	264	316	286	223	147
Total incidents	1,121	1,488	1,542	1,342	1,329	1,071	1,006	952	735	682
Gang related (%)	18.7	32.6	39.0	33.1	18.4	24.6	31.4	30.0	30.3	21.6
Burglary										
Gang-related incidents	8	49	87	75	51	49	69	71	53	31
Total incidents	1,672	1,866	1,998	1,925	1,561	1,230	1,096	1,079	1,088	941
Gang related (%)	0.5	2.6	4.4	3.9	3.3	4.0	6.3	6.6	4.9	3.3
Street terrorism										
Gang-related incidents	0	1	0	6	6	12	16	19	17	18
Shootings – inhabited buildings										
Gang-related incidents	54	40	45	37	51	38	31	24	23	23
Documented gangs	na	na	na	na	na	na	31	31	31	31
Documented gang members	na	na	na	na	na	na	na	na	na	7,191

TABLE 4.2. *Inglewood's Eight Largest Gangs (1999)*

Gang	Members (#)	Primary Ethnicity	Affiliation
Black P Stone	716	African American	Bloods
Crenshaw Mafia Gangsters	403	African American	Bloods
Inglewood Family	499	African American	Bloods
Inglewood 13	428	Hispanic	Latin
Lennox 13	1,487	Hispanic	Latin
Raymond Ave. Crips	549	African American	Crips
Rollin 60s	1,165	African American	Crips
Tepus	415	Hispanic	Latin

Family were in the northern half of the city, and Hispanic gangs, such as Lennox 13 and Inglewood 13, claimed turf in the southwestern area. Crenshaw Boulevard, located in the southeastern corner of Inglewood, was claimed by Crip, Blood, and Latino gangs, resulting in a number of conflicts between the gangs.

Gang unit data were used to assess the magnitude of the gang problem from 1989 through 1998. Gang members had been responsible for a substantial amount of the city's violence and crime over the past ten years (Table 4.1). For example, 51 to 84 percent of homicides (annually) involved at least one gang member. Likewise, about 20 to 40 percent of felony assaults, rapes, and robberies were gang related. The data also indicated that about 3 to 6 percent of all burglaries were gang related.[1] Recently, however, there had been only about twenty-three drive-by shootings annually. We examined the mean change in gang-related activity in Inglewood, comparing the average number of offenses from 1989 through 1993 with offences committed from 1994 through 1998. The overall number of burglaries had fallen, but gang members were increasingly involved in them (Table 4.3). Conversely, the overall number of felony assaults had increased over the ten-year period by 6.3 percent, but gang members were less likely to be involved. Drive-by shootings had decreased by 40 percent between the two periods. Interestingly, the numbers of gang and nongang homicides, rapes, and robberies had declined substantially, but the proportion of gang members involved in these offenses had not changed.

---

[1] However, as one reviewer pointed out, identifying a suspect in a burglary, a probable requirement for identifying a crime as "gang-related," is difficult and might account for the low gang-related proportions.

TABLE 4.3. *Mean Change in Inglewood Gang Activity*

		1989–1993 Average	1994–1998 Average	Percent Change
Homicide	Gang-related incidents	139	103	−25.9
	Total incidents	229	174	−24.0
	Gang related (%)	60.7	59.2	−2.5
Felony assault	Gang-related incidents	1,579	1,116	−29.3
	Total incidents	3,853	4,096	6.3
	Gang related (%)	41.0	27.2	−33.7
Rape or attempted rape	Gang-related incidents	112	84	−25.0
	Total incidents	378	26.2	−30.7
	Gang related (%)	30.2	32.1	6.3
Robbery	Gang-related incidents	1,984	1,236	−37.7
	Total incidents	6,822	4,446	−34.8
	Gang related (%)	29.1	27.8	−4.5
Burglary	Gang-related incidents	270	273	1.1
	Total incidents	9,022	5,434	−39.8
	Gang related (%)	3.0	5.0	66.7
Street terrorism[a]	Gang-related incidents	13	82	530.8
Shooting – inhabited building	Gang-related incidents	227	139	38.8

[a] Street terrorism, for example, is described in the California Penal Code (Section 186.20–186.33) as "Any person who actively participates in any criminal gang activity with knowledge that its members engage in or have engaged in a *pattern of criminal gang activity* [emphasis added], and who willfully promotes, futhers, or assists in any felonious criminal conduct by members of that gang, shall be punished.... "

Perceptions of the Gang Problem

The Inglewood gang unit officers all agreed that the city was facing a "major" gang problem. The officers were asked to describe the kinds of problems associated with Inglewood gang members and to estimate the percentage of total crime committed by them. All of the gang unit officers stated that gang members were involved in everything. As one officer stated, "[Gangs are involved in] everything from petty theft to murder and everything in between." Another officer reiterated that gangs were involved in "every kind of problem you can think of. I think they create terror for the community."

Asked to estimate the percentage of all crime committed by local gang members, gang unit officers' estimates ranged from 75 to 86 percent.

Although they all agreed that gang members committed the majority of crimes, two of the three officers argued that gang activity had become less violent over the past few years. The two disagreed, however, about the reason for the deescalation. One believed that a prison-based gang had called for an end to violence, because it was having an impact on street-level drug trafficking.

I would say [gang-related crime has become] less violent, but that can change at any time. What I mean by that is any little feud can spark up a war with a rival gang. We have had several homicides ... [Interviewer: Why less violent recently?] For the Hispanic gangs in particular, the Mexican Mafia had something to do with that. What they did was, they basically monopolized all of the Hispanic gangs. They wanted to get a share of the revenue from the drug sales in the streets, and at the same time, they got some kind of a truce among Hispanic gangs in Southern California. They said that they would put on a green light ... on any gang who would not comply with the Mexican Mafia's orders. Since then, crime, gang-related crime, gang-related shooting around Hispanic gangs, stopped for a while. Then several gangs rebelled against them, and we went back to the old days. But they still seem to keep a little lid on it.

The other officer suggested that new legislation directed toward gang members and career criminals was deterring gang members from engaging in violence.

That's a hard question. I don't want to say they are less violent, but they are using high-powered rifles and sophisticated weapons, but crime has gone down, murders have gone down in the county of Los Angeles. But when they do get violent, it is violent.... [Interviewer: What has the reduction in crime been caused by?] I think they think twice with gang enhancement laws, three strike laws, so I think they think twice about doing a crime, but then the volatile portion comes when they do decide to do it, they know there are three strike laws....

The most veteran gang unit officer disagreed with the other two:

[There has been] less street activity ..., but it [has] become more violent. Because now we have gang members walking up on our other gang members, where they used to shoot from a car and hit you. It would usually be a non-life-threatening wound. Now they come up, walk behind you, and shoot you in the head, so now it is more violent crime.

Likewise, there was a strong consensus among internal stakeholders in Inglewood about the gang problem and its changing nature. Nearly all of the internal stakeholders believed that the city had a significant gang problem, but that gang violence had decreased in recent years.

Most internal stakeholders explained that many of the gang problems in Inglewood were associated with street level drug trafficking and that after the drug market had stabilized, associated gang problems subsided. For example, one detective in the aggravated assault unit noted that the Mexican Mafia brought stability by requiring their street level drug dealers to maintain a low profile in order not to disrupt drug markets. A burglary detective provided a similar assessment of the current situation:

[In the past] a lot of the problems were due to the introduction of crack. They found it was more profitable to sell dope than to shoot each other, and once they got into the drug selling business, the level of violence declined.

External stakeholders in Inglewood were somewhat similar to internal stakeholders in that they believed that gangs were a major problem in their city, but they differed in that they did not indicate that the problem had diminished in recent years. Instead, external stakeholders in Inglewood focused on the present; and the tenor of their responses, when compared to internal stakeholders, suggested that the gang problem in the city was still very serious. In our discussions with them they tended to emphasize gang member involvement in violence and drug trafficking.

For instance, a prosecutor in the district attorney's office maintained that the gang problem "is very extensive. From my experience, there are times when there is a crime almost every night of a violent nature. There are...neighborhoods that are completely controlled by the gangs....They are a very predominant part of this community." Similarly, a gang intelligence officer in a California state correctional institution believed that the area had "a large gang problem." A gang coordinator with the Inglewood parole office described how he viewed the nature of the problem:

The gang problem is heavily drug based, in terms of drug dealing. At the current time, Hispanic gangs are fighting each other. Old gangsters are coming out of prison, they come back to claim their own territory from young gang members. They want to reclaim the territory for purposes of drug dealing.

While most of the external stakeholders saw gangs as a major problem in the city because of their heavy involvement in violence and drug dealing one city graffiti officer disagreed. He stated, " ...kids from high school...form little gangs, little cliques. They have areas that they hang out at....There's not really a lot of real tough gangs."

TABLE 4.4. *Albuquerque Gang Demographics (1998, 1999)*

		1998	1999
Number of gang members		7,535	5,647
Gender (%)	Male		88.9
	Female		11.0
	Unknown		0.1
Ethnicity (%)	Hispanic		81.4
	Black		8.5
	White		7.6
	Native American		1.3
	Asian		0.6
	Unknown/other		0.6
Age (%)	14 and under		0.6
	15–17		9.9
	18–24		64.8
	25–35		21.8
	36 and over		2.0
	Unknown		0.9
Street gangs (#)		260	
Primary ethnicity of gang (%)	Hispanic	35	
	Black	23	
	White	10	
	Asian	1	
	Multirace	31	

ALBUQUERQUE

In 1999, the APD's GREAT system showed that there were 5,647 documented gang members in the city (Table 4.4). This represented a 25 percent decline when compared with the number of gang members documented in 1998. Police officials explained that the apparent decline was actually the result of the gang unit having updated the department's gang database, purging a large number of inactive gang members from the system. Also in 1999, the gang intelligence system showed that roughly 90 percent of Albuquerque's documented gang members were male, while 10 percent were female. These figures are similar to those from other police agencies across the country, both large and small, that show that nine out of every ten gang members recognized by the police are male.

Gang unit records showed that few documented gang members were under eighteen years old (10.5 percent) or over thirty-six years old (2.9 percent). Rather, the majority of gang members were between the ages of eighteen and twenty-four years (64.8 percent), followed by those between twenty-five and thirty-five years old (21.8 percent). In terms of ethnicity, 81.4 percent of documented gang members were Hispanic, 8.5 percent were black, 7.6 percent were white, 1.3 percent were Native American, 0.6 percent were Asian, and 0.6 percent were of another ethnic group or mix (Table 4.4).

In 1998, Albuquerque's gang unit identified 260 local gangs. According to the unit, 35 percent were comprised primarily of Hispanic members, 23 percent primarily of black gang members, 10 percent primarily of white gang members, 1 percent primarily of Asian gang members, and 31 percent of the gangs were comprised of members from different ethnic backgrounds (Table 4.4). Of the 260 gangs, fifteen were considered by the gang unit to be significantly more influential and/or dangerous than the others. The majority of influential gangs were comprised of Hispanic gang members; all but two had more than 100 members. Furthermore, all of the influential gangs were believed by the gang unit to be involved in drug trafficking and violence (Table 4.5).

The APD had never formally tracked the number of crimes committed by documented gang members. When we asked police administrators, managers, and officers why no data were collected on gang crime, all of them referred to the amount of time that it would take to collect the information. Some of those closely involved in managing the gang unit also claimed that people within the department could not agree on a definition of gang crime. The gang unit's sergeant believed that they should use a "gang-related" definition, by which if either the offender or victim was a documented gang member, the incident would be recorded as a gang crime. The police chief believed that the sergeant's method would portray the city's gang problem inaccurately, giving the impression that the gang problem was more serious than it actually was. Instead, he wanted to use a "motive-based" definition, by which if a crime was committed for the furtherance of a gang, the incident would be recorded as a gang crime. Given the amount of time that data collection might take, and the disagreement about how to collect the data, it was simply easier for the unit not to collect the information.

The argument between the sergeant and the police chief was not inconsequential, as it has in fact been found to have profound implications for defining the scope of a city's gang problem. Cheryl Maxson and Malcolm Klein (1990) applied two the definitional approaches to homicides recorded in Los Angeles. One of the definitions required evidence of gang motivation for a crime to be recorded as a gang crime,

TABLE 4.5. *Albuquerque's Fifteen Most Influential/Dangerous Gangs (1998)*

Gang	Members (#)	Primary Ethnicity	Criminal Activity
Brewtown	113	Hispanic	Drug trafficking and violence
Rollers Only	7	Hispanic	Drug trafficking, violence, and auto theft
Barelas	254	Hispanic	Heroin sales, auto theft, and armed robbery
San Jose	895	Hispanic	Heroin and crack sales and violence
Los Padillas	163	Hispanic	Crack cocaine trafficking
18th Street	605	Hispanic	Narcotics trafficking and violence
14th Street	191	Hispanic	Narcotics trafficking and violence
Surenos	407	Hispanic	Drug trafficking, carjackings, violence
Duranes	151	Hispanic	Narcotics trafficking and violence
Los Carnales Locos	88	Hispanic	Narcotics trafficking and violence
South Side Locos	261	Hispanic	Narcotics trafficking and violence
Westgate Locos	414	Hispanic	Drug trafficking, auto theft, and violence
Uptown Kings	116	Hispanic	Narcotics trafficking and violence
Crips	165	Black	Narcotics trafficking and violence
Bloods	127	Black	Narcotics trafficking and violence

Albuquerque Police Department (1999), Gang Status Report for Albuquerque, NM.

while the other definition recorded the crime as a gang crime if either the offender or victim was a gang member. When the authors applied the more restrictive motive-based definition to the homicide data, the estimated rate of gang homicides was reduced by approximately 50 percent when compared to the more broad member-based definition.

Perceptions of the Gang Problem

Seven of the eight gang unit officers in Albuquerque believed that the city had a major gang problem. Asked to describe the types of problems that gang members caused, most officers gave general descriptions such as, "They are involved in everything." A number of them specified violence, drug trafficking, and property offenses. For example, one officer stated:

Pretty much anything from drive-by shootings to burglaries to drug-related problems to...you name the type of crime. Probably right now it's become more drug-related. I think it's financially more beneficial for them to be involved in anything that's drug-related. I think they've gone away from just, what we call the "stupid crimes," the drive-by shootings just for no reason. There's a purpose for everything they do now and we're aware of that. We see gang members that's walking around with thousands of dollars on them, Rolexes, nice clothes, nice cars. Now I think it's a profit, it's a business, that's what it is.

Another officer agreed, saying, "Everything you can think of. Homicides, drug trafficking, drive-by shootings, beatings, robberies, burglaries, and any crime you can think of, they do." Still another responded, "Everything. Everything that you can think of, but I think the biggest problem is drugs."

Estimating the percentage of total crime that the officers believed was committed by gang members, half of the officers estimated that gangs accounted for about 70 percent of the crime in the city, and a quarter of the officers believed that about 30 to 55 percent of the crime was caused by gang members. Six of the eight gang unit officers believed that gang activity had become more violent in recent years. Most officers who believed this attributed the problem to the availability of guns. One officer explained, "More violent, because the crimes that they are committing with weapons, instead of using a Saturday Night Special, they are using automatic weapons, assault rifles, and that type of stuff."

Another officer stated, "In recent years, it has been more [violent]. Everybody's got guns." Likewise, a gang unit officer agreed that the amount of gang violence attributed to gangs was high, depending on the type of gang violence, but pointed out that the department's administration did not agree with his view. He explained:

The crime stats seem to be down as far as drive by shootings and things like that, but our gang homicides are up. Geez, anywhere from three to five drive-by shootings a week. And our homicides are running probably – the chief would probably tell you like 7 percent. I would probably tell you 40 to 50 percent, at least, if not higher. At a certain part of this year, nine out of ten homicides were, maybe not gang-motivated, but a gang member was involved.

Two other officers disagreed. They maintained that gang violence had remained about the same in recent years. One stated, "I would say,

about the same. It's just changed. The sophistication level is different."
Another stated:

Violence-wise, I think it has stayed probably the same. I don't see it becoming
more violent. The reason being, is because I think that they have slowed down
on their drive-bys, so that it doesn't draw attention to the neighborhoods, so they
can be involved in more monetary crimes. See, if you are doing the drive-bys
and the shootings, then you would draw more attention to that neighborhood. If
you don't do them – but then I don't see a real large decrease, but I don't see an
increase.

There was a lack of consensus about the seriousness of the city's
gang problem among internal stakeholders in Albuquerque – with most
internal stakeholders stating that the city had a moderate to minor
gang problem. Some internal stakeholders expressed the view that while
Albuquerque had a relatively large number of gang members, violence
was not especially bad. For example, a commander in a police district
that is generally thought to have one of the area's worst gang problems
gave this moderate assessment of the local gang problem:

The extent of it – I would classify it as fairly extensive for a community of our
size. I think we probably have, per capita, more gang members than most cities
our size. The nature of it is that it's not as bad as it could be, given how many
people we do have as gang members. There is obviously some violence associated
with gangs . . . but for the number we have, things could be a lot worse in terms
of violence.

Internal stakeholders who perceived that the city had a moderate gang
problem explained that neighborhood gangs had existed in Albuquerque
for many generations. They further explained that many of these gangs
were involved in street level drug trafficking that occasionally resulted in
violence as a consequence of conflicts over control of the drug market.
One supervisor from the violent crimes unit explained:

Most of the community's gang problem has been around for a long time. As far as
law enforcement is concerned, most of it is influenced from the west coast. . . . They
wanted to control the crack market. I guess in California a rock of crack goes for
between five and ten bucks. Out here the market was twenty to twenty-five dollars.
So organized gangs saw it as an easy profit. . . and they used violence and of lot of
murders to control [the drug market].

Many of the school resource officers interviewed, who worked closely
with youth in Albuquerque, however, stated that the gang problem
in Albuquerque was relatively minor. One stated: "It's not that bad."

Another explained, "Most of the gang members that we have... [in] school are not that heavily involved in gang activity. More what you would call wannabes." Another school resource officer placed the gang problem in a historical context, indicating that that the current gang problem is not as serious as it once was in the city.

Well, I think back in 1995–1996 we did have a gang problem. We had reciprocal problems with the Crips and Bloods and whatever, and the subcultures of them. But in the last 2 or 3 years, I'd say 2 years, the gang influence isn't that much. The only kind of gangs we have are just like other students that... want to force their way of thinking on other students... they're wannabes.

A few internal stakeholders believed that the city's gang problem was serious. However, they offered few specifics in terms of the problems they caused or the types of crimes they were involved in. Their comments were similar to those below:

I think it's increasing. We do have a major gang problem. The gangs are filtering in from California, moving eastward. We also have a lot of Hispanic gangs coming from south, from over the border. We deal right now with an ever growing population of a gang called the Burritos. They're growing. They're predominantly Spanish speakers only, and they're a force to be reckoned with.

You know I can't quote you exact figures, but I know from what I've seen here that we have a gang problem that I think most people in this town are totally unaware of. I don't know.

Conversely, there was a strong consensus about the seriousness of the gang problem among most external stakeholders in Albuquerque. Specifically, external stakeholders generally believed that their city has a major gang problem. For example, an Albuquerque juvenile prosecutor made the claim: "From my perspective, I think we have a tremendous gang problem in Albuquerque. The way I see it is the amount of violence that is going on." A juvenile probation supervisor described it as a "fairly large problem," and the director of a local intervention program believed the area had "a big gang problem."

Many of the external stakeholders made reference to the substantial amount of violence that was associated with the gang problem. A director of a youth outreach program commented about the high level of gang violence, then added, " ... there's a lot of violence, period, not just gang violence." An external stakeholder from a state-level commission on crime and delinquency agreed that violence was on the increase, and attributed that to the move of gangs toward profitable enterprises:

The commercialization of gangs has probably been the most profound impact. By commercialization, I mean the profitability of drugs, the selling of things. Turf issues have always remained pretty much the same. The way they protect turf has changed because of the commercialization of gangs. With that, and I don't know if that is a term that you use, but the profit motive has brought about more violence.

One district attorney explicated the seriousness of the city's gang problem by sharing how gang violence has affected the daily lives of residents and those who he worked with.

I think that the way the gang problem presents itself mostly in the public is that they hear about the drive-by shootings. And just about the feelings of insecurity that the public has because of all the different shootings and generally they are by gang members. I think that just the confidence the public has in being able to go outside late at night. Even people around the office, they just don't feel comfortable going out at certain times, going to certain places.

Of interest was the fact that external stakeholders in Albuquerque tended not to be aware of historical changes in the fundamental nature of their city's gang problem. In other words, they rarely contextualized the magnitude of the city's gang problem in terms of prior levels of gang crime and violence. Instead, they tended to focus on current problems associated with gangs. However, when they did recognize such changes, they usually had to do with the gang problem getting worse. For example, an intensive probation supervisor described how the problem had worsened in Albuquerque:

I've been here since 1984, and I see it getting progressively worse. It seems to be more organized now with some the gangs. There seems to be a lot movement now between the gangs and the institution [prison]. It's very well organized back and forth between the streets and the institutions for a couple of gangs. The violence has gotten higher. It seems to be more indiscriminate and it seems to be younger and younger, as far as I see.

LAS VEGAS

In 1994, the Las Vegas Metropolitan Police Department Gang Unit began collecting data pertaining to gangs, gang members, and gang crime. The number of gangs in Las Vegas had increased substantially from 119 in 1994, to 164 in 1999 (Table 4.6).

Likewise, the number of gang members and associates increased almost twofold over that period. Specifically, the number of documented

TABLE 4.6. *Las Vegas Gangs and Gang Members (1994 through 1999)*

	1994	1995	1996	1997	1998	1999
Gangs	119	146	159	167	179	164
Gang members	3,508	4,263	5,098	5,805	6,232	6,608
Gang associates	1,387	1,623	2,051	2,343	2,580	2,774
Gang member ethnicity (%)						
Hispanic	34	39	41	42	43	na
Black	40	37	35	35	34	na
White	17	17	16	16	15	na
Asian	8	7	6	6	6	na
Other	1	0	0	0	1	na
Gang member and associate ages (%)						
Under 13	1	0	1	1	1	na
13–15	8	7	6	4	2	na
16–17	18	17	14	11	8	na
18–21	41	43	41	40	37	na
22–24	19	19	21	23	26	na
25 and older	13	14	17	21	26	na

Data from the Las Vegas Metropolitan Police Department Gang Unit – Annual Reports, 1994 through 1998.

gang members increased from 3,508 in 1994, to 6,608 in 1999, and the number of gang associates increased from 1,387 to 2,774.[2]

As of 1998, most documented gang members in the city were Hispanic (43 percent), followed by blacks (34 percent), whites (15 percent), Asians (6 percent), and others (1 percent). Examining the ethnicity of gang members over the five-year period from 1994 through 1998 showed that gang members had been increasingly coming from the Hispanic community, while the proportion of black gang members had substantially declined. The data showed little change in the proportion of gang members who were white, Asian, or other.

The gang unit's files also provided information on the ages of gang members and their associates. In 1998, only about 1 percent of

[2] As one reviewer rightly explained, it is important to distinguish between those who associate with gangs and gang associates. "Gang associates" in the sense discussed here refers to an administrative label placed on an individual based on the criteria that were used to document them. Conversely, a person who associates with gangs is just that, a person who is less involved in the gang or technically not a member of the gang, but is someone who just hangs out with gang members.

TABLE 4.7. *Las Vegas's Eleven Largest Gangs (1998)*

Gang	Members (#)	Primary Ethnicity
18th Street	508	Hispanic
28th Street	745	Hispanic
Lil Locos	357	Hispanic
Santana Chuco	776	Hispanic
Varrio Naked City	240	Hispanic
White Fence	207	Hispanic
Donna Street Crips	279	Black
Gerson Park Kingsmen	559	Black
Piru Bloods	213	Black
Rollin 60s	352	Black
West Coast Bloods	267	Black

Las Vegas Metropolitan Police Department, 1999. *Annual Report – 1998*. Las Vegas: Author.

documented gang members were under thirteen years of age, while 2 percent were between thirteen and fifteen, 8 percent were between sixteen and seventeen, 37 percent were between eighteen and twenty-one, 26 percent were between twenty-two and twenty-four, and 26 percent were twenty-five or older. In other words, almost 90 percent of the documented gang members and their associates in Las Vegas were adults. It appeared, however, that this was a new trend. As recently as 1994, almost one-third of gang members had been juveniles. This finding was contrary to much of the research literature, which suggests that a defining characteristic of emerging gang cities is that their gangs are largely comprised of juveniles (Spergel et al. 1994). This suggested that the gang problem in Las Vegas was far more serious and chronic than one might have expected, considering that the city had only relatively recently developed its gang problem.

According to the gang unit's database, there were eleven gangs in Las Vegas with at least 200 members; six were comprised primarily of Hispanic gang members and five primarily of black gang members (Table 4.7). Black gangs in Las Vegas typically claimed territory in the western part of the city and lived in public housing complexes. Police officials claimed that the black gangs were responsible for a disproportionate amount of street-level drug sales, particularly marijuana and crack cocaine. Hispanic gang members, located primarily in the eastern half of the city, were not as concentrated within the city as were black gang

TABLE 4.8. *Gang Activity in Las Vegas – 1994 Through 1998*

	1994	1995	1996	1997	1998
Drive-by shootings[a]	433	527	327	276	196
Drive-by shooting victims[a]	Unknown	119	140	93	66
Shooting victims, other[a]	Unknown	Unknown	Unknown	77	27
Dead gang members[a]	20	24	45	35	22
Homicides	12	18	39	32	19
Suicides	7	6	3	3	1
Other	1	0	3	0	2
Gang-related felonies[b]	Unknown	433	291	529	526
Guns recovered from gang members[b]	Unknown	246	145	283	203

[a] Data from Las Vegas Metropolitan Police Department Gang Unit Annual Reports, 1994 through 1998.
[b] Data from an unpublished report provided by the Las Vegas Metropolitan Police Department Gang Unit, 1999.

members. Police officials stated that although Hispanic gang members were involved in street-level drug trafficking, the majority of their criminal activity involved conflicts with other gangs that had claimed nearby territory.

Table 4.8 shows the gang activity that took place in Las Vegas between 1994 and 1998. In 1998, the police department collected data on 196 drive-by shootings, sixty-six drive-by shooting victims, twenty-seven non-drive-by shooting victims, and twenty-two gang members who had been killed. Of the twenty-two gang members who had been killed, nineteen died in homicides, one died from suicide, and two died in another manner (e.g., natural death, traffic accident, etc.). The table also shows that 526 gang-related felonies occurred and 203 guns were recovered from gang members in 1998.

When we examined trends in gang activity over the past five years, the analysis illustrated that some gang-related activity had decreased substantially. In particular, the number of drive-by shootings, and the number of victims injured from drive-by shootings, had decreased by about 50 percent over this period. On the other hand, the data showed that although the number of gang homicides had decreased from a peak in 1996, the number of gang homicides in 1998 was still higher than in 1994 and 1995. In addition, the number of documented gang-related felonies had increased and the number of guns recovered from gang members had been fairly uneven, increasing and decreasing from one year to the next.

Perceptions of the Gang Problem

As in Inglewood and Albuquerque, Las Vegas gang unit officers were asked to characterize the state of the current gang problem as major, moderate, or minor. Of the thirty-one officers questioned, about 45 percent believed that the city had a major gang problem and about 55 percent believed that the city had a moderate gang problem. A number of the officers who believed that the city had a moderate gang problem compared the problem in Las Vegas with their perception of the problem in Los Angeles. Most of the officers' comments were similar to the following examples:

In Las Vegas, I would say that they're a moderate problem compared to others [like] Los Angeles. I truly think that we've pretty much kept a pretty good thumb on the gangsters. We know what they are doing and we put a pretty good thumb on them. I don't think it's got out of control. A major problem would be out of control where you just have rampant robbing and murdering, and cops don't go into the neighborhood because they are getting shot at and beat up. So I think we have pretty much a handle on it, because when we find out what is going on in an area, we take our guys and we go in there and take care of the problem through enforcement or task force or whatever. We've done that a bunch of times, and I think it's working pretty good.

At this stage, in Las Vegas, I would say [the gang problems are] moderate, and within 10 years, they'll be major. We'll be a little Los Angeles.

I would say – I would not classify us – we do not have a major gang problem because we do not let it get out of control. Los Angeles, they have a major problem ... the gangs run that city. But as far as us, we are a tourist city and we cannot afford to let gangs get control here so we are very, very strict. I'd say it's a moderate problem.

Many of the officers who claimed that the city had a major gang problem implied that the problem could not be thought of in any other way. They were adamant that if a person were to think of the problem as less than "major," it would be tantamount to letting one's guard down, which might result in a more serious gang problem for the city. One gang unit officer stated, "I'm going to say 'major,' because if you take it too lightly, you can get overwhelmed. You as a department or a city can become overwhelmed by the problem if you take it too lightly."

Another officer concurred: "I want to say 'major,' because we want our community not to be overrun with gang members."

Whether officers believed that the Las Vegas gang problem was of major or moderate magnitude, most believed that the problem was the result of gang migrations to the area. The officers recognized that Las Vegas did have some indigenous gangs with a long-standing presence in the community, but most were specific about attributing much of the serious gang activity in the city to gang members migrating from Los Angeles. For example, one gang unit officer explained, " . . . I mean we had some [gang members] from here. But the majority of the hard-cores and violent crimes are people moving from other jurisdictions." A gang unit sergeant added, "Oh, there's a big problem with [gang migration]. Every guy you see here on the corner slinging rock is an L.A. gangster." Still another sergeant stated,

> . . . We do have some well-established gangs here, some well-established violent gangs. But we're also seeing all the time these California gangsters coming in. 18th Street originated in L.A., they're 200 deep here now. I swear to God, it seems like everybody is from California. Off the top of my head, the last time I had anyone from somewhere else was Salt Lake City.

When we asked the officers directly whether they believed that migration was the cause of the local gang problem, almost 60 percent responded with an unqualified "yes," and another 20 percent responded that gang migration was at least partially responsible.[3]

With regard to criminality, most of the officers explained that gang members in Las Vegas engaged in a wide variety of crimes, and that they did not specialize in any one type. When asked about the types of crimes committed by gang members, most officers gave responses similar to the three below:

> From beer skips, petty larceny, all the way up to homicide.

> I can't think of anything that they don't get involved in.

> Name it, we got it. We've got destruction of private property with the tagging. All kinds of vandalism with anything, stolen vehicles, robberies, burglaries, murders, assaults, home invasions, sexual assault. There is nothing they don't do.

---

[3] The other 20 percent indicated that they did not know whether migration had had an impact on the gang problem. However, no officers believed that gang migration had *no* impact on the city's gang problem.

A modest number of officers, while agreeing that gang members engaged in a variety of criminal activities, felt that the major problem for residents was the fear and intimidation that gangs instilled in them:

Well, the way I look at it, they disrupt the every day life. They make people afraid to walk the street at night. People, good people, living in the neighborhood who will not go out after dark. They're – a perfect example, I had a friend of mine who used to work for one of the highway rental places here in town, and he worked day shift. And he said during day shift while everybody was in school, the neighborhoods, and the nicest people in the neighborhoods, but as soon as 3:00 came, all the nice people disappeared. And then all of a sudden, all of the gang members and shitbags come out. You know, people have to – well, I grew up on the East Coast and, you know, it's a small town, but you could walk down the street and leave your front door unlocked. You know, you can't do that in this town. You can't go anywhere. You know, I think about what I'm going to do with my 3-year-old daughter when she's got to go to school. I worry about where she's going to go to school already, she's only 3 years old. What high school is she going to go to? Every high school has problems.

Well, I mean, to me, they cause, I mean, just being a regular citizen, they cause fear. I mean, we've had times when people were at the mall just shopping. Gang members go in there and steal something, and the next thing you know, they are in a shoot-out in the parking lot. So I think for the everyday citizen that just goes out and goes to the store or to work, or something like that, it's a problem. Because it could happen to anybody, anywhere.

When we asked the officers to estimate the percentage of total local crime that gang members accounted for, their responses were inconsistent. About half of the officers acknowledged that they were not sure of the answer, but a quarter of the officers estimated that about 50 percent of crime in Las Vegas was attributable to gangs, and another quarter of the officers estimated that between 5 and 85 percent of crime in Las Vegas was attributable to gangs.

The "we don't know" response contrasted sharply with the responses of officers in the other cities that we studied. Perhaps the Las Vegas officers were simply more willing to acknowledge that they did not know, possibly because such information about gang crime was not disseminated to gang unit officers, or perhaps the officers were simply not interested in the numbers.

About 65 percent of the officers agreed that gangs had become more violent in recent years, and many reported that the number of drive-by shootings and other gun-related offenses had increased. Another 20 percent believed that gang activity had decreased; these officers noted that gang crime typically fluctuated from year to year, but they were currently seeing less violence than in high gang crime years such as the early 1990s. The remaining 15 percent believed that gang violence had been stable in the past few years; none offered a basis for this conclusion.

Internal stakeholders in Las Vegas took a slightly different view of the city's gang problem. While none of the internal stakeholders spoke of the city having a major gang problem, most of them made reference to the fact that the problem had "spread" across the city. They explained that up until recently the city's gang problem was primarily restricted to the city's housing projects. In these neighborhoods there were serious gang problems that were characterized by gang turf wars, street-level drug sales, and high levels of violence.

In an effort to control the gang problem, the city closed down the housing projects where gangs were especially problematic and relocated families across the city to other housing projects. This had the unintended consequence of spreading the gang problem across the city. A lieutenant who had been with the police department for sixteen years described the situation:

The gang problem...as I saw it was pretty centralized. We had neighborhoods that were government-housing neighborhoods. We had gangs that were basically turf bound. In West Last Vegas where I grew up, I was familiar with the Gerson Park Kingsmen...an example of one of our most notorious turf gangs. It started out with things such as fights, turf battles...and evolved into more violent crimes. You know...drive-by shootings, walk-up shootings. It's interesting...about the Gerson Park Kingsmen – that entire government housing development was torn down. Through the evolution of time, we start to see the whole problem become more and more decentralized, and you start to see different gangs then develop as offshoots.

Another lieutenant provided a similar explanation:

One of the [city's] first reactions [to gangs] was to determine that a lot of the gang problem emanated out of our public housing projects. And they took people and moved them from this project to another project, to another project, to another project. So the gangs, actually the proliferation of them throughout the city, was actually facilitated by the city and county.... [But] all they did was like cut the worm into several different sections and moved it in different parts of the garden and now you have worms all over the garden.

With the geographic displacement of gang members across the city also came a change in the types of problems associated with gangs. Many of the internal stakeholders stated that turf and territory were no longer an issue for gangs and that they became more involved in street level drug dealing as well as more involved in the trafficking of narcotics. One sergeant described the current problem:

It's changed a lot. Oh, they were very territorial a few years back. There was a lot of public housing, um, in the section called West Side.... Those houses have either been town down or renovated and changed and because of it the gangs have seemed to spread out and there's more mobility. So there's different sets, you know, spread out throughout town. So the territory aspect doesn't seem to [be] quite as strong as it used to be. Some of the stronger gangs right now are probably narcotics related, what we see.... Gangs are probably the biggest suppliers in other words actually bringing in the product in to Las Vegas.

Only one internal stakeholder had a contrary view of the gang problem in Las Vegas. A lieutenant assigned to a command in a predominantly black area of the city had lived in Las Vegas for thirty-four years and had been on the force for ten years; he shared this perspective:

Well, up in the Rodney King era there were gangs. And the gangs ... basically a terror thing. You know, the Gerson Park, wherever public housing projects were. But I have never seen an organized effort at anything to where I would classify it as a gang. In some areas, there are 8, 9, 10 tough people in the area. And people tag on wearing colors, etcetera, for protection more than they are an active, organized gang. And then as far as activities, the only efforts you can really see are drug sales.

When compared to internal stakeholders, external stakeholders in Las Vegas were more likely to express that the city had a gang problem and that it was growing worse. Many of the responses from external stakeholders about the nature of the city's gang problem resembled the following comment made by a district attorney:

I've noticed that, uh, over the 8 years that I've been here in this office that the gang problem has become more and more, uh, in the forefront. Um, you know, it's noticible when your dealing with a defendant and you notice that they come from usually common areas like ... Los Angeles, the Southern California areas ... since the city has grown I've seen more and more, uh, gangs....

Another county official made a similar remark about the scope of the city's gang problem:

[Gangs] are everywhere. They're even in the nicest neighborhoods. My house got hit the other day, or my wall got done the other day.... So, I think they're a lot more mobile now.... I think their turf is getting pretty big now.

External stakeholders also differed from internal stakeholders in the extent to which they viewed gang members' involvement in drug trafficking. Specifically, external stakeholders emphasized that the gang problem had shifted from its historical turf-based orientation to today's more organizationally sophisticated, economically oriented gangs. Staff from the Las Vegas probation and parole unit tasked with supervising gang members noted:

Really, as the city got bigger, more commercialized with gaming, the gang members wanted to get more into that instead of staying on the street. They got smarter and more commercial. The majority of the gang activity we have out here are young individuals, and they're just mostly killing each other. The older gangbangers are more into the commercial stuff, getting into stuff like gaming or more professional, trying to make like they're legit. Well, that's just for a front, lets it look like they're doing something well, but underneath they're transporting drugs, they're doing more commercial stuff that we want to know about. It got more organized, much more of a business enterprise rather than a social group. Beating up each other became, it evolved into a business enterprise.

A local attorney made a similar response:

The turf concept is outdated . . . In my opinion [gangs] are becoming, rather than just street level, now becoming more sophisticated into narcotic levels. I know one case where, I know this guy was a documented leader of the 28th street gang and he was charged with attempted murder, slicing a kid at his neck with a knife. And, uh, he got like $100,000 bail on him and he's able to post it. And even though the judge wouldn't allow me to . . . find the source of the bill, he was suspected at the time because he was heavily involved with narcotics and that's how the revenue he was generating to get out of jail.

PHOENIX

The Phoenix gang unit began documenting gangs and gang members in 1990, when it documented 150 gangs and 1,778 gang members and associates (Table 4.9). By 1999, the number of gangs had more than doubled to 336, and the number of members had nearly quadrupled to 6,945. It is interesting to note that the number of documented gangs and gang members had risen steadily over this ten-year period.

Table 4.10 shows the number of gang members belonging to each type of gang, as classified by the Phoenix gang unit. In 2000, about 79

TABLE 4.9. *Numbers of Gangs and Gang Members in Phoenix (1990–1999)*

	1990	1991	1992	1993	1994	1995	1996	1997	1998	1999
Gang members and associates	1,778	2,789	3,265	3,717	3,478	3,759	4,136	5,057	6,776	6,945
Gang sets	150	253	na	298	320	381	319	357	341	336

TABLE 4.10. *Phoenix Gang Types and Affiliations (2000)*

Gang Types	Members	Associates	Total	Percent
Hispanic	5,244	352	5,596	78.7
Crip	902	87	989	13.9
Blood	161	7	168	2.4
Other black	179	7	186	2.6
Midwest	103	5	108	1.5
Other	55	5	60	0.8
No gang affiliation	3	5	8	0.1
TOTAL	6,647	488	7,115	100.0

percent of gang members and associates belonged to gangs classified as primarily Hispanic, and another 16 percent belonged to Crip and Blood gangs, comprised primarily of African American members. A few gang members and associates (1.5 percent) belonged to gangs from the Midwest, such as the Gangster Disciples and Latin Kings.

Gang unit statistics showed that most documented gang members and associates in Phoenix were adult males. Ninety-three percent were male; 7 percent were female. Only about 16 percent were juveniles. Like Las Vegas, Phoenix is a relatively new gang city, and the fact that most of its gang members were adults suggested that the problem had become more serious and chronic than was typical for new gang cities (Table 4.11).

Contrary to the finding mentioned previously, an examination of Phoenix gang crime trends indicated that the problem there did not appear to be serious or out of control. Since 1990, the gang unit had been collecting the data on numbers of gang homicides, aggravated assaults, and drive-by shootings. Gang crime was relatively infrequent early in the 1990s, increased substantially in the middle of the decade, and then declined in the late 1990s (Table 4.12). For example, gang homicides increased from three in 1990 to twenty-seven in 1994, then declined to

TABLE 4.11. *Gender of Phoenix Gang Members and Associates, by Age (2000)*

	15 and Under	16–17	Juveniles (%)	18–25	26 and Over	Adults (%)	Total Members	Total Percentages
Males	312	636	13.3	4,616	1,052	79.7	6,616	93.0
Females	80	95	2.5	296	28	4.6	499	7.0
TOTAL	392	731	15.8	4,912	1,080	84.2	7,115	100.0

TABLE 4.12. *Gang Activity in Phoenix (2000)*

	1990	1991	1992	1993	1994	1995	1996	1997	1998	1999
Homicides										
Gang related	3	11	20	21	27	21	13	11	17	4
Total incidents	128	128	136	158	231	214	186	175	187	216
Gang related (%)	2.3	8.6	14.7	13.3	11.7	9.8	7.0	6.3	9.1	1.9
Aggravated assaults										
Gang related	377	479	536	519	383	317	243	226	205	132
Total incidents	6,642	6,954	7,155	7,872	7,507	7,272	6,126	6,048	5,906	5,766
Gang related (%)	5.7	6.9	7.5	6.6	5.1	4.4	4.0	3.7	3.5	2.3
Drive-by shootings	171	118	134	155	98	114	108	86	73	28
Total violent incidents	580	888	918	865	649	519	408	385	331	232

four in 1999. Similar patterns were observed for aggravated assaults and drive-by shootings. However, for both kinds of crime, at the end of the decade, gang activity declined to all-time lows. For instance, in 1999, there were 66 percent fewer gang-aggravated assaults than in 1990, and the number of drive-by shootings decreased by about 84 percent during this period.

To further analyze the magnitude of the gang problem in Phoenix, we examined the proportion of total gang-related incidents for homicides and aggravated assaults. Depending on the year, 2 to 15 percent of homicides were found to be gang related. Over the ten-year period from 1990 through 1999, there were 1,759 homicides in Phoenix, of which 159 (9 percent) were recorded as gang related. A similar trend was observed for aggravated assault, with 2 to 8 percent of all aggravated assaults involving a gang member, depending on the year; 67,249 aggravated assaults were reported overall, with 3,417 (5 percent) recorded as gang related.

Perceptions of the Gang Problem

We asked the gang unit officers for their perceptions of the current gang problem. Seventy percent believed that the city had a major gang problem, and 30 percent described the gang problem as moderate. Although many officers offered little explanation for their opinions, a number of them who believed that the city had a major gang problem voiced concerns specifically about the impact of gang activity on the quality of life in Phoenix neighborhoods.

I'd say they're a major problem here. [Interviewer: Why?] They're a problem in the respect that they do basically terrorize their neighborhoods. And they take on their own neighbors and what-not like that. We have a lot of "shots fired" calls, and we obviously respond to them and find nothing there. We have a lot of drive-bys that we know are gang related that has no victims, and don't have enough information to really pinpoint who did it, but those are the things that happen continuously that are a major problem in the community.

I think that any type of gang problem is a major problem, and I say that because gangs are city-wide like the police department is, but in these gang-ridden neighborhoods, you have a lot of good people out there that want to get on with their lives, whether they're rich or they're poor, and be left alone. When you have one or two gang members in a neighborhood creating a disturbance, graffiti in vehicles, shooting out windows, harassing people's daughters, versus 30 gang members that are going to other gang neighborhoods and shooting them up....

The remaining officers who classified the city's gang problems as moderate emphasized two issues. One group noted that the seriousness of the gang problem fluctuated, and that currently, the gang problem was not as bad as at some other times.

Again, gang activity, it's hot and it's cold. Right now I would say moderate, but at times, it has been major.

It used to be they were a major problem. I'd say now, it's moderate. Its kinda . . . it goes in waves. I mean right now we're in the period where most of the old guys are in jail, most of the little guys are starting to get a little bit older, and in another year or two, the older guys are starting to get out of jail and the little guys are a little bit older, and they're gonna start taking their orders, and its going to be right back there, you know, where we were four years ago, just chasing everybody, which is a good time.

Another group of officers argued that the city's gang problem was moderate, but only because the gang unit was working to keep the problem from escalating.

. . . Gangs, I wouldn't consider it a minor problem, but is it the biggest problem that's happening in town? It's the type of problem that if you don't keep it in check, it can get out of hand.

I want to give it "major," but it's not at this point. I think it's one of those things that, if you don't keep a tight grip on it, it would in no time expand on its own.

When we asked about the types of problems that gangs caused, most officers commented that gang members were involved in a wide assortment of activities ranging from graffiti to homicide.

Just about the whole gamut of crimes. Stolen vehicles, drug sales, extortion, fraud schemes.

A real wide variety – drugs, intimidation, assaults, agg[ravated] assaults, robbery, murder, and about every kind of crime that's committed.

A few, however, focused on one problem area; about half of this group pointed out that gang members frequently used weapons and engaged in violence.

The biggest thing that I say they do is the drive-by shootings. Almost always their drive-by shootings target another gang member, but by virtue of them shooting from a moving vehicle, 50 percent of the time, the next door neighbor gets hit, the little baby inside the house gets hit. There's all this collateral damage from the drive-by. They're not hitting their designated target, and the bad thing with that is, these are innocent people that have nothing to do with the gang. If they drove by and shot and killed only that gang member, somehow I can understand a lot of it. But here's a kid playing across the street, or recently an old guy gardening, and he gets shot because they were aiming at the guy two houses down.

I think the street gangs are known for their weapon violations, either everyday assault, drive-by shootings, retaliation, home invasions, those type of crimes.

The other half of this group expressed concern about the fear and intimidation gang members caused for their neighbors. For example, one officer remarked:

I see...just a localized intimidation factor that some of these gangs have over their neighborhoods. You know, we've got some gangs that have been around since...that I've talked to members that have been around, you know, some guys that were in the gang in the late '50s. So you've got generations of almost control of some of these neighborhoods, and that I've seen as probably a major problem. That people don't quite understand, I mean, if you don't live in the neighborhood and they don't see it, then they don't understand that what these people go through in some of these small neighborhoods that are dominated by them.

Most officers concurred that a modest proportion of all local crime was attributable to gangs. Nearly all of them believed that gangs were responsible for 10 to 40 percent of the city's crime, a relatively small amount when compared with gang unit officers' perceptions in the other cities that we studied.

Most of the Phoenix officers agreed that local gang violence had declined over the past few years; however, they diverged on the reason for the decline. Some explained that gangs were becoming more business-like.

Less violent, they've kind of restructured themselves. They're looking more at the business end, whether it's the chop shops, the selling the dope, extortion type stuff. It's become more of a business. So we don't openly see the drive-by shooting, the stabbings that we had in the past. We still have them, but most of the time upon investigating them, we're finding out that there is a lot more of same-gang on same-gang violence. Where they're taking out somebody for ripping them off for their own dope or whatever.

Other officers believed that the decline in gang violence resulted from the gang unit's suppression efforts.

I believe in Phoenix, less violent and less numerous in occasion. [Interviewer: What's the basis for your evaluation?] I just think since the first year I was on the department working the 41 area, I can remember where on Buckeye Road, where West Side City hangs out, I can remember violent crimes there nightly, to now where that street is pretty much a ghost town except for normal citizens. Gangs are not on that road anymore, and the city as a whole, I would say that the violent crime, or the crime rate, period, as far as gang members go, has normally gone down since then through enforcement.

Another officer agreed:

I would say less violent, because we as a unit have gotten more organized and much more directed at them. We also now have the benefit of simple statutes that we can use against them, like the criminal syndicate charge and the allegation of gang activity, for sentencing. We're putting people away for a long time, and I think that's kinda sending them a message.

A small number of the interviewed officers believed that gang violence had increased in recent years. For example, one of them pointed out that the number of gang homicides had recently increased, and another commented that drive-by shootings and other weapons-related offenses were on the rise.

Internal stakeholder perceptions of the gang problem in Phoenix tended to reflect the generally held belief that the problem had moderated, and that the fundamental nature of gangs had changed. Specifically, many of the internal stakeholders in Phoenix took the view that gangs were a major problem for the city in the early 1990s but by the late 1990s the gang problem had dissipated or almost vanished. One officer made the comment:

Currently from what I see it's kinda dissolved in that [we] had a couple major sweeps and most of the major players are in jail, there's a lot [of] miscellaneous gang members hanging around with each other but right now they [are] not really doing anything gang per se, they may be out still committing crimes but nothing gang or anything like that.

Another detective made a similar observation:

A lot of that type of old traditional gang has gone away, at least in the Phoenix area from what I've seen.... They're still out there... but the vast majority of what the public and what a lot of regular law enforcement officers see is just these young street tough[s] with a given name to their block and that sort of thing.

Those that did not articulate that the gang problem had vanished explained that the gang problem in Phoenix had become less serious than in the past. A sergeant working in a high-crime precinct described the changing nature of the gang problem:

I think things have calmed down a bit. I'm with Central City only. That's all I've worked, all I know. I think things have calmed down a lot as far as the street warfare that I've seen over the years. I don't really know a reason for that. I don't know if they're going out of the precinct or things like that, but I haven't seen near the gang violence that I saw when I first came on 6 years ago. I have seen a steady kind of decrease here in the precinct.

A commander who was the former head of the gang unit provided a similar assessment of the changes over time:

Then, in 1993, I was the south precinct shift lieutenant where I was in charge of the shift three staff. Gang-related violence was pretty much at an all time high – shootings very frequently, rival gangs, open notorious shootings, cruising on South Central, and the biggest problem was rival gangs crossing paths and having shootouts in the middle of the night. I left in 1994. I came back in 1997...I noticed immediately a distinct difference between then and now. The violence had gone down. We could see it. We could feel it. The violence is still there and unacceptable, the gangs are still there, but the rivalry and everything else isn't as high.

A lieutenant from patrol was the only internal stakeholder that had a more mixed assessment of the problem. He had worked in the gang unit in its early days, and had been shot and wounded in the line of duty by a gang member.

I think the gang problem has gotten a lot worse that it has been, but in a lot of neighborhoods where we got special grants and special programs, and especially with the growth of the gang unit over the years, we move better on gang problems, and in some areas it has gone down and some areas it has gone up. In some areas, Hispanics gangs, all gang activity, has probably gone up in general, but in some neighborhoods it has decreased. Black gangs have definitely gone up....

In Phoenix, while external stakeholders were split in terms of whether the gang problem was worsening, they tended to generally see the gang problem as more serious when compared to internal stakeholders. For example, an assistant county prosecutor assigned to the gang prosecution unit described the problem as follows:

I think it's very extensive. We have a number of gangs within Maricopa County, but predominantly the Phoenix metropolitan area. The nature of it is probably, there are a couple of different realms, a lot of the gang activity is focused around the drug dealing aspect of it, and the gangs have their focus in dealing drugs. And the gang activity is done to protect that aspect of it.

Another gang coordinator gave a similar response, but voiced concern about the age of newer gang members and their involvement in violence.

Here in metropolitan Phoenix...I think it's growing. I think the nature of it has changed in that the youth that are getting involved are much younger...a lot of the older ones are in prison but they're coming out now and I'm seeing them come back to the street and kind of recruiting and reorganizing. Our youth are younger. I think they're more violent.

Other external stakeholders in Phoenix believed that the gang problem was becoming less serious; however, none of them believed that the gang problem was minimal or nonexistent. Instead, these stakeholders tended to point to the fact that the gang problem in the city had been more serious in previous years but that the gang problem had subsided as of recent years. For example, the director of a program that works with gang members felt that the gang problem had been "curtailed somewhat," and attributed this to proactive prevention and intervention programming.

Likewise, a former Phoenix police officer who had taken a management position with another nearby police agency explained that in the mid-1980s gang membership increased in Phoenix and with it gangs become more organized, and more neighborhoods became affected by gangs. However, he emphasized that by the mid-to-late 1990s the gang problem had subsided and that gangs were no longer the problem that they once were.

SUMMARY

The measurement of gangs, gang members, and gang crime is far from perfect, and relying on any one data source to gauge a community's gang problem is hazardous, at best. For that reason, in trying to assess the magnitude and nature of the gang problem in our study communities, we examined official data on the numbers of gangs, gang members, and gang crime. However, we supplemented this with information with interviews obtained from gang unit officers as well as internal and external stakeholders. Although there were some inconsistencies, an examination of data from these various sources led to the following conclusions.

All of the study cities had experienced dramatic rises in the number of documented local gang members. Documented gang members in each of the cities were typically male (90–99 percent), minority (85–100 percent) adults. Gang members lived in poor neighborhoods with a high proportion of minority residents, often times in multifamily housing complexes.

The data also suggested that since the early 1990s, the number of gangs had increased in all three of the cities for which we had data. We found that police agencies in all four of the cities rarely analyzed data on the social and organizational composition of gangs, other than tracking the number of gang members in each gang. However, two of the agencies (Albuquerque and Las Vegas) had performed some modest analyses examining the primary ethnicity of gangs and the types of crimes some gangs were more inclined to commit.

Analysis of each department's gang crime data showed a general decline in gang violence. The only exception was Albuquerque, where the gang unit, which was responsible for the collection of gang intelligence, had not collected data on gang crime because of differences in opinion between the gang unit and the chief of police about how to define gang crime. The units that did collect gang crime data, collected data on a very small number of offense categories. This had the unintended effect of creating a stereotype that gang crime was nonversatile.[4] With this said, we found that among the units that collected gang crime data, the data indicated that the magnitude of each city's objective gang problem varied substantially across the sites with Inglewood having a relatively sizeable gang problem, Las Vegas having a moderately sized gang problem, and Phoenix having a relatively minor gang problem.[5]

In addition, we found that the majority of the officers' perceived the magnitude of their local gang problem to be greater than indicated by the official gang crime data recorded by their department. Except in Las Vegas, the vast majority of officers in each unit perceived that their city had a major gang problem, that gang members engaged in a wide variety of criminal behaviors, and that roughly 30 to 70 percent of all local crimes were probably attributable to gang members.[6] Data collected by the gang units indicated, however, that gang members actually contributed to a relatively small proportion of local crime (except Inglewood), and that each city had experienced a reduction in gang crime, particularly violent crime, in recent years. Consequently, the gang units we studied were operating in a somewhat paradoxical context: more gang members, a heightened perception of local gang problems, but fewer (and in some cases, very few) actual incidences of gang crimes.

---

[4] We would like to thank Malcolm Klein for bringing this issue to our attention.

[5] Anecdotal data obtained in Albuquerque suggested that its gang problem was moderate to minor – somewhere between Las Vegas and Phoenix.

[6] Las Vegas is excluded because most of those officers stated that they did not know the proportion of crime that was committed by gang members, and that such information was not pertinent to their jobs. However, most officers in Las Vegas did believe that the local gang problem had grown worse in recent years.

The misperception of the magnitude of the local gang problem held by many of the gang unit officers has the potential for misinforming policy makers about the nature and scope of the problem. Gang unit officers in all of the study sites were responsible for collecting, processing, and disseminating gang intelligence for the police department, as discussed in Chapter 3. Furthermore, gang unit officers often times served as "experts" on gang-related matters, and educated their institutional environment about the nature and extent of their community's gang problem. The information shared by gang unit officers, including their misperceptions of the problem, may in turn be used by policy makers to make decisions. In fact, all of the gang units we studied played some role in educating local politicians (either formally or informally) about their community's gang problem. Our findings thus suggest that data obtained from gang unit officers may lead to erroneous assessments of gang problems, which in turn may misinform policy agendas.

We also found important differences between internal and external stakeholders with regard to their perceptions of the gang problem. External stakeholders as a group tended to view the gang problem as more serious than did the internal stakeholders. Specifically, external stakeholders were more likely to either express that their city had a major gang problem, that their city's gang problem was worsening, or that the types of problems engaged in by gang members were of a more serious nature than did internal stakeholders. Additionally, when external stakeholders spoke about their city's gang problem, they were much more likely to enunciate the desperation of the situation.

One possible explanation for the differences in perception could be the differential contact and involvement with gangs and gang members of the two kinds of stakeholders. Although their respective gang units played a role in nominating individuals included in both our internal and external stakeholder groups, those who were *external* stakeholders probably had more direct contact with gangs. Several external stakeholders were in positions dedicated almost exclusively to dealing with gang members. For example, the group included prosecutors who had been assigned gang-related cases; correctional officers who had worked solely on gang intelligence; probation and parole officers who had supervised caseloads of gang members; and representatives of nonprofit gang-intervention organizations.

Internal stakeholders had varying, but generally limited, contacts with gangs. Typically, such contacts only occurred incidentally as the stakeholders carried out other police functions, perhaps patrols or investigations. With the exception of those in criminal justice policy agencies, the external stakeholders' work worlds were "gang filled," while gangs were only one segment of the work environment for internal stakeholders. Quite possibly, external stakeholders perceived the gang problem and related violence as more extensive because they had more extensive contacts with gangs.

It is also possible that external stakeholders, who by definition are outsiders, were more susceptible to influence from the media on high-profile gang incidents, as well as to gang unit lore from gang unit officers and others inside the police department. Such sources of information, in addition to their own work-related contacts with gang members, may have caused external stakeholders to perceive the gang problem as more serious.

Another commonality was that internal and external stakeholders tended to be much more focused on the types of crime engaged in by gang members in their city. In particular, there was a consensus among internal and external stakeholders that gangs in their community were heavily involved in drug sales, drug trafficking, and associated violence. Gang unit officers, on the other hand, went out of their way to make the point that gang members were generalists in their offending patterns.

In summary, we found that the scope and nature of each community's gang problem varied, but that there was a general decline in the level of gang crime across the study sites. We also found that each group (i.e., gang unit officers, internal stakeholders, and external stakeholders) had varying perceptions about the magnitude and nature of their community's gang problem and that few were able to accurately assess their city's gang problem when compared to their police agencies official data – even those who collected and compiled the data themselves.

As pointed out by Decker and Kemp-Leonard (1991), effectively responding to gangs requires a thorough understanding of the problem. The findings presented in this chapter show that the different groups of actors in each of the study sites lacked a common understanding of the local gang problem, and each group's perception varied according to their role vis-à-vis the gang problem. This finding suggests that: 1) policy responses to gangs are necessarily guided in part by myths rather than objective facts, and 2) conflict about appropriate responses to gangs may be inevitable given the absence of a shared understanding of the nature of the local gang problem among the gang unit, and internal and external stakeholders.

5

Form, Function, and Management of the Police Gang Unit

> Specialized units pose special risks for corruption. They have tradition-ally operated independently from the ordinary chain of command, target offenders who are perceived as "bad or dangerous," often engage in dan-gerous operations, and may work together as a cohesive group for many years resulting in the development of strong internal loyalties. Because of these factors, specialized units risk the development of a subculture, with their values separate and apart from those of the department, that will resist oversight and supervision by the department. Further, specialized units pose special risks that are inherent in their missions, including the use of exces-sive force, other civil rights violations (such as selective enforcement), and corruption (such as theft and bribery).
>
> – Erwin Chemerinsky, Report of The Rampart Independent Review Panel-Executive Summary, (unpublished manuscript), 2000b: 17.

In this chapter we explore the police response to gangs by examining the organizational structures, operational functions, and management of specialized police gang units. First, we describe how police depart-ments structure or organize their resources to control gangs, focusing on where the gang units were placed within the police departments, administratively and physically. Second, we describe the functions or operational strategies of the gang units. In other words, with a broad stroke, we describe what the gang units were doing, or at least what they were supposed to be doing, according to departmental guidelines and expectations. Here we place special emphasis on the intelligence gathering and sharing function of the gang units, because we found this function to be highly valued by others in the gang unit's environment. Third, we discuss the organizational configurations of gang control efforts. Specifically, we examine how gang units were functionally, spatially, and temporally differentiated. Last, we describe how the police gang units were managed. In particular, we focused on the existence and adequacy of formal written policies and procedures, formal and informal goals and objectives, unit performance measures, and especially the nature and extent of managerial supervision within the units.

ORGANIZATION OF GANG CONTROL IN POLICE DEPARTMENTS

As we discussed in Chapter 1, specialized police gang units, at least in part, are created to focus departmental resources, energy, and skill on a community's gang problem. The creation of a specialized unit to respond to a community's gang problem would appear to make sense (Huff and McBride 1990). First, as a means of achieving specific goals, the organizational tool of specialization has been used by police for well over a century. Local police agencies, for example, share the mission of *protecting and serving* the public. But since the creation of police, discrete divisions or units with distinct goals have been organized within local police agencies for contributing to that mission. For instance, a patrol bureau is responsible for patrol and a detective bureau is responsible for investigations. As such, specialized units, such as a homicide units, burglary units, vice units, or even gang units, allow the police to assign personnel and resources to focus on one goal or purpose.

Second, public agencies commonly organize their resources according to specific clientele. School districts, for example, serve students of specific ages. Although some schools teach young children, others teach adolescents, and still others teach adults. Likewise, hospitals serve patients who have different health needs. One ward might serve pediatric patients, another might address burn victims, and another might focus on emergency medicine. Police agencies have also used specialization to serve specific "client" groups. For instance, vice units work with prostitutes and johns, narcotics units work to combat drug use and drug sales, and traffic units enforce traffic laws.

Third, since the industrial revolution, work based on performing particular processes or tasks has been thought best to be grouped together. Classical organizational theory (Blau and Meyer 1971) posits that greater effectiveness can be achieved when workers perform fragmented or highly specialized duties. Effectiveness is increased because specialized workers become more skilled at performing the specialty task. Thus, in theory, they become more efficient, which in turn increases the productivity of the organization.

It should not be surprising that police departments have chosen to create specialized gang units to focus, consolidate, and coordinate their gang control efforts, because a number of reasons have been offered to suggest that specialization is an effective and efficient means of organizing resources. However, not all of the gang units that we studied organized their units in the same way. Specifically, their administrative locations, organizational configurations, functions, and management structures varied considerably from one department to the next.

This is at odds with much of the police research that suggests that on a general level, police agencies organize their resources similarly with regard to specialized units. For example, many large police departments have homicide units, auto theft units, and property crime units. These are typically located within an investigative division or detective bureau, and they are usually configured in similar manners – most often comprised of officers or detectives who report to a sergeant or some other supervisor. The units normally have an official mandate and specific goals, objectives, and performance measures; for example, they are often evaluated based on clearance rates.

Additionally, these units have specific roles or functions within their departments, such as being responsible for investigating specific crimes, and they are not normally responsible for ancillary functions. For instance, they are not responsible for speaking to the public about the type of crimes they investigate; they are not responsible for directed patrols to deter individuals from committing the type of crimes that they investigate; and they are not responsible for collecting, processing, and disseminating intelligence on those who have committed the crime or might commit the crime in the future. Most specialized units have clearly defined roles, and the activities that their officers perform are similar, specific, and focused, regardless of which police department is their parent organization.

Contrary to this widespread uniformity among police special units, we found that the organization of gang control varied substantially among the four police departments selected for this study. In each of the four cities, we found police gang units located in different administrative groups within their police organizations (Table 5.1). In Albuquerque, after having been shuffled around the police department from patrol to

TABLE 5.1. *Gang Unit Organizational Locations and Staffing*

	Albuquerque	Inglewood	Las Vegas	Phoenix
Administrative Location of Gang Unit	Career Criminal Section	Robbery and Assault Section	Organized Crime Bureau	Organized Crime Bureau
Physical Location of Gang Unit	Substation	Headquarters	Off-site	Off-site
Police supervisors assigned to unit	1.0	0	8.0	7.0
Sworn officers assigned to unit	3.0	3.0	41.0	31.0
Civilians assigned to unit	0.5	0	11.0	1.5
Total personnel	4.5	3.0	60.0	38.5
Squads assigned to intelligence	1.0	1.0	1.0	0
Officers assigned to squad	3.0	3.0	11	0
Civilians assigned to squad	0.5	0	11	0
Squads assigned to enforcement	0	0	2.0	4.0
Officers assigned to squad	0	0	15.0	24.0
Squads assigned to street investigations	0	0	2.0	1.0
Officers assigned to squad	0	0	11.0	2.0
Civilians assigned to squad	0	0	0	1.5
Squads assigned to prevention	0	0	0	0
Officers assigned to squad	0	0	0	0
Squads assigned to task force	0	0	1.0	1.0
Officers assigned to squad	0	0	4.0	5.0

investigations, the gang unit finally was placed in the career criminal section, located in the Special Enforcement Bureau. One supervisor stated that the gang unit was placed there because it complemented the mission of the section. Other key players in the decision argued that it was in that section because the section supervisor was a friend of the new gang unit supervisor, and he took the unit as a favor.

Inglewood's gang unit was administratively located in the department's robbery and assault section. As in Albuquerque, the gang unit's organizational placement was the result of necessity rather than because of any clear organizational strategy. Because the Inglewood gang unit was staffed with only three officers, and the span of control in the department was one supervisor for every five officers, police managers argued that it would be a "waste" to assign one sergeant to supervise the three officers.

Both the Las Vegas and Phoenix police departments had placed their gang units administratively within their organized crime bureaus. In Las Vegas, the Gang Crime Section was organizationally located together with the criminal intelligence and special investigations sections. In Phoenix, the gang unit was similarly located with the intelligence and investigation squads (both of which focused on organized crime), a vice unit, and an Internet crimes squad. In each case, the gang unit had been placed in an organized crime bureau because of that bureau's existing capacity to collect and process intelligence. Police managers in each department explained that when the gang unit began to focus substantial time on intelligence gathering, administrators moved to avoid recreating information-management processes that were already being conducted successfully by other units in the police department. Each department insisted that its intelligence should be collected and stored according to protocols established by the federal government – protocols already being applied in the organized crime bureaus. Therefore, managers argued, because similar processes were going to be conducted and the same protocols would be observed by the gang units, it only made sense to place the units within the organized crime bureaus, where the information-management infrastructure was already in place.

The physical location of the gang units also played a role in the organization of departmental gang-control efforts. Inglewood's gang unit was located in the middle of the police headquarters building, next to the offices of all of the detectives, and just one story above all of the patrol officers. The unit had one of the largest spaces in the police department, and their offices were consistently open to other police officers. The unit's physical location facilitated interaction and information sharing among gang unit officers and detectives working in the criminal investigation bureau as well as patrol officers.

In Albuquerque, the gang unit was located at the Southeast Substation, where all units belonging to the criminal career section were housed. The substation was in the middle of an industrial section of the city, with almost no pedestrian or vehicle traffic. Although the Southeast Substation's address and phone number were in the telephone book, the gang unit's location at the substation was considered confidential information. The unit's address was not disclosed to the public, and even many in the police department were unaware of its location. This resulted in no community members and few officers, other than those assigned to the substation, visiting the gang unit's office and interacting with unit officers.

Both the Las Vegas and Phoenix gang units were located in off-site, secret locations. The Las Vegas gang unit was housed in the back of a county office building in the middle of downtown, and the office required the use of a PIN number to enter. The Phoenix gang unit was also downtown, and an elevator key was necessary for access to the ninth floor of the office building where it was located. In each case, gang unit officers were generally the only ones working from the off-site location. Other police officers, if they even knew where the gang unit was located, needed assistance to enter the gang unit's office due to enhanced security procedures. As a consequence, the gang units were physically located where contact with anyone outside the unit would be limited, including contact with the public and with other members of their own police departments.

Officers in Albuquerque, Las Vegas, and Phoenix gave several explanations for why the gang units were located in secret locations. Some pointed to the fact that they worked undercover and did not want to be exposed to the public, in particular to gang members. Other officers stated that they used unmarked vehicles and did not want their vehicles "burned," making them too obvious to gang members. Many officers stated that they had been placed in secure, off-site locations to protect them from gang members who might retaliate. In many conversations with officers, we heard that at the end of the day (or night), they simply felt more comfortable knowing that gang members would not be waiting for them after work.

GANG CONTROL FUNCTIONS

We found that police gang units generally engaged in one or more of three principal police functions: intelligence, enforcement, and prevention and education. The relative emphasis placed on each function varied from department to department. The Inglewood gang unit was a single-function unit, generally engaging only in activities related to intelligence. Two of the units, Albuquerque and Phoenix, carried out activities related to more than one of these functions, and the Las Vegas gang unit was comprehensive, assuming at least some responsibility for activities related to all three functions. In the following sections, we briefly and broadly describe the different functions assigned to each police gang unit. A more thorough discussion of how each gang unit actually spent its time and their various forms of programming is discussed in Chapter 7.

Intelligence

Police officials and researchers have identified intelligence – gathering information about gangs, gang members, and their activities; developing and maintaining gang databases and tracking systems; and disseminating data – as one of the most important functions carried out by specialized gang units (Bureau of Justice Assistance 1997; Jackson and McBride 1996; C. Katz 2003; Katz, Webb, and Schaffer 2000). Indeed, in early 2005 the chief of the Chicago Police Department attributed a substantial proportion of that city's 45 percent decline in homicide to the use of gang intelligence and the sharing of that intelligence with other police units (*Chicago Tribune* 2005). Our research in the Inglewood, Albuquerque, Las Vegas, and Phoenix police departments indicated that each of their gang units did, in fact, perform an intelligence function. However, the importance of this function to the gang units and gang unit officers varied substantially.

In Inglewood, intelligence gathering and dissemination was, for the most part, the sole activity assigned to the department's gang unit. Key stakeholders in that department, such as detectives working in the robbery and burglary units, attributed substantial value to gang unit intelligence that supported their investigative processes. Information such as monikers (street names), legal names, addresses, known associates, photographs, and gang affiliations were perceived as very useful in conducting investigations, and detectives were quick to cite instances when intelligence from the gang unit had been instrumental in solving a crime and leading to an arrest. Almost all of the internal and external stakeholders in Inglewood made comments similar to the following one made by a robbery detective:

For example, the last robbery that I worked was committed by someone named Penguin at a bar. I went to the gang unit with the question, "Who hangs out at the bar on East 13th who has the name of Penguin...." The gang unit was able to go through its intel file and pull a photo and give it to the victim to see if it's the same guy. This happens over and over again.

Stakeholders in Inglewood also repeatedly reminded us that the intelligence provided by the gang unit was an invaluable resource for proactively addressing community crime problems. Stakeholders stated that it was not unusual for the gang unit to inform them about an ongoing criminal conspiracy or about forthcoming violence – information that the gang unit typically obtained through their street contacts. As such, it was not surprising to find that the gang unit officers placed high value on the importance of collecting and processing intelligence given the amount of positive feedback that they often received (Chapter 6).

Like Inglewood, Albuquerque's gang unit was responsible for the collection, processing, and dissemination of gang intelligence, but it was also responsible for enforcement functions. Stakeholders in Albuquerque affirmed the importance of the unit's intelligence function by tying assessment of the gang unit's value directly to the amount of information that the unit provided to others.

A great example is an apartment complex up in Westgate. We had a drive-by. We got people in custody. We call the gang unit out. They want to know what's going on with our people, and they'll be able to give us some information regarding who we are dealing with. So they bring their little computer and tell us, "Yeah, we have these people in the system."

Many stakeholders in patrol and area command units recalled that in earlier days, the original gang unit had been valuable to the department as a dependable source of intelligence on gangs and gang members. However, it appeared that as the unit became more autonomous and institutionalized it had focused less on intelligence and more on suppression, and as a result, stakeholders tended to devalue the unit's contribution to gang control efforts. For stakeholders in Albuquerque, the gang unit's most valuable commodity was the information it gathered and shared. For this reason, when the gang unit was resurrected, intelligence again became the unit's primary function.

On the other hand, just because a gang unit had a formal intelligence function did not necessarily mean that the function was a central focus of the unit. For instance, in both Las Vegas and Phoenix, gathering and processing gang intelligence was formally considered to be one of the most important functions of the unit, and was reported to be important by gang unit officers (Chapter 6). In practice, however, civilian staff in both units processed and disseminated most of the gang intelligence, and gang unit officers spent relatively little of their own time on intelligence-related activities (Chapter 7).

This could be accounted for in part by the fact that the organizational culture of both units placed greater value on the enforcement function than on intelligence. But they may also have spent relatively little time on intelligence because many of them were unfamiliar with how to use their gang database system or a computer. In Phoenix, for example, officers routinely waited hours or even days for a civilian to retrieve information from the gang unit's database because they were not comfortable using the computer. In Las Vegas some referred to feeding intelligence information into the system as putting data into "a black hole in space." As a consequence, responsibility for processing and disseminating gang intelligence was almost exclusively left to the gang unit's civilian staff.

Gang unit stakeholders in both Las Vegas and Phoenix spoke of the need for good intelligence. Many of them brought up examples of how gang intelligence could be useful for solving crimes involving gang members and for suppressing gang crime. However, while stakeholders recognized the potential advantages of using the intelligence possessed by the gang unit, many stakeholders were critical of the fact that such intelligence was generally unavailable to them, and that they lacked access to the information they thought was contained in the intelligence system as well as general information possessed by the gang unit. A Las Vegas patrol lieutenant gave this account:

Well, like I say, sometimes getting information from them is difficult . . . unless you know somebody up there, sometimes getting information can be really difficult. We went through one phase when I first came out here that I didn't like seeing in my area. . . . You know, they would come in and they would serve a warrant, or give a sweep, like I said, or something like that. And we'd be totally clueless that they were even here. You know, we'd start getting phone calls about guys in military uniforms. This I'd think was a hoax. . . . I've always told them you can come and play in my backyard, but at least you can give me the courtesy to let me know you're here.

Another Las Vegas patrol lieutenant noted that "[the gang unit is] isolated from the rest of the police department...they work down-town...not much interface. A new officer wouldn't know where to call for help."

Similarly, stakeholders in Phoenix acknowledged the many benefits that could be obtained from the gang unit's intelligence, but complained about the fact that the unit was physically and operationally isolated from the rest of the department and from the larger community. A Phoenix patrol officer underscored the problems of isolation and its negative impact on communication:

I think the main thing, which we've addressed a couple of times, is their distance. That's something, I just don't understand why we have that. It just creates that gap. In fact, it's hard to get hold of them. It's just a phone call, but to sit down and talk to them and say, "Hey, we've got this problem, you know." If they were out at the station, I could grab them in the hallway and just give them a quick one-minute spiel on my problem. That's the main thing I see, the distance. If I were to prioritize, it would be number one, the distance.

A stakeholder in another Phoenix precinct made a similar comment:

The main thing is just have that communication between us, and right now. Obvi-ously they're not going to be able to just transfer these guys out to the precinct, but if they're going to keep the distance, at least do a once-a-month briefing. A lot of the bureaus do that, like we just had one from burglary and the motorcycle cops, so I think we ought to have a mandatory one each month, just real quick, 5 minutes. You can be real informal. Just come in and say, "This is what we're working on." We want to help them out, but I can't remember the last time they came in and did a briefing. It's pretty unfortunate. We have all these officers. We have 260 officers at this precinct who'd love to help them, but we just don't have the communication, and without that, you're not going to get much done.

As such, while intelligence was a formally stated core function of both Las Vegas and Phoenix's gang unit, factors associated with organiza-tional culture, information technology literacy, and physical and oper-ational isolationism necessarily limited the role that intelligence played in each unit. In general, negative stakeholder perceptions related to the intelligence function tended to be expressed in terms of problems with information sharing and communication. Interestingly, it appeared that stakeholders nearly uniformly assumed that the intelligence generated by their gang units was of adequate quality. We heard very little from stakeholders that questioned the accuracy or currency of their unit's intelligence.

Enforcement and Suppression

Gang units' suppression and enforcement activities are those most likely to capture the imaginations of the public and the media, as well as that of police officers looking for action on the streets. Symbolically, suppression activities communicate to the public that their police department is taking the local gang problem seriously, and is mounting a forceful response. Whereas the intelligence function gave value to gang unit activities and legitimized the existence of the unit, from the perspective of many stakeholders, especially internal stakeholders responsible for investigation, enforcement activities legitimized the unit in the eyes of the public, the media, and fellow police officers. Enforcement actions gave outsiders a degree of confidence that the unit was doing what a gang unit ought to do.

Suppression activities in the units that we studied were typically restricted to directed patrols in known gang areas. This meant that the majority of their enforcement activities were focused on minority public housing districts and on parks and parking lots in the poorer neighborhoods that gang members were believed to frequent. Many of the officers explained that patrolling gang areas allowed them to keep an eye on gang members and gang activity, while at the same time providing them with the opportunity to develop personal relationships with gang members for the purpose of establishing a thorough intelligence network.

The importance of suppression activities was a central value in the gang unit's work group culture, even though the amount of time actually spent on such activities varied immensely from one gang unit to the next. The one exception to the centrality of suppression in the gang unit ethos was the situation in which the unit performed a single nonsuppression function, such as intelligence, such as we found to be the case in Inglewood. The gang units in Las Vegas and Phoenix stood in marked contrast to Inglewood. As discussed in the preceding section, although the Las Vegas and Phoenix gang units had responsibility for intelligence, most of their resources were focused on enforcement. Compared with intelligence gathering, suppression activities were highly visible; when covered by the media, suppression actions publicly demonstrated that the department was combating the local gang problem.

Of special interest was the finding that some of the gang units that we studied were devoting relatively little time to criminal investigation activities. The gang units' involvement in criminal investigation tended to be indirect, performed largely as part of the intelligence function. As we mentioned previously, detectives in most of the sites that we studied were quick to point out the value and use of information provided by the gang unit in solving cases involving gang members. As a consequence, gang unit officers were occasionally called in by other specialized investigative units to assist in the investigation of crimes involving gang members.

In two of the four sites, Las Vegas and Phoenix, the gang units had the primary responsibility for investigating serious gang-motivated crimes, with the exception of homicides and kidnappings. Gang unit officers in these units maintained that their expertise with gangs placed them in a unique position to investigate and solve crimes. The officers also believed that their involvement in gang-related investigations was essential for gathering worthwhile and timely intelligence. This resulted in interunit conflict in the Las Vegas Metropolitan Police Department. There, the gang unit wanted investigative responsibility for gang-motivated homicides, but the homicide bureau wanted to retain investigative responsibility, maintaining that their crime-specific expertise was required to investigate and solve homicides, whether gang motivated or not.

Prevention and Education

The prevention function filled by the gang units that we observed was nearly nonexistent. In describing gang unit activities, we found that prevention and education was, at best, a residual category that included all activities other than intelligence or enforcement. Interestingly, none of the gang units had participated in this country's most well-known prevention effort, the Gang Resistance Education and Training (GREAT) program. We found that in all four departments, the community relations unit or bureau conducted these kinds of formalized prevention efforts.

When we asked officers in the gang units why their units were not responsible for prevention and education, they stated that although they believed these activities were worthwhile and should be performed by someone in the department, they thought that prevention and education should not be the responsibility of the gang units. Officers in all of the units agreed that enforcement-related activities should be their primary focus. Some officers argued that education and prevention activities would conflict with the purpose and other functions of the gang unit, while others stated that their unit's resources were already strained, and they could not afford to be distracted from their "real job" of combating gang-related crime.

As will be discussed in Chapter 6, these views were further reflected when we asked the officers to rate the importance of enforcement, intelligence, and education activities. In two of the units, Inglewood and Phoenix, performing prevention talks and providing information to citizen groups about gangs ranked as the two least important activities that the unit performed. Similarly, in Albuquerque and Las Vegas, these two activities were ranked in importance to the gang unit just above dealing with gang graffiti, which received the lowest score in both departments.

However, with this said, while gang unit officers were not formally responsible for the training of police officers on matters relating to gangs in the department, this responsibility typically fell to gang unit officers. For example, officers in each of the units studied were often asked to give a gang class to new recruits at the police academy and when requested provided presentations to other officers on an ad hoc basis. In most of the study departments the gang unit officers were thought of as the residential gang experts, and any gang training administered by the department was through the gang unit.

DIFFERENTIATING ORGANIZATIONAL CONFIGURATIONS

We found that each of the gang units had a distinctive organizational configuration designed to facilitate their mandated function(s). In particular, we found that the organizational configuration of police gang units could generally be placed along a continuum of complexity based on the number of functions that the unit performed and how those functions were organized within the unit. At one end of the continuum was the single function gang unit, where responsibilities and tasks were not functionally, spatially, or temporally differentiated. A good example of this organizational configuration was Inglewood's gang unit. The unit consisted of three officers who were assigned to collect, process, and disseminate gang intelligence for the entire police department, during a single daytime shift (10 a.m. to 6 p.m.). Although the unit did occasionally engage in auxiliary functions, for organizational purposes, it was mandated with a single function – intelligence – for which all of the officers in the unit were responsible. In fact, the unit's organizational configuration was so simple that the department did not believe that the unit required an immediate supervisor.

Further along the continuum was a somewhat more complex organizational configuration. This type of unit was responsible for multiple functions, but functions were not differentiated among the officers in the gang unit. This type of gang unit tended to perform two functions, such as intelligence and suppression, with one being primary and the other secondary. Here, we define the primary function as the focal activity of the unit, the one on which most of the unit's efforts and resources were expended. The secondary function usually received far less attention and fewer resources, and was viewed as less important by gang unit officers. This type of unit also expected all of its officers to engage in all gang unit functions. In other words, gang control activities were diffused evenly throughout the unit, to be conducted by all officers.

The APD's gang unit was a good example of this type of unit. The Albuquerque unit was responsible for a combination of intelligence and auxiliary investigative activities, with the emphasis on intelligence. The unit was staffed with one sergeant, three officers (at the time of our observation), and one part-time civilian volunteer. All gang unit officers were responsible for gathering, processing, and disseminating gang intelligence, and were required to assist detectives with criminal investigations involving gang members. However, there was some functional and spatial differentiation of responsibilities within the gang unit. First, the sergeant assigned the civilian volunteer to process gang intelligence. In particular, the civilian collected all field investigation (FI) cards on documented gang members and entered the information in the gang unit's computerized intelligence system. Second, gang unit officers were assigned to particular command areas and were responsible for conducting intelligence and investigative functions in their assigned areas. As such, they were to disseminate gang intelligence to the area commander and to other officers who worked in their areas, and they worked with the detectives who were assigned to investigate crimes in the same area.

The Albuquerque gang unit was not temporally differentiated, with all of the officers working the same hours. On Tuesday, all officers worked from 10 a.m. to 6:30 p.m., primarily to focus on paperwork and liaise with day and swing shift personnel. Wednesday through Saturday, the officers worked from 3 p.m. to 11 p.m., the period perceived by gang managers to have the greatest amount of gang activity. During these days officers were to liaise with swing shift officers and target gang members for the purpose of collecting intelligence.

Next on the continuum was the Phoenix Police Department gang unit. This unit was assigned two functions: intelligence and enforcement. To perform these functions, the unit was staffed with 39.5 full time equivalent personnel; 31 were sworn officers, 1.5 were civilians, and 7 were supervisors. The activities of the gang unit were functionally, spatially, and temporally differentiated. In terms of functional differentiation, the unit was comprised of six squads. Four were dedicated to street enforcement; each squad was staffed with about six officers. These officers were primarily responsible for investigating serious gang crimes; their secondary function was to collect gang intelligence, performing directed patrols in known gang areas. The four squads were in turn spatially differentiated, with three squads assigned to one of three precincts – Maryvale, South Mountain, or Central City – and one assigned to both of the northern districts, Desert Horizon and Cactus Park. In terms of temporal differentiation, all of the squads worked from 3 p.m. to 1 a.m., but two of the squads were assigned to work Wednesday through Saturday, and two worked Saturday through Tuesday. All four squads worked during what managers perceived to be high-peak gang activity hours, and all worked on Saturday, the day that gang activity was thought to be greatest.

The fifth squad was dedicated to street investigations, and was staffed with two officers and 1.5 civilians. This squad was functionally differentiated, in that its two civilian staff were responsible for processing and disseminating the unit's gang intelligence for the entire city, while the two sworn officers worked with the district attorney's office to collect evidence on all cases previously submitted by the gang unit. The two sworn officers in the street investigations unit also had secondary responsibility for investigating serious gang crimes. However, they only performed investigations when the gang crime took place during hours not worked by the enforcement squad, and if they were not too busy responding to requests by the county attorney's office or administering the gang ROP. All of the officers and civilians in this squad worked Monday through Friday from roughly 8 a.m. to 4:30 p.m. Managers stated that this squad worked the day shift, during the week, because their positions required them to work with stakeholders (e.g., the county attorney's office, detectives) who also worked these hours and days.

The sixth squad was part of a federal gang task force. The gang unit allocated five officers and one sergeant to the task force, that also included ten FBI agents, one parole officer, one investigator from the State Department of Corrections (DOC), one officer from the Mesa Police Department, and one officer from the State Department of Public Safety (DPS). The task force was responsible for gathering intelligence and conducting investigations on highly organized gangs throughout the metropolitan area. These officers worked various hours and days of the week, depending on the nature of the investigation.

At end of the continuum, opposite the organizationally "simple" unit, is the organizationally "complex" unit, which is functionally comprehensive and highly differentiated. This gang unit performs intelligence, enforcement, and prevention, with each of these functions being assigned to highly specialized squads or details within the unit. The Las Vegas Metropolitan Police Department's gang section might serve as an example of an organizationally complex gang unit. Las Vegas's gang section was responsible for intelligence and enforcement functions, and performed some prevention and intervention-oriented activities. These functions were covered by forty-one sworn officers, eleven civilians, and eight supervisors, each of whom was assigned to one of six teams.

Fifteen of the Las Vegas officers were assigned to one of the two enforcement teams. The teams were primarily responsible for two functions: enforcement and intelligence gathering. In particular, they were assigned the task of performing highly visible, directed patrols in known gang hot spots and collecting intelligence on gang members, gangs, and gang activity from gang members, patrol officers, and residents. Likewise, eleven officers were assigned to one of two investigation teams. These teams were charged with investigating all gang-motivated crimes, with the exception of homicides, sexual assaults, and high-profile takeover robberies, such as casino robberies. When officers assigned to the investigation teams were not investigating gang-motivated crimes, they supplemented the efforts of the officers on the enforcement teams.

Gang unit managers and the intelligence squad analyzed data on drive-by shootings to determine the hours that officers would be assigned to work. In particular, they were interested in increasing the probability that gang unit officers would be on duty during the hours that drive-by shootings most often occurred. This was intended to increase the enforcement squads' presence during peak gang activity to increase deterrence, and decrease the likelihood that the investigative squads would be "called out," in order to decrease overtime pay for investigating gang crimes. As a result, both of the enforcement and investigations squads worked from 3 p.m. to 1 a.m. One enforcement team and one investigation squad worked Wednesday through Saturday, and the others worked Sunday through Wednesday.

Eleven officers and eleven civilians were assigned to the gang intelligence unit. Within the unit were three squads or details: intelligence, case submittal, and graffiti. All officers and civilians worked Monday through Friday from about 8 a.m. to 5 p.m. Similarly to Phoenix, these hours were chosen because the tasks performed by the personnel required them to connect with stakeholders who worked during these same hours (e.g., county attorney's office, business owners).

Seven officers and eleven civilians worked within the intelligence squad, which was responsible for gathering, processing, and disseminating gang intelligence. Civilian staff worked with sworn officers to process all collected gang intelligence, maintain the gang information system, and disseminate gang intelligence to those who requested it. Additionally, sworn officers in the intelligence squad occasionally presented prevention-oriented talks to school-aged youth, as well as to groups of community members, and they provided gang members with employment opportunities.

Located within the gang intelligence unit was the case submittal office staffed with two sworn officers. These officers were responsible for preparing all gang cases, by both patrol and gang unit officers, for prosecution. This included case screening, sorting paperwork, evidence disposition, and search and seizures. As such, these officers tracked all gang cases through their conclusion and liaised with the county attorney's office. Two officers were assigned to the graffiti detail. These officers were responsible for investigating all cases of gang graffiti, gathering intelligence on individuals who engaged in gang graffiti, and reporting gang graffiti to city services for removal.

Last, the gang unit assigned four officers to the Southern Nevada Gang Task Force. The task force was a cooperative effort involving the DEA, the Las Vegas Metropolitan Police Department gang unit, Nevada Division of Investigation, and the Henderson Police Department. The task force was charged with enforcing drug laws as a means of targeting gangs involved in high-level drug sales. In particular, the task force targeted drug organizations that supplied drugs to street gangs, in order to reduce the supply of drugs to the community. These officers, for the most part, worked from 8 a.m. to 5 p.m., Monday through Friday, unless an investigation required an alternate schedule.

GANG UNIT CONTROL AND MANAGEMENT

We examined gang unit control and management in the four departments that we studied by focusing on four topics: the existence and adequacy of written policies and procedures, the degree to which measurable goals and objectives were formally established, unit performance measures, and the extent to which personnel were supervised. Although our examination is not a comprehensive audit of gang management, we do examine several useful indicators of the managerial quality of the units.

Written Policies and Procedures

An analysis of interview data from gang unit officers, supervisors, and departmental executives, as well as a review of departmental documents, showed wide variations in the existence and adequacy of written policies and procedures governing the gang units that we studied. Inglewood's gang unit was at one extreme with no written guidelines and no formal documentation of the unit's functions, the activities that it was to engage in, or even a general statement of its mission or purpose. The only written policies that we identified concerned the documentation of gang members and gangs, and these had been developed by the Los Angeles County Sheriff's Department. As a consequence, in the absence of written guidelines, the Inglewood gang unit's function was largely determined by departmental culture and traditions that had been developed over time by previous gang unit officers.

One of the three Inglewood gang unit officers had been with the unit for more than twenty years, since its creation. He provided the unit with stability and continuity in terms of expectations and functions. For example, a wide and deep consensus about the gang unit's function was evident from interviews with gang unit officers, police executives, and internal and external stakeholders. In particular, nearly everyone was in agreement that the primary function of the gang unit was to collect, process, and disseminate gang intelligence. Almost no other function was ever mentioned. As a result, the officers in the unit were not conflicted about priorities or their role and function within the department.

Similarly, in Albuquerque, no written policies or procedures existed for the gang unit, other than a few departmental documents that defined gangs and gang members. However, as stated in Chapter 4, at the time of our study the gang unit had been only recently resurrected. Interviews with police supervisors indicated that when the unit was created, there were few expectations about what the unit would do. The precise function of the unit was largely left up to the newly appointed sergeant who, in the beginning, directed officers toward activities involving intelligence gathering and dissemination. The sergeant also assigned a civilian volunteer to process gang intelligence. As such, although the unit did not have an official mandate or policies or procedures to facilitate operational activities, the unit's supervisor assigned tasks with a common theme – intelligence – to particular personnel, guiding the unit toward specific objectives.

After a short while, a consensus developed within the gang unit and among police executives that the function of the Albuquerque gang unit was twofold. First, the gang unit was responsible for gathering, processing, and disseminating gang intelligence. Each gang unit officer was assigned to a particular command area, where he was responsible for collecting gang intelligence and disseminating it to that area's commander. Second, gang unit officers were responsible for assisting investigators in their assigned areas with criminal investigations involving gang members. As such, although gang unit officers did not have primary responsibility for gang investigations, they were responsible for working with investigators when their assistance was requested.

Unlike the Inglewood and Albuquerque departments, the Phoenix Police Department did have written SOPs, about four pages in length, that were regularly revised to provide guidance to the gang unit and its personnel. The department's SOP also clearly outlined the purpose of the unit and many of the specific functions that were to be carried out by the squads in the gang unit. The Phoenix Police Department's SOP stated that five functions and responsibilities were to be performed by officers assigned to street gang enforcement squads, and seven were to be performed by officers assigned to the street gang investigations squad.

Although the squads were assigned some similar functions, each had its own unique functions as well. For example, both squads were responsible for gathering and disseminating gang intelligence and for using that intelligence to identify geographic areas with a substantial amount of violent gang activity. Both were also responsible for making presentations to law enforcement officials on the nature of the local gang problem. However, although the street gang enforcement squad was responsible for coordinating and collaborating with other officers in the department to solve gang crimes, the gang investigation squad was also responsible for conducting investigations, case management, and collaborating with the county attorney's gang/ROP detail.

The Phoenix Police Department SOP governing the gang unit also discussed the role of the gang unit's sergeant, and provided general direction to gang unit personnel. The SOP covered issues relating to the operation of vehicles, and set out detailed policies and procedures governing notification of the parents of juvenile gang members who had been contacted by gang unit officers. Many of the gang unit personnel possessed documents that detailed the state law governing documentation of gangs and gang members by law enforcement agencies. Overall, the Phoenix gang unit was fairly well governed by written policies and procedures, with the department SOP clearly stating the purpose and functions of the unit squads, as well as providing policies and procedures to guide daily operations.

The Las Vegas Metropolitan Police Department's gang unit had the most comprehensive policy and procedures manual. Approximately fifty pages in length, it focused on three major issues: 1) organizational objectives and goals, 2) general policies and procedures, and 3) specific procedures. Additionally, the manual provided definitions on gangs, gang members, and gang crime.

The Las Vegas gang unit's policy manual thoroughly discussed the configuration of the unit, detailing its rank and organizational structure, and providing a detailed description of each unit or squad or detail's function. For example, the manual stated that the unit would be comprised of five sections: the gang intelligence unit, a case submittal office, investigative teams, enforcement teams, and the Southern Nevada Gang Task Force. As discussed in the prior section, the intelligence unit was responsible for gathering, processing, and disseminating intelligence; the case submittal office prepared gang cases for prosecution; the investigative teams were charged with investigating gang-motivated crimes; the enforcement teams were charged with gathering intelligence and patrolling gang hot spots; and the task force was responsible for targeting gangs involved in high-level drug trafficking.

In addition to providing gang unit officers with guidance as to their functions and the activities that they were to perform, the Las Vegas unit's policy manual described general issues pertaining to the coordination of training, the operation of the section's library, the management of criminal intelligence information, and records retention. It also provided information pertaining to officer uniforms, property assigned to officers, personal appearance, and the issuance of departmental vehicles. The manual dedicated considerable space to specific procedures for disseminating gang intelligence, handling confidential informants, maintaining investigative files, making media releases, establishing seizure logs, and obtaining search warrants. Overall, Las Vegas's gang unit was unique among the four that we studied in that its SOP was thorough and detailed in its presentation of policies and procedures governing gang unit officers.

Documenting Gangs, Gang Members, and Gang Crime

One major activity undertaken by police gang units is documenting gangs, gang members, and gang crime, and each of the study departments had established written policies for the documentation of gang members and gangs. The Las Vegas and Phoenix gang units also had formal policies for defining gang crimes.

Albuquerque (in the early 1990s) and Inglewood (in 1989) adopted the Los Angeles County Sheriff's Department's Gang Reporting, Evaluation and Tracking (GREAT) system for its departmental gang information system, and along with it, the Sheriff's Department's criteria for documenting gang members. Both departments were still using those same criteria at the time of this study.

In Arizona, in 1994, the state legislature implemented several gang-related definitions for the purpose of establishing a statewide standard for documenting gangs and gang members. In that same year, the Phoenix Police Department adopted the criteria established by its state legislators in an effort to be consistent with other agencies across the state and to increase the utility of gang intelligence within the state. Las Vegas was the only department that did not rely on an outside agency or institution to establish its criteria for documenting gang members. Rather, in 1993, the unit created its own criteria.[1]

As seen in Table 5.2, all four of the gang units relied on many of the same criteria to document gang members. For example, all four agencies

---

[1] Although all four gang units were responsible for documenting gang members, other criminal justice agencies participated as well. For example, in Las Vegas, parole and probation officers specializing in gang members' cases were occasionally involved in documentation. They did so by completing FI cards, checking appropriate fields, and providing other required information. The completed cards were then turned in to the police gang unit. We were unable to determine the extent of documentation by parole and probation officers.

TABLE 5.2. *Police Gang Unit Criteria for Identifying Gang Members*

Albuquerque	Inglewood	Las Vegas	Phoenix
Self-admission	Self-admission	Self-admission[a]	Self-admission
Tattoos associated with gangs	Tattoos associated with gangs	Tattoos associated with gangs[a]	Tattoos associated with gangs
Clothing and colors	Clothing and colors	Clothing and colors[b]	Clothing and colors
Possession of gang graffiti	Possession of gang graffiti	Use of hand signs associated with gangs[b]	Reliable informant
Use of hand signs associated with gangs	Use of hand signs associated with gangs	Reliable informant[b]	Identified as a gang member by other law enforcement agency
Reliable informant	Reliable informant	Prior arrests with known gang members[b]	Any other indicators of street gang membership
Associates with known gang members	Associates with known gang members	Statements from parents[b]	Identified as an associated by physical evidence (e.g., photo, letter)
Prior arrest with known gang members	Prior arrest with known gang members	Participation in gang related crime[a]	
Statements from family members	Statements from family members	Any other circumstance when an officer can articulate obvious gang membership[a]	
Identified as a gang member by other law enforcement agency	Identified as a gang member by other law enforcement agency	Identified as an associated by physical evidence (e.g., photo, letter)[b]	
Attendance at gang function	Attendance at gang function		
Identified by other gang members	Identified by other gang members		

[a] Denotes status as a gang member.
[b] Denotes status as a gang member associate.

used self-admission, tattoos and clothing associated with gangs, and intelligence from reliable informants as criteria for documenting gang members. Additionally, three of the four units used hand signs associated with gangs, prior arrests with known gang members, and prior identification by another police agency as grounds for documentation.

Although both Albuquerque and Inglewood used criteria such as possession of gang graffiti, association with known gang members, attendance at gang functions, and identification by another gang member to document gang members, Las Vegas and Phoenix used physical evidence and any other indications that would suggest gang membership for that purpose.

Both Las Vegas and Phoenix had two classifications of gang members for documentation purposes. In Las Vegas, the criteria for documenting gang associates and gang members were different. As seen in Table 5.2, primary evidence, such as self-admission, wearing a tattoo associated with a gang, or participation in a gang crime, was needed to document an individual as a gang member. Secondary evidence, such as statements from parents or a reliable informant, could only be used to document an individual as a gang associate.

In Phoenix, gang associates had to meet only one of the state legislature's criteria to be documented, while gang members had to meet two or more of those criteria. The difference between gang associates and gang members was primarily one of the information's usefulness in court. In particular, intelligence and records on gang associates could not be used by prosecutors in court, while intelligence on gang members could. Furthermore, gang associate records had to be purged from the unit's gang database after being retained a shorter time than gang member records. (Issues related to purging are discussed in Chapter 7.)

Three of the four gang units defined gangs in similar terms. As seen in Table 5.3, Albuquerque, Inglewood, and Las Vegas used almost identical criteria; a gang was defined as 1) a group of three or more persons, 2) with a common name, and/or common identifying signs or symbols, and 3) with members who were engaged in crime. Phoenix's definition, created by the state legislature, was a variation using similar criteria. In Phoenix, a gang was defined as 1) an association of persons who had at least one criminal street gang member, and 2) whose members engaged in the commission, attempted commission, facilitation, or solicitation of any felony act. Although Phoenix's definition was perhaps broader, in that it did not require a certain number of members or a name or

TABLE 5.3. *Police Definitions of a Gang by City and Gang Unit*

Definitions:

Albuquerque	An organization, association, or group of three or more persons, formal or informal, that has a common name, and/or common identifying signs or symbols, whose members individually and/or collectively engage in a pattern of criminal activity.
Inglewood	A group of three or more persons who have a common identifying sign, symbol, or name, and whose members individually or collectively engage in or have engaged in a pattern of criminal activity creating an atmosphere of fear and intimidation within the community.
Las Vegas	An ongoing organization, association, or group of three or more persons, whether formal or informal, who have a common name or common identifying symbol, whose members individually or collectively engage in a pattern of unlawful or criminal activity.
Phoenix	An ongoing formal or informal association of persons whose members or associates individually or collectively engage in the commission, attempted commission, facilitation, or solicitations of any felony act, and that has at least one individual who is a criminal street gang member.

Defining Criteria:	Albuquerque	Inglewood	Las Vegas	Phoenix
Three or more members	X	X	X	
Common name, signs, symbols	X	X	X	
Pattern of criminal activity	X	X	X	
Association of persons one of whom is a criminal street gang member				X
Members engage or attempt to engage in or facilitate a felony				X

other identifiers common to all members, it did require the group or its members to be involved in felonious activity.

Two of the gang units had formal, written policies defining gang crimes. The Phoenix Police Department's definition was motive based, more restrictive than definitions used in many other police departments, but was clear and concise: "Any criminal act committed for the purpose of promoting gang status or personal status in a gang."

Las Vegas's written policy defining gang crime was also motive based, but the examples accompanying it were of gang-related and

gang-motivated crimes. It was also somewhat more complex and difficult to interpret:

Crimes committed by gang members or associates, which by the nature of the
crime would tend to *benefit the gang or the status of a gang member* within the
gang. Examples include drive-by shootings; crimes committed as a part of an
initiation for membership into a gang; or any violent street crime confirmed to
be *related and/or gang motivated*, including *all gang incidents* associated with
weapons and violent crimes *involving juvenile gang members* [emphasis added].

Furthermore, the policy clearly stated that any violent crime involving
a juvenile gang member would, by definition, be considered a gang
crime. In Chapter 7, we will discuss how these definitions affected the
recording of gang crime and the assignment of officers to investigate
particular crimes.

Formal Goals and Objectives

We found wide variations in the gang units' formal goals and objectives. Neither the Albuquerque nor the Inglewood gang unit had formally established goals or objectives. When gang unit managers in these
departments were asked to define their unit's goals and objectives, they
were unclear about what we wanted to know. Some answered by discussing their unit's assigned functions; others listed common activities.
For example, Inglewood managers stated that the unit's goal was to
collect and disseminate gang intelligence (a function). In Albuquerque,
executives stated that their goals were to perform intelligence-related
activities and to assist other detectives with gang-related investigations
(also functions). Managers of these units were guided by the functions
assigned to them, rather than to the purpose and expected outcomes
of their work, and by the corresponding activities and processes that
needed to be performed by the gang units.

Although Phoenix had no goals or objectives stated within their SOPs,
the unit did have two administrative mechanisms for which unit goals
had been set. The first was a monthly management report for the bureau
commander, generated by the lieutenant in charge of the gang unit.
Implicit in that report were nine goals that were to be achieved by the
gang unit, monthly and annually:

1. Adjust case clearance rate on assigned gang follow-up investigations.
2. Number of gangs successfully targeted for criminal investigation.

3. Efforts to include community notification in [number set annually] percent of gang investigations.
4. Notify area managers within eight hours of any significant organized crime bureau operation in their area.
5. Percentage of parental follow-up contacts by gang squad's following documented street contacts.
6. Efforts to improve morale.
7. Provide a minimum of eight hours per year of formalized training for [number set annually] percent of all organized crime bureau personnel.
8. Number of documented efforts to improve internal communications within the bureau.
9. Develop innovative ways to absorb unanticipated costs, identify budgetary savings, and overall budget management.

Second, as part of Operation Safe Streets (Chapter 7), the Phoenix gang unit established five goals and objectives that it strived to meet every summer (May 15th through August 15th):

1. Reduce gang-related violent offenses by 3 percent during the summer months.
2. Investigate 90 percent of the violent crimes involving criminal street gangs during the hours of Operation Safe Steets (OSS2000).
3. Respond to 100 percent of the citizen complaints of criminal street gang activity in their neighborhood within five working days.
4. Maximize the enforcement of all weapons violations though the use of "Project Exile," while utilizing all appropriate federal and state charges.
5. Reduce the perceived fear that criminal street gangs have on the community by providing constant feedback of OSS2000 enforcement efforts to the affected neighborhood associations and Block Watch groups through the Precinct Area Team Managers (Phoenix Police Department 2000:1).

At the end of each summer, the unit submitted a report to police executives, as well as to area commanders, documenting the success or failure of the unit's efforts.

Over the year, the Phoenix gang unit set objectives and performance measures related to unit processes and outcomes, focusing on process-oriented measures such as the number of gang investigations and gangs targeted, the number of training hours provided to officers, and the number of efforts to improve internal communications within the bureau. The unit also set outcome-based objectives such as the reduction of gang violence and of fear of gangs within the community. Of interest was the fact that the gang unit in Phoenix had not referenced collecting, processing, or disseminating gang intelligence in any of its goals, objectives, or performance measures, although intelligence was one of its primary functions.

Las Vegas was the only gang unit of the four to have formal goals and objectives within its SOP. The goal of the gang unit as set out in the department's SOP was as follows:

The Gang Investigation Section (GIS) of the Organized Crime Bureau (OCB) of the Special Operations Division (SOD) will be responsible for the lawful collection, analyzation, dissemination of intelligence information, and the follow-up investigation of gang-motivated crime, except crimes involving homicide, sexual assault, or high profile takeover robberies, such as casino robberies.

The objectives of the unit were also contained in the unit's SOP:

The objectives of the Gang Investigations Section are to suppress street gang criminal activity through lawful arrests and prosecution, and to deter street gang criminal activity through the lawful collection, analyzation, and dissemination of intelligence information. Specific annual objectives will be written as per 5/102.32 of the Department Manual.

As noted in the preceding text, the gang unit also had yearly objectives. For the period of our observation, the gang had these five objectives:

1. Through enhanced collection and communications and improved use of automated systems, the Gang Investigations Bureau will analyze and disseminate gang intelligence information such that a minimum of 55 percent of cases submitted for prosecution include such information.
2. Through criminal investigations, use of technology, advanced surveillance, and coordination with other agencies and department sections and bureaus, the Gang Investigation Bureau with (sic) affect an increase in the number of weapon cases submitted for prosecution on violent gang members by 5 percent from previous year statistics.
3. Through seminars, public presentations, the citizen academy, and media exposure, the Gang Investigation Bureau will affect an

increase in the number of community groups educated on street gangs by 10 percent from previous year statistics.

4. Through comprehensive, historical, and financial investigations, the Gang Investigation Bureau will participate in a multijurisdictional task force such that three violent gang organizations are investigated toward pursuing federal and state prosecution.

5. Through interaction with patrol, proactive visible police presence, community interaction, tactical enforcement activity, and involvement in the Department of Housing and Urban Development's Operation Safe Home, the Gang Investigation Bureau will affect a decrease of weapon-related gang violence in selected gang corridors by 5 percent from the previous year statistics.

The Las Vegas gang unit's goals and objectives were generally comprehensive, and the objectives were updated annually. As in Phoenix, Las Vegas's objectives related to both unit processes and desired outcomes, focused on increasing investigative use of gang intelligence, decreasing gang violence, the number of targeted gang investigations, the number of presentations to the public, and the number of weapons cases submitted for prosecution. Also as in Phoenix, however, Las Vegas did not focus on issues related to the collection or dissemination of gang intelligence.

Expected Outcomes

During our interviews with gang unit managers, we asked about the outcomes that they expected from their gang units, formally and informally. More than half of the managers in each department cited the reduction of gang crime as an important outcome. However, after gang crime reduction, managers became less consistent in their expectations for their gang units. In Albuquerque, gang unit managers also expected the gang unit to reduce fear of crime and increase perceptions of safety, whereas in Inglewood, managers were also interested in increasing alternatives for youth. In Phoenix, managers stated that the gang unit should be increasing intelligence collected on gang members, and in Las Vegas, managers sought a reduction in the number of gangs and gang members and an increase in the number of gang convictions.

Accordingly, regardless of the units' functions, goals, or objectives, the consensus of all gang unit managers in all four departments was that gang units should achieve reductions in gang crime. Of interest was the fact that desired outcomes reported by the managers were not necessarily connected to unit capacity or functions. For example, no explanation was given for why a single-function unit (Inglewood) should achieve the same outcome(s) as a more comprehensive unit (Las Vegas). In addition, in both Albuquerque and Inglewood, the primary designated function was to gather and disseminate gang intelligence, activities that were not directly related to changing citizen perceptions of crime and safety nor to providing opportunities for youth, the outcomes sought by the Albuquerque and Inglewood gang unit managers.

Performance Measures

Of the four departments, only Las Vegas had formal (written, codified) performance measures to gauge unit success, tracking the numbers of gang members, reported drive-by shootings, deceased gang members, cases submitted, cases cleared, arrests (by type), seizures, cases initiated and assisted, weapons and narcotics recovered, and field interviews. The Las Vegas gang unit also required specific measures for tracking the success of its graffiti detail: the numbers of taggers, arrests, charges (by type), citations, search warrants, seizures, requests for service, classes instructed, cases handled, and field interviews, and the total amount of damage caused by graffiti. As we will see in the following text, however, just because the unit had formal performance measures it does not necessarily mean that they were always used.

We interviewed managers about the measures they used, formally or informally, to evaluate gang unit performance and requested examples of how the evaluations were documented. Gang unit managers in all four departments generally agreed on the importance of using the amount of gang crime in the city as a performance measure. Although all gang unit managers (with the exception of Albuquerque) monitored in some way the amount of gang crime in their cities to evaluate unit effectiveness, we found that this particular measure was not necessarily used to assess the performance of the unit. When the cities did experience increases in gang crime, the changes were not necessarily attributable to lack of gang unit success. Police executives recognized a multitude of reasons for gang crime to increase, many of which were unrelated to the efforts of the gang unit.

While gang unit managers started using other performance measures, few corresponded to the units' assigned functions, and some relied upon data that the departments did not have the capacity to generate. For example, in Albuquerque, managers stated that they used the amount of reported graffiti cases submitted to the county attorney, and "gang statistics" to evaluate the gang unit. We found the use of these measures problematic in several ways. First, Albuquerque's gang unit was not responsible for submitting cases to the county attorney, only for assisting other detectives in the investigation of gang crime. Second, Albuquerque's gang unit was not typically responsible for issues involving gang graffiti. Third, neither the Albuquerque gang unit nor the department produced data showing trends in gang membership or gang activity, nor did they produce reports about gangs, gang members, or gang activity. In fact, the agency did not regularly collect data pertaining to gang crime trends, making evaluations based on such statistics impossible.

In Inglewood, managers stated that they evaluated the gang unit by measures such as citizen perceptions of safety and city council satisfaction. However, the primary function of the unit was to collect, process, and disseminate gang intelligence – a function with little direct impact on fear of gangs or the city council's satisfaction with the department's response to gangs. Furthermore, while managers stated that they used citizen perceptions of safety and council person satisfaction, such data was rarely collected. When it was, the results were so general in nature that even measurable changes could not in any way be directly attributed or related to unit activities.

Because both were charged with collecting and disseminating gang intelligence, we might have expected that Albuquerque and Inglewood gang units would be evaluated by process measures that required tracking the numbers of individuals documented or of responses to requests for intelligence. The units could have also used surveys to collect data about gang intelligence "consumer satisfaction." In short, unit managers could have determined how often the unit's intelligence was requested, how often it was used, and whether the intelligence collected by the unit was useful to others.

Both Phoenix and Las Vegas used process and outcome measures more in line with their respective functions, although they were both lacking the consistency and emphasis that we would find within other units in the same police departments. For example, both units were responsible for directed patrols, yet the number of arrests made by the gang units were not actually tracked for their performance evaluations. Likewise, few of the managers mentioned clearance rates as a measure of success, even though both units had primary responsibility for investigating gang crimes.

Once again, we would have expected emphasis to have been placed on measures related to collecting and disseminating gang intelligence, a core function of both units. Most managers did not indicate that their units were evaluated on measures such as the numbers of field interviews or stops or of gang members documented, or how often the unit responded to requests for intelligence. Interestingly, we did observe that some of this information was collected, albeit unknown by managers. For example, in Phoenix, the civilian staff in the intelligence squad tracked the annual number of requests for gang intelligence, the source of requests, the type of intelligence requested, and the amount of time spent responding to requests. These process indicators were used to illustrate the amount of intelligence that was disseminated and the amount of work performed by the unit. Likewise, in Las Vegas, we found that the gang unit tracked performance indicators such as the numbers of field interviews conducted by officers and of gang members documented, along with the unit's clearance rate. It was unclear why gang unit managers were unaware that these data were available for use in evaluating unit performance.

Not only did the managers that we observed fail to use the quantitative aspects of the intelligence function (e.g., number documented) in assessing gang unit performance, but we also found no indication that they took into consideration the quality of intelligence produced by their gang unit. The absence of any emphasis placed on the quantity or quality of intelligence in assessing gang unit performance was surprising given the valued attached to the intelligence function by internal and external stakeholders.

Supervision of Gang Unit Personnel

During our observations and interviews with gang unit officers and managers, we inquired about the supervision of the gang unit officers. In particular, we focused on the amount of supervisory attention given to gang unit officers by their immediate supervisors, and the extent to which managers perceived that they had control over their officers. We found variations from one unit to the next.

In Inglewood, gang unit officers reported to a sergeant in the robbery and assault section, rather than having a supervisor within the unit. This resulted in their not being supervised on a regular basis. During our observations, we never saw this supervisor, nor was he referred to in any way. When we asked directly about the gang unit supervisor, the officers gave responses such as, "Well, we really don't have one," or "We have one, but it's only a formality. He really does not have much to do with our unit." With a little further probing, we learned that the officers contacted their supervisor only when something special was needed or an issue was viewed as particularly important. As two officers in the unit explained:

> They don't supervise our daily activities. It's not like they are over our shoulder or anything. When there is something really crucial or very, very important that is going on or some type of detailed project that we are doing, they are very much aware of it. But we are a well-disciplined unit. Not much discipline or supervision is needed. . . . Like I said before, most of the gang investigators here, we all have our own projects or assignment that we have to do, and the only time that we really need a supervisor around is when we have problems, or we need to get through some red tape, or if it is a big project where we are all involved.

> Units like our gang unit and our narcotic units are very loosely supervised, because on a day-to-day basis, we have so many different things we do that a supervisor really can't keep track of us. We are in here one minute, then we are out on the street. The next minute, we will be back in here again. So it's hard for them. They just want to know what we are doing, and we brief them on what we are doing, why we do it, and when we have questions. We are pretty much a self-supervised, self-motivated unit. . . . It's chain-of-command, we start from our sergeant and it goes up if it has to. . . .

Supervision of gang unit officers was more directed in Albuquerque than in Inglewood, but the supervising sergeant still provided his officers with a great deal of freedom. He explained:

> I tell my detectives that we give them a badge and we give them a gun, and they're adults, and I want them to make their decisions on their own. A lot of time they do that. They are out there on their own and everything else, but I am here if they need supervision. If they need to ask questions and stuff, I am always available to them, but I try not to mother-hen them or micro-manage what they are doing. I like them to go out and be the liaison between the area commands and the area of town that they are working. I can't do that for them.

Observation of the Albuquerque gang unit, however, indicated that this sergeant was in fact involved in the day-to-day activities of the gang unit. He had regular contact throughout their shifts, ate most meals with them, worked beside the officers on investigations, and backed them up in the field. Interviews with the officers confirmed our observations. Gang unit officers in Albuquerque told us that they were often with the sergeant in the field, and that he was included in most field activity. Interestingly, the officers did not experience his participation as supervision, but rather as his working *with* them on the streets. One officer stated:

I wouldn't necessarily say it's supervision, per se, as you need somebody watching over your shoulder for everything you do. It's more that he's involved in everything we do because he wants to be. He likes to work just like everybody in this unit. One reason they were chosen was because they worked. That was one of the big criteria. Did you work in the field? Did you actually go out and do stuff, or did you sit back and take calls all day long and not bother to be proactive whatsoever? He is a really proactive supervisor who likes to know what's going on, get involved, and assist you and address any issues or problems that occur.

Another officer concurred:

Pretty much, most of the time our sergeant's with us side-by-side. If we request him to go with us, he'll be right there with us. A lot of times he'll ask us, "Hey, do you guys have anything going on?" If we say yes, he wants to come along. He acts more as a part of the team when we're out in the field. If we develop the operation plan, it's our operation plan, and he helps, but yet he's always our supervisor.

In Las Vegas, the amount of supervision officers received differed according to the squad to which he was assigned. Officers in enforcement squads received substantial supervision. In the field, the sergeant patrolled the same area as his squad, working all stops, interrogations, and arrests with his officers. As a consequence, there was constant oversight of enforcement squad officers. The following statement by an enforcement squad member represents many of the views we heard:

[Supervision is] almost constant, because our sergeant is actually just another member of the team. He goes out with us, he does enforcement with us, he shows up on calls. He's with us just about all the time. So there's always . . . it's not just as a supervisor, he's a member of the team. He goes out there with us and takes care of business, and then if there is a need for a supervisor, he's right there.

When we asked the officers why the sergeant rode with their squad and constantly supervised their work, some explained this was a relatively new arrangement. They noted that the sheriff and his executive team had increased supervision of officers after a 1997 incident in which two gang unit officers engaged in a drive-by shooting, killing a gang member. The police department hoped that increased supervision would reduce future problems that might be associated with the gang unit.

Observations and interviews indicated that officers in the other Las Vegas gang unit squads worked under substantially less supervision. They noted that intense supervision was both impossible and unnecessary. First, officers assigned to the intelligence unit, graffiti detail, and case-submittal office all noted that their positions required them to work multiple assignments or cases, taking them in different directions than other officers in their units or squads or details. As a consequence, they pointed out, little supervision occurred due to the nature of their jobs. Second, many of the officers in these units saw themselves as experienced detectives who had been assigned to the unit because they were self-motivated, needed little direction, and were responsible. As such, they and their supervisors felt that they did not need to be closely supervised, as they related to us:

I can only answer that question for the two squads I've been on. I went to an investigative team for a time, and supervision was there, but it was loose. And because you've got six guys that are investigating not only six different cases, but they may have two or three cases apiece, so they got to go different directions to do different things. So in that case, the supervision is a little looser, yet everybody's involved in knowing what each other is doing.

Not much. I mean the whole purpose of coming up here is you are detectives. You are supposed to be self-starters, self-motivated. And they require, most of us require, little supervision or no supervision. That is the whole purpose of why you come up here.

As a result, many officers in Las Vegas only had contact with a supervisor when they were assigned a case and when they needed managerial assistance.

Compared with supervisors in Las Vegas, Phoenix supervisors spent less time with their officers. Our observational and interview data suggested that most officers in the unit, regardless of assignment, had minimal supervisory contact. Most of that was in the form of briefings once or twice a week, or for administrative reviews (e.g., reviewing paperwork, case wrap-up). Officers pointed out that although they had daily contact with their supervisor, it was typically informal, such as general work-related conversations or discussions about their personal lives. When we asked officers about the amount of supervision they had, here's what they had to say:

I think very minimal, everybody up here is supposed to be and is very minimally supervised because of the jobs that we have. Sometimes we won't see our supervisor for a shift, sometimes for a couple days, depending on what you're doing. However, if we do need something, we can basically rely on supervisors to take care of what we need or whatever, be it job related or personal reasons. You know, for days off or something's going on, our supervisors are really good with that.

Very little, you are self-supervised a lot. You'll see your sergeant in the beginning of the shift and then as you need him throughout the night, you know then if there's a shooting or something you'll see him out there. But otherwise you're pretty much on your own.

We also asked gang unit managers whether officers in the gang unit knew their ideas and viewpoints regarding gang control efforts. The question was intended to focus on the formal and informal expectations that gang managers had for their units. In Albuquerque, managers were split; some believed that the officers were well aware of their viewpoints and ideas, and others did not. One commander, who had just recently returned from a lengthy leave of absence, believed that his officers were generally unaware of his viewpoints regarding the gang unit. The chief of police was unsure, while the lieutenant in charge of the unit was confident that the officers had a strong understanding of his perspective and viewpoints.

The chief of police noted that he spoke with the sergeant in charge of the gang unit on occasion, and that he expected the sergeant to pass along the information. However, when asked directly, he was unclear about the extent to which that actually happened:

I never say "yes" to those things. Too often I get embarrassed. I guess I would like to think that [the sergeant] has talked them. I think they generally know. It is generally understood. It is a very proactive group. It's not social work. It's knowing who the gang members are, trying to diffuse problems as they occur. If you get one kid shot, then you are going to have another kid shot by the other gang. It is just a matter of time. And what do we do to intervene to make sure that that doesn't happen.

A manager in charge of the gang unit (along with other units) met frequently with his unit officers, both before they were assigned to the unit and afterward, to ensure that they understood the direction that the gang unit was heading and his expectations. Asked whether the officers knew what was expected of them, he responded:

Yes, because we had a meeting with members of the unit before we expanded it and told them that this is the direction that we are going to take. And basically [we] asked them if they would like to stay and if this was something that they would be interested in. And if they did stay, everybody would be held in the same standard. As we had the interviews, we explained, before we ever started asking questions, the overview of how the gang unit was going to perform.... [Interviewer: How much contact do you have with the gang unit officers?] I try to go out with the different groups at different times, so not a lot.... [Interviewer: You just have more contact with the sergeants?] More with the sergeants, but I talk with the detectives when I run into them in different parts of the building, and I go out with them on different operations. It is kind of difficult for the one person that is mainly doing administrative stuff during the day to be out at night.

In Inglewood, the chief of police, as well as gang unit supervisors, noted that they did not think that gang unit officers had a strong sense of their ideas or viewpoints on how the gang unit should operate. The following comments were made by two of the commanders, when we asked about their influence on the gang unit, and whether gang unit officers were aware of their viewpoints on how the gang unit should operate and what its priorities should be:

I don't know. Let me put it this way: If they do, it is probably through the chain of command, because, one of the things, I have been busy with so, so many things on the plate this year, that quite frankly I have not had occasion to go around to all the units and kind of impart my wisdom. I do have my first mandated supervisors' meeting on June 2. And we will have first lines, who originally included the gang unit. If anybody does not know my philosophy about not only police work, but gang suppression and everything else, by that, then that won't be my fault any more. So you kind of have to do it within the chain, but I will see . . . some of the . . . guys, and we will discuss it in the hall. Because that is the good thing about a small department. I know everybody. Whether they know my philosophy, I think they know they have my support, and they know that I think what they do is very important.

No, I would say they don't. I don't have enough time to devote to it, to sit down and talk to them.

Almost all of the managers in Las Vegas and Phoenix were confident that the officers in their units or squads knew their perspectives on gang control. In both units, as new individuals came into the unit, managers would meet with them one-on-one to explain their expectations and to present their vision of the unit's history and the direction in which the unit was headed. The lieutenant in charge of the Las Vegas unit on occasion had gone as far as to document his vision and disseminate it to unit officers, requiring a signed statement from each one asserting that he had read it:

I talk about it to them all the time. Whether they say they know them or not . . . we discuss it with the sergeants, we discuss it with officers, and we discuss it on a regular basis. This is what we're doing, this is my vision for this thing, let's do it. And sometimes you have to go, "This is my vision, read it and sign it, so you understand it," but I prefer not to do that.

In Phoenix, the lieutenant talked to each of his officers and attended briefings and other meetings, ensuring that the officers understood their priorities and were in alignment with the direction of the unit:

Yes, we have very open lines of communication for the detective level and the sergeant and at my level, and I attend a lot of their briefings, and I'm usually up to date on all the investigations they've logged in and their enforcement efforts, and if there's any major enforcement effort that's going to take place, such as serving a search warrant or this or that, I'm usually notified of it. Those are usually review-and-approve anyway, and I've talked to a lot of these guys on a one-on-one basis, and also in briefing and group basis, and they're very aware of what our priorities are. I don't call them *my* priorities, 'cause its *our* priorities, *our* in the gang enforcement unit.

Of special interest in both units was the fact that officers worked directly for sergeants, which led to additional reinforcement of the managers' views and expectations. In Las Vegas, because some of the sergeants worked in the field with their officers, a regular dialogue occurred about what they wanted from the officers. One sergeant stated, "Do they know my personal feelings? They know my personal feelings as far as how I want my squad to work and what I expect out of them, and how to conduct themselves out there." Similarly, the sergeants in Phoenix gave responses like the following: "Yeah, right from the bat I had a fresh squad...and you just sort of just laid it on the line. This is what I'm looking for, this is what I expect from you."

SUMMARY

In sum, we found that the four gang units that we studied varied substantially in terms of organizational structure, function, and management. With respect to organizational structure, we found that the police departments were not uniform in the organizational locations of their gang units. Not only did they vary in where they placed the gang units into the departmental organizational structure, but also those placement decisions had more to do with administrative convenience than with organizational planning or operational strategies.

We found that all of the gang units except Inglewood were located off-site. The locations were kept secret and their facilities were kept secure. As a result, the gang units we studied were generally unavailable to the public, community leaders, fellow police officers, and other criminal justice officials. Gang unit officers claimed that the secrecy and additional security was necessary to keep gang unit officers safe from attacks from gang members, and to keep their identities and vehicles from being known to gang members so that they could continue to conduct criminal investigations. Nevertheless, the physical isolation of three of the units hampered their intelligence sharing and interunit communication. As a result, the value of the gang unit to stakeholders, especially internal stakeholders, was diminished because intelligence was the commodity most sought after by these stakeholders.

We also found that the gang units differed in their functional, temporal, and spatial characteristics. We were able to place them along a continuum of complexity based on the characteristics of the unit. At one end of the continuum was the least complex or differentiated unit – the *simple gang unit*. This unit performed a single function, such as intelligence, and was responsible for a specific geographic area, with officers all working during a single period of time. Next along the continuum was a slightly more complex pattern of differentiation and specialization. This type of gang unit tended to perform two different functions, such as intelligence and suppression, with one of the functions being primary and the other, secondary. Here, we defined the primary function as the focal activity of the unit and the one upon which most of the unit's efforts and resources were expended. The secondary function usually received far less attention and fewer resources, and was considered less important by gang unit officers. In addition to functional differentiation, this type of unit was more spatially and temporally differentiated than the simple gang unit. At the other end of the continuum, opposite the organizationally simple gang unit, was the complex unit. This unit was functionally comprehensive; it performed intelligence, suppression, and prevention activities, with each function receiving a different level of effort and resource investment. The complex unit was comprised of several squads and details that were responsible for specialized tasks. Each squad and detail was also responsible for particular geographic areas, and for coverage during particular time periods. The comprehensive unit was organizationally and operationally run almost like an independent police department that solely focused on gangs and gang problems. This continuum of gang unit complexity based on differentiation should be thought of as an ideal type, with different gang units placed at different points along the continuum. In reality, none of the gang units that we studied fit any of the three points on the continuum perfectly; rather, they approximated these types.

Although all of the gang units we studied were responsible for an intelligence function, the emphasis placed on intelligence varied greatly across the study units. Inglewood officers took seriously their role of collecting, processing, and disseminating intelligence, and they valued this function highly as did their stakeholders. Our data analysis yielded similar results, albeit to a lesser extent, in Albuquerque. In Phoenix and Las Vegas, however, the intelligence function was met with less enthusiasm by gang unit officers even though it was highly valued by their stakeholders. Officers in both of these units were unable to use computers to access intelligence, and as a consequence, they typically left intelligence responsibilities to civilian staff. This had a negative impact on the quantity and quality of intelligence that was disseminated to others.

Unlike the gang unit officers (with Inglewood being the exception), the most important gang unit function for internal and external stakeholders in each of the four study sites, was intelligence gathering. From the stakeholders' points of view, such intelligence enabled investigations and suppression activities, and when that intelligence was shared, it facilitated their own agencies' responses to the gang problem. Although generally positive about their gang units and the functions they performed, stakeholders were able to identify problems and to make recommendations for improving the gang units' performance. Typically, these problems and related recommendations had to do with communications and the sharing of intelligence and information, and the organizational arrangements that isolated the gang units. These problems tended to be seen as intertwined. In particular, stakeholders were critical of the fact that it was often difficult for them to obtain intelligence from the gang unit and they attributed this problem to the physical and social isolationism that the gang unit self-imposed on itself.

With the exception of Inglewood, the gang units studied tended to place the greatest value on enforcement or suppression activities. This was the case in those departments with a relatively more serious gang problem to address (i.e., Albuquerque, Las Vegas), as well as those with a less serious gang problem (i.e., Phoenix). Communities with serious gang problems present gang units with the greatest opportunities to devise, experiment with, and engage in enforcement activities, whereas communities with less serious gang problems present fewer such opportunities. We found that this was largely a consequence of community, political, and media demands placed on the police department. As such, enforcement strategies and tactics were often employed in an effort to maintain legitimacy from those in the gang units' and police departments' environments. It is also worth noting that enforcement activities were critical to the gang unit work group culture, regardless of the actual amount of time spent by officers on enforcement activities or the other official function(s) of the unit.

None of the units studied placed much value on gang crime prevention as a function performed by their respective unit. As will be discussed in Chapter 7, Las Vegas's gang unit was the only unit observed engaging in prevention activities. Interestingly, however, all of the police departments participated in the GREAT program and sent officers from units other than the gang unit to local schools for the purpose of delivering the GREAT curriculum. Although officers in the gang unit believed that such prevention activities should be carried out, they felt strongly that it should not be their responsibility.

Last, we found that the agencies varied with respect to the control and management of their unit's and officers, and that each department's degree of control and management was largely related to the unit's organizational complexity. Specifically, the simple gang unit had almost no written policies or procedures, no formal goals or objectives, and no performance measures, and was almost never supervised. On the other hand, the most complex gang unit had numerous written policies and procedures, specified objectives and goals, and clearly delineated performance measures, and it more closely supervised its officers. Those agencies with multifunction gang units fell somewhere near the middle in their levels of control and management of their gang units.

We found that the gang units that we studied were characterized by some noteworthy organizational features that had important implications for their functioning. For example, SOPs guiding the units were absent or underdeveloped, with Las Vegas being the only exception. The units lacked formal goals, objectives, benchmarks, and unit performance measures that could be used to gauge their effectiveness. In addition, administrative oversight, formal organizational control, and managerial direction for the gang units was largely absent, and unit supervision was minimal. Certainly, there were exceptions, but the overall absence of stronger organizational controls coupled with the physical and operational isolation of the units (except in Inglewood), and lack of consistent performance expectations created an environment in which the units were largely self-directed, determining their own goals and objectives, setting operational priorities, and crafting their own tactical practices.

6

The Gang Unit Officer

> Joining the gang squad and becoming immersed and expert in street gang affairs soon bec[omes] very serious business and the core of [a gang unit officer's] existence. There are peculiarities about elite units like a gang squad that can create caricatures of its members.
>
> – Malcolm W. Klein, *Gang Cop*, Alta Mira Press, 2004: 91

We were interested in how the individuals who policed gangs had influenced their agencies' responses to the gang problem. We approached this by focusing first on gang unit officers' personal characteristics and on their prior assignments and experiences within their police departments. Next, we examined how they became gang unit officers – the selection process and how that process affected the types of officers who were assigned to gang units. Third, we looked at the training that officers received, both training that was specific to their assignments and any other gang-related training or education they might have attended. Related, we examined the problems that the gang unit officer faced after they initially became a gang unit officer. Finally, we focused on the status of being a gang unit officer and explicate the perceived roles that gang unit officers play in their department and community.

OFFICER CHARACTERISTICS

The ethnic or racial characteristics of the officers in the police gang units that we studied varied across units, but reflected the composition of their parent departments and not necessarily their community. In Las Vegas and Phoenix, roughly the same proportion of whites,

TABLE 6.1. *Characteristics of Gang Unit Officers by City*

Characteristics	Albuquerque (*n* = 8)	Inglewood (*n* = 3)	Las Vegas (*n* = 30)	Phoenix (*n* = 22)
Ethnicity				
African American	0.0	33.3	13.0	0.0
Hispanic	50.0	66.6	4.3	14.3
White	37.5	0.0	82.6	85.7
Asian	12.5	0.0	0.0	0.0
Gender				
Male	87.5	100.0	91.3	100.0
Female	12.5	0.0	8.6	0.0
Average Age	33.3	39.0	34.5	33.3
Marital Status				
Single	25.0	0.0	16.7	15.0
Married	75.0	100.0	76.7	80.0
Divorced	0.0	0.0	6.6	5.0
Parent of children	50.0	100.0	62.1	66.6
Education				
High school	37.5	0.0	61.5	25.0
Associates	25.0	100.0	26.9	30.0
Bachelors	37.5	0.0	26.9	40.0
Masters	0.0	0.0	3.8	5.0
Military experience				
No	75.0	33.3	73.3	42.1
Yes	25.0	66.6	16.7	57.9
Average years in dept.	13.4	11.2	8.2	7.8

Hispanics, and African Americans served in the gang units as served in the police departments. Although whites were somewhat underrepresented in Albuquerque, approximately the same proportion of Hispanics worked in the gang unit as served in the department. The Inglewood unit had a disproportionate number of Hispanics, but the unit was staffed with only three officers, making comparison with the larger department relatively meaningless.

Gang unit officers were mostly male. Of ninety officers assigned to the four gang units, only three (3.3 percent) were female: two in Las Vegas and one in Albuquerque. Most gang unit officers were relatively mature and experienced. They tended to be older, married, and parents of children. The average officer was thirty-three years old or more and 75 percent or more were married (Table 6.1).

Gang unit officers varied from one city to the next with respect to education, tenure in policing, and policing and prepolicing experience.

The Phoenix officers, for example, were more likely to have a college degree than their peers in the other police departments: About 45 percent of gang unit officers in Phoenix had a bachelor's degree or higher, compared with approximately 38 percent of officers in Albuquerque, 30 percent in Las Vegas, and none in Inglewood. The officers also differed in prior military experience; those in Inglewood and Phoenix were more likely to have had some form of military experience compared with officers in Albuquerque and Las Vegas.

We found some differences among the units in average numbers of years served in their departments. In Phoenix and Las Vegas, gang unit officers had served for an average of eight years; in Inglewood and Albuquerque, gang unit officers had served an average of eleven and thirteen years, respectively. The scope and nature of the officers' prior experiences within the police department differed accordingly. In Phoenix, for example, almost all gang unit officers had come directly from a patrol unit, with no other experience, including investigative experience, within the police department. In Las Vegas, although all gang unit officers had worked in patrol, about one-third of them had also served in a problem-solving or community-oriented policing unit, and one-third had previously worked in a bike or foot patrol unit. As in Phoenix, almost none of the gang unit officers in Las Vegas had had any prior investigative experience.

Officers in Inglewood and Albuquerque, on average, had had much more varied experiences within their police departments before coming to the gang unit. For instance, in Inglewood, all three officers had worked in patrol, as well as in some other unit, before coming to the gang unit. Two of them had worked in investigative units, and one had worked on the anticrime team. Likewise, in Albuquerque, two of the officers had served only in patrol before being assigned to the gang unit, but the other six had worked in units such as domestic violence, organized crime, narcotics, and property and violent crime. Accordingly, gang unit officers in Inglewood and Albuquerque had served more time in the police department, including more time in units other than patrol, and had more investigative experience than gang unit officers in Phoenix and Las Vegas.

BECOMING A GANG UNIT OFFICER

All four of the gang units had official policies and procedures in place for selecting unit officers; all were roughly equivalent. In all units, an officer had to have spent at least three years in patrol before being permitted to transfer into the gang unit. In fact, this was the only requirement for applying. When positions opened in the units, the units began accepting applications, and interested officers submitted transfer requests. The units then requested resumes from the applicants.

In Albuquerque and Phoenix, gang unit managers ranked applicants based on reviews of their personnel records. Managers considered prior work experience, disciplinary histories, foreign language aptitude, and prior evaluations. Officers who ranked high remained in the candidate pool. In Inglewood and Las Vegas gang unit managers did not prescreen applicant's personnel records; instead they reviewed them during the applicant's oral board.

Oral boards were conducted by all four of the units. In Las Vegas and Phoenix, gang unit sergeants and a lieutenant conducted oral boards, while in Albuquerque and Inglewood, a gang unit sergeant conducted oral boards along with other department supervisors. The oral board members in all departments developed and administered the interview questions. In each department, the names of applicants who scored highest on the oral interviews were then submitted to the chief's office to be considered for transfer.

Although official policies guided the processes, a number of factors were taken into consideration during the final selection of officers for the gang units. When department managers were asked about selection factors, four most desirable characteristics emerged from their answers: self-motivation, previous experience with gangs or the gang unit, the ability to speak a foreign language, and ethnic diversity.

Managers in Phoenix, Albuquerque, and Inglewood maintained that they looked for self-motivated officers. During the selection process, they said, they sought officers who would not require a great deal of oversight and who would be aggressive in the field. Many supervisors gave responses similar to the one in the following text.

I know they want somebody who is willing to work hard. Past employment record has a lot to do with that. If you are considered a worker, then obviously you have got a better chance than somebody that is not considered a worker.... [Interviewer: Define a worker.] Somebody who makes self-initiated arrests, handles, in a patrol sense, handles their beat, doesn't expect somebody else to do their work for them. Self-reliance, where you don't need to be standing over the person as a supervisor, constantly. Just somebody who is willing to go out and do the job.

Managers in Phoenix, Las Vegas, and Inglewood tended to select officers who had worked with the gang unit before. This work could have taken different forms, such as special assignments with the unit or attendance at gang unit training, or sharing information and sending FI cards to the unit. In Phoenix, for example, a number of gang unit officers had previously worked with the unit as Operation Safe Streets officers during the summer. In both Las Vegas and Inglewood, we observed patrol officers working with gang unit officers, performing data entry or riding with the officers in an effort to learn and to develop a relationship with gang unit officers. These officers were enhancing their chances of being selected for the unit in the future. Managers in these units made comments like the following:

Certainly if in someone's background it comes through that they have shown an interest in the gang unit by frequently contacting the gang officers, or the gang officers have firsthand knowledge of the quality of work of the officer.... We don't want somebody who has never shown an interest and just, "oh, something's available, I think I'll apply." Hopefully that person will be eliminated in the process.

We found that officers who spoke the language of local non-English-speaking gang members or their parents were given preference by all four of the gang units. Of eight gang unit officers in Albuquerque, four spoke Spanish and one spoke Vietnamese. As one officer explained:

The only reason we purposely selected a Vietnamese officer ... because we've seen an influx of Vietnamese gangs in Albuquerque, and we didn't really have a way to address that, because we can't talk to them. So we purposely chose that officer. He was an outstanding officer....

Although fewer officers spoke Spanish or another foreign language in the other units, it was nevertheless a desirable qualification.

... it is sometimes a very big problem. A majority of gang members in this city are Hispanic. With Hispanic gang members comes the Hispanic language. And if you don't speak that, then it's very difficult to do any – I think it is advantageous to have officers in that unit that reflect the gangs that they are working. Certainly if we are dealing with Latino gangs, being Latino or certainly being able to speak Spanish. There have been officers that can bridge that, particularly if they have the language skills, but it just is kind of a natural kind of thing. So I would certainly be cognizant of that.

I could tell you one of the most important things that they try to look for is somebody that's bilingual, somebody that speaks Spanish.

Not only were all gang unit managers interested in selecting officers who could speak the primary language of gang members and their parents, but they were also interested in ensuring that their units reflected the ethnicity of these individuals. Many of the managers pointed out that having officers of the same ethnic backgrounds as gang members gave the unit a competitive advantage.

I am very pragmatic about what I need in this unit. And if I need female officers because female officers give me another advantage and another way to attack things, then I recruit female officers. And when I do recruitment, I recruit what I need. I mean, you can't have an all-white gang unit when you have 42 percent of the gangsters in Las Vegas are Latino, and 33 percent are black, and 28 percent are white, and the rest are [Asian]. You have to have a diverse group. It is very difficult to be an all-white police group. I actively recruit minorities, females, and foreign language officers. Actively recruit, and it has nothing to do with affirmative action. It's just because that is what I need. I need those types of officers, so I go look for them.

However, Las Vegas officers pointed out that it sometimes had been difficult to get minority applicants, in part because of the unit's reputation for being white. One officer explained:

Of course, there are a lot of officers that don't want to come up here, because there's not too many black police officers up here, or Hispanic officers or female officers or detectives up here. So they don't feel comfortable coming up here. . . .

There's a lot of officers that try to put people up here that they have common ground with them, because they want to feel comfortable working with them, and they haven't been around anybody else that is a minority or individuals that do things different than they do. So they feel uncomfortable by it, and those individuals are up here, they don't want to come here, because they know those individuals are up here.

As a result, Las Vegas gang unit managers and officers stated that they occasionally used a targeted selection process aimed at bringing minority officers to the unit. One officer explained:

We have had selection processes were they have specifically targeted and stated – unofficially, of course – that we are going to bring up a female this time, or we're going to bring up a Spanish-speaking officer, or we're going to bring up a black officer this time. So it has played a role, it hasn't worked out real well. [Interviewer: What has the intent been?] It's political, it's public perception. Public perception is – okay, you have this gang unit, but you don't have an Hispanic or a black or a female on there, they must all be racist. Obviously, every police department across the country is getting the backlash from what L.A. has done. So politically, the people upstairs, the administration, has looked at it and said, "Well, let's try to even this out," but it hasn't worked.

In Phoenix and Las Vegas, many gang unit managers and officers agreed that an applicant's complaint record was one of the most important factors in the selection decision, and that an officer who had received even one sustained complaint for excessive force would not be interviewed. In Las Vegas, gang unit managers looked for excellence in documenting and recording information. Because a primary function of the gang unit was collecting intelligence, they needed officers who would be meticulous at this.

Perhaps the most interesting finding, however, turned out to be a qualification that was missing from the lists of gang unit managers in Phoenix, Las Vegas, and Albuquerque: *prior investigative experience*. In Phoenix and Las Vegas, the investigation of street gang crime was a core function of the gang units. We were surprised to find that new gang unit officers were not required to have even minimal prior investigative experience, given the seriousness of the crimes that they would be required to investigate.

GANG UNIT OFFICER TRAINING

The training that gang unit officers received varied by unit in quantity, quality, and substance. This section summarizes training practices and experiences in each of the four units studied.

Inglewood

Inglewood gang unit officers were the best trained of the four units. All Inglewood officers had received training on gangs as part of their academy training.[1] They were exposed to gang trends and taught how to identify gang members and submit gang intelligence. Next, all officers appointed to the gang unit were required to attend a forty-hour training session conducted by the California Gang Investigators Association. This training formally educated officers about profiling gang members, filing considerations, writing reports, and preparing for court and case presentation. It focused on issues related to gang organization,

---

[1] We were unable to observe gang training provided to Inglewood gang unit officers, or any of the other gang units. Anecdotal evidence suggests, however, that while these officers did receive training, that training was not as sophisticated or thorough as we might expect or desire. Our conversations with many gang researchers over the years indicate that most "gang training" involves the telling of war stories, rather than serious academic attempts to increase the amount of knowledge about gangs, gang members, and gang crime.

recognizing gang activity, investigating gang activity, and procedures for documenting gang members.

Once assigned to the gang unit, new officers were paired with the most senior officers in the unit for on-the-job training. This was informal, with the new officer shadowing the experienced officer for several days. During this period, the senior officer would explain the role of the unit, the technical aspects of collecting, processing, and disseminating gang intelligence, and other issues pertaining to gangs and the gang unit.

Inglewood officers continued to receive formal training as long as they were with the unit. Their training took place in a number of venues. First, they were required to receive twenty-four hours of continuing academy training each year, and some gang unit officers reported that they used this opportunity to take courses relating to gangs. Second, the California Gang Investigators Association conducted a monthly meeting at which members took turns training other members; all gang unit officers were expected to participate. Third, a number of area criminal justice agencies provided training that on occasion focused on gangs and the gang problem, and gang unit officers were invited to those sessions. Although most advanced training was optional for gang unit officers, many noted that they did regularly attend gang training, largely because it was available through a number of sources.

Albuquerque

In Albuquerque, few gang unit officers had had any gang-related training before being appointed to the gang unit. In addition, no courses or methods had been established for training officers once they were assigned to the unit. When we asked about the training that officers had received after coming into the unit, none reported having received any department-sponsored training, formal or otherwise.

Instead, officers explained, they attended national, state, and local conferences focusing on gang-related issues. Each year, the Albuquerque Police Department allocated a predetermined amount of money per officer for training. Some gang unit officers said they used their share to attend one out-of-state conference and a few state training sessions. Others did not travel out-of-state for training because of the high costs; instead, they used their training funds for state and local training so that they could attend more courses. This training, however, could be of any type. Gang unit officers were not required to attend training related to gangs, gang investigations, or to their responsibilities in the gang unit.

Phoenix

In Phoenix, several gang unit officers reported receiving training on gangs before being assigned to the unit. Many of the officers stated that they had been interested in gangs and, as a consequence, had trained on issues related to gangs. A number stated that although they had been assigned to patrol at the time, they had requested assignment to areas with high levels of gang crime. This assignment, they argued, had given them on-the-job training in the form of exposure to gang members, as well as to gang unit officers.

Additionally, almost 40 percent of the gang unit officers stated that they had attended at least some gang training seminars prior to being assigned to the unit. Most of this training was conducted by other officers from the gang unit or other units in the police department. Just over 10 percent of the officers assigned to the gang unit had earlier served as liaison officers between the gang unit and the patrol division; they had received sixteen hours of training from the gang unit while in that role. About a quarter of that training time was spent learning to use the department's gang database system; the remainder focused on issues related to local gangs and gang unit policies and procedures.

Once officers had been selected for the Phoenix gang unit, they were required to attend the same training that the gang liaisons had attended. Afterward, they were permitted access to the unit's gang intelligence system. In addition, several reports and manuals about gangs, gang members, and gang activity were available for new gang unit officers. The handbooks also addressed officer safety, communication, and interviewing and interrogating gang members, and they provided instruction on "how to research gang members."

Almost all of the Phoenix gang unit officers stated that they had received additional training after joining the gang unit. Officers attended local gang training seminars conducted by other metropolitan area criminal justice agencies, and occasionally attended national conferences related to gangs. Interestingly, however, the Phoenix police department did not pay for gang unit officers to receive additional gang-related training. Officers paid their expenses out-of-pocket, even seminar fees and travel costs. The unit commander attempted to assist by leaving officers on salary while attending training, so they did not lose vacation time.

Given those obstacles, we were surprised that so many officers had attended gang training conferences. Officers commented that the training was often useful, and that they minimized costs by carpooling and sharing hotel rooms. Remarkably, only four Phoenix officers indicated that they had received no training after being assigned to the gang unit. Those officers remarked that they had received on-the-job training by just being on the streets.

Las Vegas

In Las Vegas, many gang unit officers had received gang training as part of their academy coursework. In particular, the academy featured a section titled *Gangs in Clark County*. During this session, new officers were exposed to gang trends and gang identification, and they were trained to communicate more effectively with young people in general, and with gang members specifically. Most Las Vegas officers indicated that they had also attended several departmental training courses on gangs, such as *Black Gangs*, *Asian Gangs*, *Hispanic Gangs*, and *Gang Trends*. Several had attended national or regional gang conferences before being selected for the gang unit. Gang unit officers who had prior gang training indicated that they had taken the courses because of a general interest in gangs – and as part of their strategy for getting into the gang unit.

In addition, Las Vegas gang unit officers, like all others in the department, were required to receive twenty-four hours of training annually, but gang unit personnel had added requirements. During their first six months, they received training in such things as cultural awareness, crime scene preservation and investigation, interview techniques, informant management, and computer skills. By their third year in the gang unit, officers were also to have attended courses in verbal judo, gangs in Clark County, advanced firearms training, drug detection, time management, and video photography.

Training Quality

We asked gang unit officers to rate the quality of their training on a scale of 0 to 10, with 0 = poor and 10 = excellent. Although we had found that training requirements varied significantly between units, there was little variation among the units in how officers perceived the quality of their training. For instance, on average, officers in Inglewood rated their training at 8.5, Albuquerque officers at 7.5, Las Vegas at 7.45, and Phoenix at 7.85. In general, officers expressed satisfaction with the training received, but added that the material covered in most courses had not changed much since the first time that they had encountered it. Some noted that national conferences were more interesting, in part because the material was less repetitive than at the department and local levels. The following responses were typical:

Some are better than others, I think the ones in state, they're not the best, but it's better than nothing. When you send yourself out of state, like now we have a unit in Anaheim, for the national gang conferences, those are generally better. They pull people from all the major cities, Chicago, Detroit, New York, all over the country, and they talk about their gang problems. 'Cause then you're learning things, whereas these gangs here, when they teach local classes, it's kind of the same thing over and over. You can go to one and you've been to ten of them.

It depends on where the seminar is. If it's a national seminar, I would say 10. If it's an interstate (sic), basically, I feel that interstate (sic) conferences are basically spearheaded by our department. I would, that's about seven or eight, because most of the time we are teaching it.

Other gang unit officers in all departments thought that training was generally of good quality, but that the best training was gotten on-the job, working in the field.

I would say, you know, I'd say most of the stuff that I have learned from gangs has been just from working with them and being out in the field. So I would say, the gang-related classes . . . probably a six.

. . . in the initial stage when I first came up, the training was very good and it helped me, it provided a lot of information for me. And now as I'm in my, I don't know, my last – not last, but in the last two or three years, it's not – it's just kind of going over the same stuff, over and over again.

REALITY SHOCK: ENTERING THE GANG UNIT

We asked all gang unit officers to tell us about any problems they encountered when they first became gang unit officers. A small number of them, primarily in Phoenix and Las Vegas, stated that they had had no problems when they assumed their new positions. This was the exception rather than the rule, however. Most remarked that they either had problems related to changing work environments or with learning to perform in the new position.

Adapting to a New Work Environment. For some officers, the primary problems encountered after transferring to the gang unit were associated with the new working environment. As a group, these officers tended to identify three challenges. First, a number of them had difficulty adjusting to working as part of a team. Before transferring, many had worked alone as patrol officers or detectives. Once assigned to the gang unit, they acquired a partner or began to work closely with a group of other officers. The following comments are representative of those made by officers in all of the units:

I think the toughest thing coming to the gang unit from patrol, you're paired up with another officer, and you may have different work ethics or different work things that you do. I think that that would be the toughest thing to overcome, but after you kind of get a thing going on that you get along well, work well together, that's good. But sometimes you don't work well together, and you're kind of stuck together.

I think – I don't know how every department in the nation works, but this unit is a very close-working, close-knit type of a unit. I think that one of the problems I had is, I had to learn to fit into what my role on this team was. And I was no longer an individual police officer pushing a black-and-white every day, that I had to learn my role, so this team would succeed and not just Officer [X] succeeding.

Some officers had difficulty adapting to working in a different geographic area. As patrol officers, many had worked specific beats and precincts, and had become intimately familiar with the community and streets. Once in the gang unit, they had to know the entire city, or at least those areas where the gang unit frequently worked. We heard statements such as the following:

The hardest, for me what was hard, was coming from Maryvale, I got assigned to the 25 squad which handles Central City, and I knew nothing about Central City. I'm real familiar with Maryvale. Central City is different streets, different people, different types of people, where Maryvale didn't. I think when I found out I was coming to gangs, I assumed that I would go to the 21 squad, who handles Maryvale. But once I got here, I went to the 25 squad because the man.... So now I have to learn a new area so, and it makes it hard when you're doing, like a traffic stop. It's hard to concentrate on what you need to do with a traffic stop when you also have to look at street signs. I think that was the hardest thing as far as the actual dealing with people.

It just took time to learn gangs from other areas. 'Cause when you're in patrol, you work one specific geographic area. And when you come into the gang unit, you work the whole city of Las Vegas. It just takes time to learn the other areas of town that you are not familiar with, and the other types of gang members or gangs that you are not familiar with. So it's just a learning process of learning the other areas and everything.

Some officers found working with gang members, their families, and friends to be more challenging than expected. It took time to come to an adequate understanding of the unique populations they encountered on

the job. A few found they needed to adjust their demeanor and develop
new communication skills in order to succeed.

I think, see, I came from Illinois, so there wasn't that many Hispanics, learning
the Hispanic culture and then how tight the family is, the family structure, the
language barrier, I think that was probably the hardest thing.

Well, number one was approaching these gang members who are known to be
violent and carry guns and everything, and approaching them with an outwardly
lackadaisical appearance, because the thing that I saw is the more authoritative
you are in your approach, the less cooperation you're going to get. But the way the
guys I trained with up here, their approach is very subtle, in an effect, and almost
a mutual respect. And I saw that when you approach them like that, instead of,
hey, put your hands up, here, do this, do that, you'd get a lot more information.
In fact, most of the times, they start volunteering information about rival gang
members and everything else. So I think it was just dropping guard a little bit. You
know, dropping that authoritative figure and trying to relate on a more one-to-one
basis.

Learning a New Job. Some officers responded to our question about
problems encountered when first becoming a gang unit officer by
describing their difficulties with finding and absorbing new information related to the job. For some, the information they needed centered on working with the gang population; others had needed more
or clearer information about procedures, practices, and even technical
skills. Many officers stated that before coming to the unit, they had
had little working knowledge about gangs, so the sheer quantity of new
information presented a challenge.

I wouldn't call them problems, I would just say, having to adjust to a new assignment. One of the things that I experienced was that I was overwhelmed with all
the gang slang, language, with monikers, having to remember so many different
faces, names, monikers, where the gangs hang out, and all that kind of stuff.

I would say . . . knowing the members; getting to know the gangs. Getting to know
where they, particularly, where they hang out. Once you know that, getting to
know the specific members. Like being able to go up to you and say, "Hey, John,"
instead of "What's your name?" Or another hard part is getting to know the
signs, getting to know somebody is a gang member who doesn't necessarily want
to admit that they are a gang member. . . .

The most frequent responses to our questions about adjusting to the
assignments had to do with new gang unit officers' problems with learning *how* they were to perform their duties. Some officers explained that
for some time, they had lacked confidence that they understood their
unit's policies and procedures, how to conduct criminal investigations,

and how to use the gang database. Very few officers associated this kind of problem with lack of training, however. Instead, they regarded it as a normal hurdle that they initially faced – a problem that was resolved with time, patience, and on-the-job experience and training.

I'm still learning, basically at this point, how to sub out cases, how to work the computer, for example The computer in a patrol car is different than the computer in the office. Obviously, those are some of the steps that I need to take to learn. So it just takes time and experience.

When we became detectives and started submitting our own cases, I had no knowledge of that. I have never done anything like that, like a search warrant or an arrest warrant, and I had to learn all that. I was computer illiterate and had to learn computer processing and stuff. [Interviewer: Was it all sort of on the job learning?] Yes. At home I spent a lot of my personal time trying to update my knowledge on computers and stuff like that.

GANG UNIT OFFICER STATUS

In all four gang units, officers had the title of detective or investigator. These titles were not indicative of promotion, by departmental standards gang unit officers were the same rank as patrol officers. In two departments, officers assigned to the gang unit did receive pay increases, however. In Las Vegas, officers received an 8 percent raise while assigned to the gang unit, because the unit was designated as hazardous duty. Likewise, in Inglewood, gang unit officers received an extra 3 percent in pay upon assignment to an investigative position. Phoenix and Albuquerque did not give officers extra pay for assignments to the gang unit.

Officers in every unit remarked that although the designation of detective or investigator was technically not a promotion and did not represent an increase in rank, it could be viewed from some perspectives as the equivalent of a promotion, in that the titles sometimes conferred status within the department.

It's not considered technically a promotion. . . . The nice thing about the unit, it gives you a lot of freedom that you don't usually have as a policeman or patrol officer. While again it's not technically considered a promotion, in the minds of most police officers, myself included, it's kind of an elite group of detectives and people who live here. Most officers would really like to work here.

Officers varied in their perceptions of whether special status was attributed to being a member of the gang unit. A number of them argued that the gang unit was just like any other unit in the police department.

Although being a detective offered some special status, particularly among younger and newer officers, most thought of themselves as simply participating in one of a number of specialized units in the department. This sentiment was echoed in all of the units, but it was particularly strong in Las Vegas, where few officers felt that being a member of the gang unit gave them special status.

I like to compare to when I was in the military, my brother, my youngest brother, used to always ask me, "Who's better, the Marines or the Army, the Navy or the Army?" And each one is good at what they do, you can't generalize and say who's better. The Army can't do beach landings like the Marines can, and the Marines can't do an extended land deal like the Army can. So I personally don't think I am any different than a patrol officer. I just do a different job.

A number of officers in each unit, however, pointed out that their *knowledge* of gang-related issues gave them special status within the department. Their contact and work with gang members, who were more likely than most to engage in violent crime, gave the officers access to information, and therefore, insight, that others in the department did not necessarily possess.

Probably the knowledge of knowing almost everybody on the street, because our job is to contact and talk and become personally involved in these gangsters' lives, their family lives, their mothers, their school lives, so we get to know the people. We don't know them all, I mean there is just too many of them to know, but we know most of them, the ones that are the most active, and we know a lot about them, and they talk to us, and we know a lot of what is going on in the street. And so we are kind of like an encyclopedia here of what is going on in the city, and everybody comes to us because of it....

A number of the gang unit officers commented that they enjoyed special status within the department because of the many benefits they received while in the unit. For example, some noted, no supervisors looked over their shoulders; they were self-directed in the field; they worked in individual cubicles; and the gang unit was physically located in a separate facility, apart from the rest of the department. Other officers mentioned that special status came with wearing a uniform that differentiated them from others in the department. In Las Vegas, the officers wore Battle Dress Uniforms (BDUs), and in Phoenix, Inglewood, and Albuquerque, officers wore plain street clothing – typically jeans, a polo shirt, and tennis shoes. In Phoenix and Las Vegas, gang unit officers were permitted to take assigned undercover vehicles home. Still other officers told us that being in the gang unit gave them a sense of belonging to a special group, as opposed to being just one of many, as they had been in patrol.

Difference just as far as filing and keeping track of items and having your own little space to work, so I mean, it seems like a little thing to stick us in a cubicle, but that cubicle is – I think it's very beneficial, it gives you that sense that they're treating you more like an adult. You got your own phone line, your own voice mail, you've got a personal vehicle that it's either take home or you drop off by your house, by a city facility, so you've got that.

The people in my class, they look at us now and see how we've changed. Kind of like not many officers can wear gold rings and dress the way they want when they go to work, drive undercover cars. Pretty much we answer to our elite chain of command, we're almost – you can call it separate from the rest of the department. You can see where we're at now, we're in our own building.

We also asked gang unit officers how their peers outside the unit perceived them. Regardless of the department, we heard commonalities in their responses. Namely, almost all of the officers focused on the perceptions of *patrol* officers, and they rarely mentioned other detectives in the department in this context. Furthermore, although most officers made broad statements about the generally positive relationships that existed between the gang unit and patrol, officers tended to focus on the negative perceptions of their units. Several of them commented that most other officers in the police department did not know what the gang unit did. The following response exemplified their claims:

They don't know anything about the gang unit. They don't know anything that goes on here. All they do is see us out there once in a while, and they don't see us because we are back in here doing something. They don't know what our job entails. But that's no different than any other position. No one knows, because no one takes the time to find out. Not everybody, but most people don't take the time to find out, what are the narcotics guys doing, what do gang guys do, or what somebody else is doing. They all have their own perception of what they should do.... and what they are doing, and what they are not doing. So nobody really knows....

Some gang unit officers believed that a lack of familiarity with the gang unit and its functions and processes led to frustration and resentment among patrol officers. For example, they pointed out that when patrol officers contacted the gang unit for assistance, help was often refused because the gang unit officer would determine that the request was unrelated to gangs. An officer in Phoenix explained:

There's a lot of misconceptions about what gang squad does and what we're responsible for. Patrol's a very busy detail and they like as much assistance as they can, it's just a lot of them don't realize what our duties are, what we're responsible for, and what we can and cannot do. What was their perceptions? Oh, the gang squad is lazy. That we are not willing to assist them in their investigations, which, you know, which I knew was not true while I was on patrol and would attempt to pass on my thoughts on gang squad rep.

The most common response given by gang unit officers, particularly in Phoenix and Las Vegas, was that patrol officers viewed gang unit officers as arrogant and egotistical. Many thought that patrol officers were jealous of gang unit officers and resented their status because the patrol officers had not been selected for the gang unit at some time, or simply because the gang unit officers were different. Some suggested that this problem was not isolated to the gang unit, but was also an issue for other specialized units in the department.

Some of them believe that we're *prima donnas*, and others envy us and want to be in our position. I think there's a lot of times, because of the situation by the gang unit being so many gang members out on the street and so little gang officers. You know, we don't have that much time in the day to go run to every patrol officers' meeting. And a lot of times they'll stop a gang member and they want us to respond to a location and we can't, because we're busy. And because of that, they think we're too good, you know, screw 'em.

You know, and then we're – we're dressed different. We have a different uniform than a patrol. Any time you have the, I believe, the segregation like that, you're going to have problems, you know, even though I don't disagree with them. Gang members treat us different than they treat patrol officers, and so I believe that there is a purpose for us being, you know, differently identifiable, whether it's in our cars or in our uniform or whatever. You know, and any time you have the specialty detail tag, there's going to be problems, you know.

Well, like I touched on it before, I mean some of them think that we're cocky, we've been called "knuckle draggers," you know, most of us here, we hit the weight room more often than maybe some of these other units do, so they always call us the "no neckers" or something like that. I think they probably perceive us as maybe egomaniacs. Some patrol officers are eager to talk to you and, myself personally, I can get along with anybody, so I don't mind giving out info or helping people. Some of these other guys, you know, hold things in themselves so, you know, it's a fine line, and it's depending on who the officer is or the unit is, you know, some of them don't like us, and some of them do.

Conversely, the common thread in the answers of officers who perceived that their unit was viewed positively was their unit was responsive to patrol officers' needs.

[They think of us] as a resource. They know that we know the gangsters. They hear of a particular problem and they come to us with it, and if they know of a subject that is running from them or something like that, and they can identify them, nine times out of ten, a basic description from a gang member that we are familiar with, we can drop out of the top of our head, "that is so-and-so from whatever gang," so we start writing up warrants. They use us a lot as a resource.

It's a mixed bag. And it's dependent on – mostly upon how well we communicate with them, and how accessible we are to them when they ask for assistance. Do we blow them off, or do we go out there and talk to them? I suppose it would be the same as when you are a police officer, and you are asked for information from a citizen. It's going to be the same kind of perception. If you blow them off, they are not going to have a very positive perception of you, and they are going to resent you. It's the same thing here, and it's the same when I was on the private sector. We had a difficult time sometimes alienating the store staff, you know, not responding to their needs. When you did that, you ended up not having information flung in your direction, which was sometimes pertinent, keeping you from being able to do your job. Many of the leads that we get are from patrol officers, because they are out in the field all the time, on a day-to-day basis, and they have more access and there's more of them. If you go to briefings, talk to them . . . you don't even have to teach them anything, just be accessible to them. I found that they seem to respond real positively to it, and we get information flowing to us instead of around us.

Responses from Albuquerque gang unit officers generally resembled those in the preceding text. However, Albuquerque officers believed that the gang unit's reputation had changed dramatically from that of the gang unit of years past. Almost all of them related that the prior gang unit had had a poor reputation among other officers, which was one of the reasons that the gang unit had been disbanded by the police chief. They noted that former gang unit officers had not worked hard, and when they did, it was not necessarily related to gangs. According to the officers, that gang unit had developed one of the worst reputations in the department. Almost all of them noted, however, that officers across the department were quickly gaining respect for the newly created gang unit.

. . . It used to be that they had a notorious view of not really working, when the gang unit wasn't full. They had 17, 18 officers. They were under different sergeants, and the sergeants were more of a type to say, "just show a force and go bug a bunch of gangbangers," but they weren't really perceived as, at least myself when I was in the field, I didn't perceive them as actually working very hard. It was hard to get most of them to come out to your scenes to do anything. But hopefully, now we're changing the perception because we're going out. We're going to the briefings. We're talking to the field officers. We're getting called out at least by the field more.

Well, we kind of have – it's a mixed emotion, I think, because the last gang unit that we had, a lot of people didn't take very well. They weren't very – all I can say is, in the short time that I was in the department and there was a gang unit, they weren't very respected in a lot of ways, because they weren't very proactive. They just kind of – they didn't do a whole lot of work. So right now it's been very, very good. A lot of officers that I know, especially that have come out near my academy, are very anxious to get over there with me. I mean 10, 15 guys really came to me and said, "How do I get to your unit."

Stakeholder Perceptions of the Gang Unit

We were further interested in exploring how the gang unit was viewed by their peers, outside of the unit, and whether these views were congruent with the gang unit officers perceptions of themselves and their unit. As such, to further explore the reputation of our study gang units we asked all stakeholders several questions pertaining to their relationship with the gang unit.

Inglewood's internal stakeholders assessed the relationship favorably. The gang unit was in close physical proximity to most internal stakeholders, a difference from other study sites where gang units were located in separate facilities. Detective stakeholders gave examples of their ability to obtain intelligence from the unit, illustrating the positive relationship. One Inglewood robbery detective said that he used gang unit intelligence "... especially about younger guys [he] didn't know." He talked about taking monikers he had picked up in the course of investigations to the gang unit for suspect identification. A homicide detective also commented that a good relationship existed "... primarily because the majority of the homicides [that the homicide unit] investigate[s] involve gang members." He also reported using gang unit intelligence to develop suspects. A local prosecuting attorney also commented on his positive relationship with the gang unit.

Oh, Inglewood is great. I mean, I am very demanding and I am constantly bothering them for things, but they are very receptive and work very hard for me. I will have a filing of a case. For example, Monday I had a case that was a sheriff's homicide, but the shooter is an 18th Street. The expert that is the best on that is an Inglewood police officer, so I basically have to subpoena him, and get him to do a bunch of work.

Albuquerque internal stakeholders were nearly uniform in describing their units' relationships with the gang unit. They used language such as "it's a great relationship," "I think it's an excellent relationship," "probably pretty good," or just "good." One commander, who responded that "it's good," went on to say that "anyone just needs to pick up the phone and get a hold of those people, and they'll be available."

A sergeant with the violent crimes detail who described the relationship as "excellent" told us, "I went through academy with the [gang] sergeant, and the detectives are constantly calling me, 'Hey, are you doing this case?' They're always willing to assist or to take over a case if it's gang related." A sheriff's representative to the Albuquerque gang task force characterized their relationship with the gang unit this way: "We work together hand-in-hand." Likewise, an intensive probation supervisor described it as "very good: just an open line of communication back and forth, the sharing of information," and went on to describe this aspect of their relationship:

They're very familiar with the people that we're supervising, so it's only natural that we talk back and forth. They'll come across our folks...I had one of my guys...we have a big low-rider car show in northern New Mexico. And our folks in intensive supervision are not allowed to travel any place outside a 70-mile radius...so [they] went up to the car show, and the gang unit was familiar with one of my guys and had him arrested....

Las Vegas stakeholders were more moderate in their perceptions of their gang unit. For example, a few stakeholders had very positive views of the gang unit. A Las Vegas county code enforcement officer who described the police department as: "...the best he had ever worked with; the gang unit took advantage of the information that he provided and wrote tickets on his behalf for ordinance violations, which he saw as "a major coup...to have police officers writing tickets for us." Most stakeholders, however, provided much less positive feedback about the gang unit. A Las Vegas prosecutor noted:

Yeah...we've gotten at odds a couple of times...a case gets submitted to our office. It's not trial-ready. Our screening department rejects it or sends it back for further investigation. The police department gets upset and they go to the media. "We have this great case, and I can't believe the D.A.'s not prosecuting it."

One lieutenant described the relationship as "improving":

Gotten better. In the past, the gang unit did not share info. Weren't around when you needed them. Over last year, the unit has been more service oriented. They have assigned liaison officers so patrol knows who to contact for gang issues. We also have their pager number. It has been helpful. They have expertise and suggestions. The gang unit comes out and investigates and frees up resources in patrol. We cannot afford the time they can.

Likewise, the director of a Las Vegas probation and parole district admitted that their relationship "could be improved." The supervisor described "butting heads a little bit" with the gang unit over the unit's attempts to take advantage of a probation and parole search clause that exempts the probation agency from the requirement of a search warrant.

They would like us to provide them with much more information and much more access than we can. But, you know, that's what I'm saying. We have our days and we don't have our days. We have days when it comes like that and we butt up, and then we have days when we're able to give them what they want.

Phoenix internal stakeholders gave varied answers when asked whether they were satisfied with the gang unit. Some responded, "Oh, yes, very much," "yes, very much so," or just plain "yes." As one detective put it, "Oh, yeah...I pick up the phone and can have access to anything they have and vice versa." A lieutenant working as an area manager reported:

Yes, right now. I have no complaints. I'll tell you, when I first got here 4 years ago, I had a number of complaints. Since I was out of shift three, I never saw them, and I'll call them and they were working different hours, so my service level was not nearly what I expected, but when [the precinct commander] got here, he changed that, he changed the service level, he changed their hours so that they cover until three in the morning, so when I needed them, they came.

A Phoenix graffiti detective also described the relationship in positive terms: "Very good, it's a matter of a phone call, and I can have anything that they have and have it on a 'right now' basis." This characterization given by a former homicide detective was similar:

I would characterize the relationship as very open, and one in which communication was easy, and that's what's so important to me as an investigator, because there's no way that I can keep up on every street gang....

On the other hand, other stakeholders voiced dissatisfaction with the gang unit. For example, a patrol officer in a high-crime district was more negative in his assessment of the relationship of patrol with the gang unit:

At times, it can be distant, and we could forget they're out there, and they could forget we're out there. We hear them on the radio now and again during traffic stops and things like that. I have probably weekly contact with them, again, like I said, because I know a lot of the guys. The average patrol guy, I don't think we have many contacts at all with them. There's not much communication between us.

Similarly, a patrol officer attributed his dissatisfaction with the relationship between patrol and the gang unit as stemming from lack of communication, suggesting that he would prefer contact "like maybe once a month, have them come to a briefing and just give us a 5-minute spiel on things that we're working on in the community, give us a pager number." An officer working on one of the Neighborhood Enforcement Teams expressed the most negative feelings, and recommended reorganizing the gang unit:

No, I'm not. I'm not satisfied, I'm not content with it, and one of the things is that because I'm looking to be squad detective, so obviously I'm trying to do face time and understand what they're doing. If I had my way, I would rather see the gang squad melted back in patrol just because Phoenix needs the manpower so badly ... there's no reason why I should as an officer, or any other officer, shouldn't be able to do gang investigation simply because we don't have a black uniform or are not assigned to that unit.

THE ROLE OF THE GANG UNIT AND THE GANG UNIT OFFICER

In the following sections we discuss the role of the gang unit and gang unit officers from three perspectives: gang unit officers and internal and external stakeholders. We were interested in how the gang unit officers perceived themselves and the role they played in their police department and community. We were also interested in ascertaining the degree to which officers within a unit shared common perceptions of their role and whether their perceptions were congruent with those of internal and external stakeholders.

Gang Unit Officer Perceptions of Their Role

Gang unit officers appeared united in the perception of themselves as crime fighters, regardless of their units' formal mandates. Our observations suggested that the gang unit officers perceived their units not as responding to *crime*, so much as responding to *groups of individual*s whom they believed to be deeply involved in criminal activities. Although this may be a fine distinction, it is meaningful. Gangs and gang members, not just their criminal acts, were viewed by the officers as the threat, and gang unit officers believed that their mission was to protect the community by combating those gangs. Unlike patrol officers and investigators, gang unit officers tended to see themselves as engaged in a fight not merely against crime, but against evil and its perpetrators.

This unity of perception across study sites was reflected again in the remarkably similar ratings of the importance of various unit activities

TABLE 6.2. *Ratings of Enforcement, Intelligence, and Prevention Activities by City*

	Albuquerque	Inglewood	Las Vegas	Phoenix
Investigate gang-related activity	5.00	4.66	4.97	5.00
Directed patrol at known gang hot spots	4.75	5.00	4.74	4.43
Deal with gang graffiti	3.31	3.33	3.21	3.14
Perform gang sweeps of known gang members	4.29	4.00	4.37	4.50
Deliver prevention talks with respect to gangs	3.63	3.00	3.94	2.62
Provide information to citizen groups about gangs	3.92	2.67	3.92	2.98
Work with other agencies on gang-related issues	4.75	4.67	4.77	4.26
Work with other units on gang-related issues	4.88	4.67	4.67	4.74
Collect and process gang-related intelligence	5.00	5.00	4.81	4.95

Ratings: 1 = unimportant; 5 = very important

given by gang officers in all four units. Table 6.2 shows the average ratings of gang unit officers of various unit activities. The officers used a five-point scale, with "1" representing activities that the officers believed were unimportant, and "5" representing activities that the officers believed were very important. Officers ranked collecting and processing gang-related intelligence and investigating gang-related activities as the most important activities, in all four of the gang units. The official mandates of all of the gang units supported the selection of intelligence as a top-ranking activity. Asked to elaborate, officers from all units routinely stated something to the effect of "that's what we are here for," "that's what we do," or "it's critical," although several officers in Inglewood and Albuquerque ranked gang investigation as a highly important activity, somewhat at odds with their official mandates. In Inglewood, gang unit officers were formally responsible for gang intelligence and nothing else, and in Albuquerque, gang unit officers were not assigned primary responsibility for investigating gang crime, but were to assist other officers with investigations.

After intelligence gathering and investigating gang activity, gang unit officers across the units agreed that working on gang-related issues with other units within their departments and in other agencies was their next most important activity. The officers indicated that their intelligence was often valuable to other units and agencies, and indicated that their experience with gangs and gang culture often assisted others in solving crimes. Officers mentioned that gang members were involved in a variety of activities, sometimes crossing jurisdictions, which made interagency cooperation especially important.

That's [interagency cooperation] very important, I'd like to shove that one up there towards a five, because, too, especially because the way gangs – gangs cover the gamut of crime. We've had gangs doing money laundering, producing counterfeit money, all gangs are into drugs or drug sales, so we need to be working with our DEB, our fraud groups, so yeah, it's important.

Well, we hear about this and we're like, fuck this, those two guys offed him. And so things just weren't adding up. So we're not working the homicide, but homicide calls us and let's us know what they know. I do some research and find out that those two guys have been identified three times in one year with the dead guy. Now you know what that homicide investigator's solution to that was? "They fucking lied to me, I'm going to go out there and jam their ass." When in reality, if he knew the gang culture, if he had walked that night and said, "Man, what's up with this, I want to get the fuckers as much as you do." They'd said, "Yeah, he's Jose, we know them from here."

Well, as it turns out, those two fuckers shot him and now they're in Mexico. But the whole case in point is when you use traditional investigative techniques, shit that has worked in the past and always worked, sometimes you don't realize that it's not still working. And a lot of these detectives take that approach, and these fuckers will clam up and they won't say a fricking word. So they need to be educated, but they don't think they need to be educated. So, I think that it is very critical that that process is ongoing throughout the department, especially since I would venture to say that well over half of the crimes committed in this community are committed by gangs.

However, as will be discussed in the next chapter, despite the importance they attached to interagency cooperation the gang unit officers, other than in Inglewood, rarely had contact with others outside their own units.

Directed patrols and gang sweeps were viewed, in general, as the next most important gang unit activities. Inglewood gang unit officers ranked directed patrol as one of its most important activities, giving it an average score of five, while Las Vegas officers generally rated directed patrol as less important than many other activities. These findings are interesting, given that Inglewood's gang unit was not mandated to perform direct patrols or sweeps, while in Las Vegas, the majority of gang unit officers were specifically assigned to do them. The officers' perceptions of the importance of these activities in these two units did not appear to match their formal responsibilities.

Regardless, many gang unit officers noted that directed patrols or sweeps were regular and important activities for the unit. Although the majority of officers in each unit ranked these two activities relatively high in importance (four out of a possible five), most did not necessarily believe that the activities were effective. Instead, the officers appeared to rank these activities high in importance simply because they performed them regularly; they were part of the job.

[I'd rank them as] three or four, maybe. Because we'll never leave them [alone]. They know we're there. We're just in their back pocket, agitating them. I'd say probably a four, because they need to know we're still alive.

Three. [Interviewer: Why is that a three?] . . . We've got tunnel vision. What I mean by that is, we hit the same exact spots everyday, that we know to be hot spots. Well, that's ineffective, very ineffective. What about everywhere else? What about these apartments over here that we never go to? How do you know that people aren't hanging out over there? You just don't know unless you go. So I think it's important and you should hit them a large majority of the time, but you also need to hit everywhere else that you don't hit. [Interviewer: Do you hit the hot spots on a predictable basis?] No, but it is pretty much in the routine. I mean, like you know where you are going to go next. You don't even have to ask. [Interviewer: So they know when you're going to show up, sort of?] We don't hit it the same time or even the same day. I'm just saying, like if on Monday we're going to go to this side of town, and we're going to start at this location, we know where we're going to go after that. And we might do the same thing over here and over here, but we would hit it on a Monday one week and a Friday another. The times of the day are completely unpredictable, but the locations are sometimes – I think it's definitely important, but I also think everywhere else is important, too. Making car stops. That's where everyone keeps their guns and drugs.

Dealing with gang graffiti was ranked as the least important activity in Albuquerque and Las Vegas, as the second to least important activity in Phoenix, and within the bottom half in importance in Inglewood. Likewise, officers in each of the gang units gave some of the lowest ratings to educational activities. Many officers noted that the gang unit did not have time to perform these kinds of duties, or that other units were responsible for them. With graffiti, many simply noted that such crimes were fairly minor, and that individuals engaged in these crimes were young, inexperienced, and not very dangerous. Many officers made statements such as the following:

> Well, because dealing with it, well, because I don't see a lot of gang graffiti. I see a lot of tagger graffiti, but not so much gang graffiti. And gang graffiti is mostly done by young punks that are not heavy into the gang yet, and it's hard to catch them at it, and it's difficult to find out who is doing it. It takes too much time, and it's a misdemeanor offense.

Internal Stakeholder Perceptions of the Role of Their Gang Unit

We asked internal stakeholders about how they perceived their gang unit's role and the emphasis that their unit placed on each function. Generally, we found strong consensus among internal stakeholders within each site, and found that with the exception of Phoenix stakeholders, internal stakeholders articulated clear roles in this domain; with emphasis primarily being placed on each unit's intelligence function, and secondarily on their enforcement function. However, in several instances, they did not distinguish between the broader role of the police department and the more specialized role of their gang unit; and they often times had a one-dimensional view of their gang unit when it was in fact was much more complex than they gave credit.

For example, in Albuquerque, an area commander noted, "The role of the police department in general is to monitor and to gather intelligence. It's diverse in nature. The ultimate responsibility for the police is to do everything in our power constitutionally to restrict the gang's illicit activities." An Albuquerque school resource officer described the police role as "to solicit good intelligence," as did a sergeant with the violent crimes unit, who then went on to describe the primary function of the gang unit as maintaining intelligence as a tool for the rest of the department. The sergeant further noted that gang units should also be involved in investigating gang-related crime.

A few internal stakeholders in Albuquerque offered a different perspective on the role of the gang unit. For example, a commander of a different area was clear that the appropriate role for the department was suppression:

> I wish I could tell you that our primary responsibility is to stamp it out and get rid of it, but being a realist, I know that's not going to happen. Our primary function is within all constitutional guidelines and conduct of human decency, our job is to

make sure that the gang activity is controlled so that it doesn't negatively impact the quality of the life of the average citizen of Albuquerque. That's basically what our job is. However we go about doing that, primarily it's in response to criminal activity. But however we go about doing that, we go about doing that.

And a few other officers in the APD articulated the gang unit's role in prevention-oriented activities. For example, a sergeant in a violent crime unit stated, "We do quite a bit of prevention as police officers. We jump into that intervention stage when kids are actually in that lifestyle and they want to get out.... "

Inglewood stakeholders pointed to their gang unit as the appropriate police response, and they described the unit's role as "keeping on top of it," and gathering and maintaining intelligence on gang members that "saves hundreds of hours of investigation time.... " For example, one detective from the department's assault unit said:

The principal functions of the gang unit then are intelligence and gathering, having information and networking with other agencies to share information and to get intelligence from them. The gang unit needs to engage in field work to get intelligence. Gang officers need to go to addresses sometimes to gather that kind of information and to be of assistance providing intelligence.

Likewise, a departmental crime analyst noted that the gang unit's function is clearly related to intelligence.

The gang unit's [role] has not changed much over time. They provide briefings and monthly interdepartmental meetings. They participate in the county association of gang officers in the state unit as well. The gang unit is really an intelligence unit, ACT or patrol are the folks responsible for making arrests. The gang unit has special rapport with gang member. The gang unit is intelligence, not enforcement.

Las Vegas stakeholders listed intelligence and suppression as the principal roles of their unit in addressing the gang problem. According to one lieutenant, their role is to "ID the problem to stop the problem." However, the lieutenant also acknowledged that police needed to work with the community to solve the problem. He thought that they needed to develop employment opportunities because "arrest is a band-aid approach."

Another Las Vegas lieutenant described two roles for the department that were similar to those of other internal stakeholders:

One collects intelligence information, trying to identify who, you know, who the gang members are, who their associates are, and what they're doing is gaining intelligence information on their activities. Also the enforcement aspect to keep as much pressure on gang members and arrests, interviews, what have you, as many gang members as we can take off the street through arrest for whatever lessens violence on the streets.

Phoenix internal stakeholders were somewhat at odds with stakeholders in the other sites in that they primarily focused on their gang unit's suppression function. When we interviewed stakeholders in Phoenix about their perceptions of their gang unit's role many gave responses similar to the following made by an area commander:

Obviously, we have to protect the community. Our role is to enforce, to [disperse] the gangs. We have a lot of low-income areas, like I said, for instance, the Garfield neighborhood. We have a gang in there that's the Garfield Gang, and we also have a younger gang that's affiliated with it called the 9th Street Gang. What they do is, they're intimidating the elder people. They're robbing them on the streets. They're doing home invasions. They're stealing their property and coercing them not to call the police. Otherwise they return and hurt them, physically, bodily harms. Obviously, we can't have that. Our role is basically, squash these gang problems like that.

Very few of the internal stakeholders in Phoenix, however, perceived the role of their gang unit solely in terms of intelligence. Instead, most would first affirm the role of suppression in the unit and then explain the unit's role in gathering, processing, and disseminating gang intelligence. For example, one detective from the Arizona Department of Public Safety explained:

They have the patrol, the uniform gang and enforcement control, you don't see much undercover [work] ... and they are really good at gathering intelligence. They have their officers specialize, they have one officer specialize in each street gang, and that officer really knows membership and really like the expert, gang expert, if I need to find out about a certain gang I call Phoenix and they get me in touch with that gang detective and usually we can get the information. . . .

External Stakeholder Perceptions of the Role of Their Gang Unit

We also asked external stakeholders about their perceptions of the role of their gang units. In Albuquerque most external stakeholders focused on the gang unit's intelligence-related activities. An intensive probation supervisor observed that "they [gang unit officers] do a lot of gathering of intelligence and data. It really helps us." A juvenile court prosecutor described the police role as "not only trying to keep the incidence of gang-related crime down, but also to gather information regarding the gang to have this base of information available." Another Albuquerque prosecutor stated:

I see their role as getting out, intermingling with these guys. Kids will do stupid things, you know, and it's not too harmful giving them a break, getting the trust going, obtaining information about more serious types of cases, trying to prevent a lot of stuff, as opposed to just reacting to it once they commit the crimes.

Almost all of the external stakeholders in Inglewood agreed with their colleagues in the other cities that the intelligence function was an important role for police. For example, a gang specialist in another criminal justice agency stated: "The principal function of the Inglewood gang unit is the intelligence function, and that's a lot of the value to my agency, in that we interface based on sharing of intelligence information." A parole officer similarly explained, "I see their job mainly as updating gang information, keeping their own officers updated on what's going on in the gang situation and writing up-to-date intelligence lists."

Only a few external stakeholders in Inglewood believed their gang unit should place emphasis on functions other than intelligence. For instance, a graffiti officer saw suppression, rather than intelligence, as the principal role of police:

So they got to keep on top of the neighborhoods, just keep patrolling certain neighborhoods, and getting a lot of graffiti, a lot of drug problems, just keep a check on those areas, because eventually you will get them out and maybe even arrested.

In Las Vegas, external stakeholder perceptions of the role of their gang unit varied substantially when compared to other sites. For example, several external stakeholders explained that the primary function of their gang unit was intelligence gathering. Many of them gave responses similar to a local prosecutor:

I mean, they go out there every day. They see gang members. They develop relationships. They're talking to these kids. They're learning a lot of valuable information: gang alliances, youth gang rivalries, which gang is not getting along with what gang, who's joining a gang, who just got jumped in. I mean they're learning a lot of stuff. And you're documenting really the basic characteristics and traits of many gangs on the nightly basis that they're out there.

Other external stakeholders focused much more on suppression being the primary role of the gang unit. Several leaders from a Las Vegas youth outreach group made the following statement:

They made a whole section, Metro's SED used to be small. They grew with the gang problem. And they've got a whole section that's all SWAT and their whole effort is just to focus on gangs. They have a detective division and the enforcement. If something goes on and one particular gang is acting up, they will go out there and target that gang. And they're high-profile guys. BDU, military type thing, to let them know that there. If these guys get out of line, they're on them real quick. Metro does a real good job.

Still other external stakeholders in Las Vegas believed that the primary role of the gang unit was prevention. For example, a district attorney explained that while the gang unit engaged in a substantial amount of intelligence-oriented activity, they were also heavily involved in outreach work.

I know that the police department in, in their, program is, they're trying to outreach and get to these kids before, uh, they join a gang. And although admirable as it is I don't know if the role of the police department [should be to] suddenly take on a role of a parent . . . I think that it is ambitious for a police department to be so proactive on a kid when they only see a kid once or maybe twice a week.

External stakeholders in Phoenix largely agreed that suppression was the primary function of their gang unit. One gang prevention coordinator said, "Suppression. Some gang intelligence gathering, but I think that's really lacking and probably because they got kind of started late on it." A probation officer similarly stated, "I would say largely enforcement and I kinda know how they are set up. I would say largely enforcement with going out making these guys, gang members, you know they get them off the streets. . . . "

A director of a nonprofit youth service organization in Phoenix also thought that the local gang unit's proactive role was useful and explained that "Traditionally their role is enforcement and protection [of the community]." But he also explained that the unit has begun to reach out to the community.

I believe the gang squad is actually taking a more proactive approach, a more one-on-one, if you will. Because they're actually dividing themselves up, going into the community, and allowing themselves to be approached by some of these individuals, thereby instilling trust in the community, whereas if someone gets wind of an activity that maybe someone's planning, they'd be more comfortable in coming to them somewhat anonymously, saying, "I hear this is in the wind right now. This is what someone is telling me about." So that way, they're a little more informed.

Interestingly, none of the external stakeholders in Phoenix mentioned intelligence as being a core function of the gang unit.

SUMMARY

Typically, the gang units we studied were all-male, ethnically diverse enterprises of veteran officers, who saw themselves as crime fighters. Unlike many other specialized police units, gang unit officers saw themselves as not only engaged in fighting crime, but also fighting groups of evil perpetrators. The gang units promised officers unusual action and excitement stemming from the perceived opportunity to take off the gloves and fight crime and an evil enemy – an image embraced and perpetuated by gang unit officers. Gang sweeps and specialized enforcement tactics promised relief from the tedium of patrol, even when the centerpiece of a gang unit's formal mandate was intelligence gathering and dissemination. The job also offered, in some of the departments, involvement in the investigation of crimes against persons, which some viewed as a potential stepping stone to homicide units. Gang unit officers noted that the status of the gang unit was enhanced by many day-to-day benefits. The units were often located off-site, and officers were self-directed, free from supervision. They wore plain clothes or special uniforms. All of these things, the officers believed, gave them a sense of working with and belonging to a special group.

However, we found that most of the gang unit officers entered their assignments with limited preparation for policing gangs, which is consistent with other research on officer movements in and out of highly specialized units (Manning 1977). They received much of their gang-related training after they began working in their units, and much of it was best described as on-the-job training. Although officers stated that they were generally satisfied with their training, lack of training proved a significant problem when they first began their jobs. Formal in-service training for officers in the gang units was hit-or-miss (Inglewood being the notable exception), even though most officers expressed a keen interest in learning more about gangs and gang-related policing procedures. The lack of training was even more pronounced for investigators in the two gang units that had primary responsibility for the investigative function. These officers typically had no prior investigative experience and were not trained in the investigation of crimes. This omission was significant, given the major crimes investigated by gang unit officers.

The dearth of specialized training for gang unit officers had ramifications for their departments, other criminal justice agencies, and their communities. Regardless of training, officers assigned to gang units were automatically labeled as experts on gangs and gang issues. Stakeholders in and out of the police departments assumed that membership in the gang unit conferred expertise, and that the officers were repositories of information on gangs. This gave gang unit officers special status within the police departments, as well the communities, and also gave them considerable influence on gang-related policies and procedures, as well as on matters related to strategic planning.

Furthermore, gang unit officers were called upon to train and educate others on gang matters. Often they conducted trainings or educational sessions for police, probation and parole officers, prosecutors, school officials, community leaders, citizens, and the media. Although we did not set out specifically to evaluate the quality of the training received or delivered by gang unit officers, or their knowledge about gangs, we were nonetheless struck by the lack of depth in their education and training in this area.

Gang unit officers felt that they were the objects of some resentment from officers outside the unit. Some stated that other officers did not understand what the gang unit did or its official functions, and when gang unit officers failed to meet their expectations, patrol officers and detectives became frustrated. For example, officers in all of the units mentioned that patrol officers would frequently contact them for assistance on non-gang-related incidents. When gang unit officers were unable to help them, the patrol officers reacted with anger and resentment. Gang unit officers also mentioned that those outside the unit viewed them as arrogant and egotistical. Gang unit officers believed that some other officers' perceptions were the consequence of jealousy, in some cases, perhaps because they had been refused a position in the gang unit.

While gang unit officers saw themselves primarily as crime fighters they recognized that it was their knowledge about gangs, and the intelligence that they processed that defined their status and role within their police department and community. Interviews with stakeholders substantiated the claims made by the gang unit officers. Stakeholders, in general, saw the primary function of their unit's as collecting, processing, and disseminating gang intelligence (Phoenix being the exception). Other functions were viewed as secondary in importance. Stakeholders who had positive assessments of their gang unit attributed it to the fact that the gang unit provided them with worthwhile information and that the information was easily assessable. On the other hand, stakeholders who did not have a favorable opinion of their gang unit saw their gang unit as difficult to extract information from and generally unhelpful in terms of providing gang intelligence.

In summary, some of the key features that shape the gang officer role are the combination of the lack of training, supervision, written guidelines, and a strong officer culture that emphasizes the gang unit officer's job as crime fighting and the belief that they are engaged in a struggle to combat evil groups of people committed to engaging in crime and harming the community. This, we found, lead to role conflict in that those in the gang unit's institutional environment placed high value on the intelligence that the gang unit officers processed, and evaluated their performance, at least in part, on the quality and accessibility of the intelligence.

7

On the Job

As a rule policemen assume that the gang must be suppressed – must be broken up. They fail to understand that boyish energies, like tics, suppressed at one place are sure to break out at some other. And when the breaking up of the gang has been accomplished, there is usually no attempt to provide substitute activities for the boys. Under ordinary circumstances, then, the "cop" becomes the natural enemy of the gang.

– Fredric M. Thrasher 1927

This chapter focuses on the actual work of gang unit officers, as we describe what the gang unit officers were doing in the four cities that we studied, how they were doing it, and why, from the officers' perspectives, they were performing their jobs as they were. We also examined how gang unit officers spent their time over the normal course of a work day. We described the numbers and types of individuals that the gang unit officers came into contact with, how those contacts were initiated, and the various strategies and tactics that we observed being used by the gang unit officers in the field.

HOW THE GANG UNIT OFFICERS SPENT THEIR TIME

We directly observed officers at work in the four cities that we studied. For collecting and analyzing the data that would help us determine how the officers were spending their work time, we chose the *time diary strategy*. This approach enabled us to record activities in the open-ended fashion used by many ethnographers and time use researchers, and allowed us to code our observations for analysis afterward. This methodological strategy offered the flexibility that we needed to arrive at a clear understanding of the actual nature of the gang unit officers' work.

Once our activity data were collected, and after an initial qualitative analysis of the types of activities that the gang unit officers engaged in and the roles they played in the field, we identified and described seven general categories to further examine how the officers allocated their time: Enforcement, investigations, intelligence, education/prevention, administrative, en route, and non-police-related.[1]

- *Enforcement.* Directed patrol, field and traffic stops, hot spot operations, and backup for other officers and units.
- *Investigative.* Surveillance, locating suspects, interviewing (witnesses, victims, and suspects), processing crime scenes, and similar activities related to conducting criminal investigations.
- *Intelligence.* Collecting information from gang members, community members, business owners, and the public; documenting gang members; exchanging information with officers and other criminal and non–criminal justice personnel.
- *Education and prevention.* Counseling at-risk youth, attempting to find employment for gang youth, educating the public about gangs and gang activity, and other similar activities.
- *Administrative.* Field preparation, report production, evidence processing, meeting with court officials, testifying in court, and job training. (This category was constructed similarly to Parks et al. 1999.)
- *En route.* Travel to and from official destinations. (This category was constructed similarly to Parks et al. 1999.)
- *Non-police-related.* Activities unrelated to official police business, for example, meals and snacks, personal errands, and restroom and other breaks. (This category was constructed similarly to Parks et al. 1999.)

The four gang units that we studied differed substantially in how officers spent time (Table 7.1). For the most part, the differences reflected variations in the principal function(s) assigned to each unit. In spite of the differences, however, we found that the kinds of activities performed by each unit, with the exception of Inglewood, were fairly similar. In this section, we compare the amount of time spent by each unit on various functions, and we discuss how the units performed each function.

[1] For specifics regarding how the data were coded in the field see Chapter 2, page 39.

TABLE 7.1. *Average Minutes per Eight-Hour Shift Allocated to Activities*

Activity (primary)	Inglewood	Las Vegas	Albuquerque	Phoenix
Enforcement (total)	57.68	155.20	127.64	144.72
Directed patrol	35.04	98.43	57.53	90.51
Investigation	22.64	56.77	70.11	54.21
Intelligence	207.81	12.51	81.63	69.17
Education/prevention	0.00	3.96	0.00	0.00
Administrative	65.26	106.08	90.95	98.17
En route	28.84	45.25	99.40	52.43
Non-police-related	102.96	135.63	64.15	81.37
Orientation of observer	17.45	21.37	16.23	34.14

Enforcement

As Table 7.1 shows, three of the four gang units dedicated a disproportionate amount of time to enforcement. The Albuquerque, Las Vegas,
and Phoenix gang units each spent an average of about two to three
hours a day on enforcement, compared with Inglewood, which spent
only about one hour a day on enforcement activities. To understand the
enforcement role of the gang units, it is important to note that none of
the gang units were responsible for responding to calls for service. It
was each officer's prerogative to respond or not. As a result, gang unit
officers only responded when there appeared to be an opportunity to
assist with a gang-related investigation or to collect gang intelligence.

With few exceptions, in fact, officers were generally free to perform
only the gang control activities that interested them. They received little
direction about what to do, or about when or how their activities were
to be performed. They were left to conduct their activities as they saw
fit, with little or no oversight. With this said, gang unit officers generally engaged in two types of enforcement activity: directed patrol and
investigation.

Directed Patrol. All of the gang units allocated some portion of time for
directed patrols. Las Vegas and Phoenix gang units each spent an average
of about 1.5 hours a day on directed patrols, whereas Albuquerque
averaged just under one hour a day, and Inglewood averaged just over
thirty minutes a day (Table 7.1). Directed patrol was almost exclusively
carried out in known gang hot spots. As a result, gang unit suppression
efforts were typically directed toward minority neighborhoods, public
housing complexes, and parks frequented by gang members.

In Albuquerque, Las Vegas, and Phoenix, directed patrols in such areas served two general purposes. The primary goal was to suppress gang crime. Officers in all three units believed that gang members were aware of their presence in the targeted areas, and that this deterred gang violence. The officers stated that directed patrols often yielded arrests of gang members, which in turn caused those arrested, as well as their gang member friends, to think about negative consequences associated with gang life.

The second purpose of directed patrols in known gang areas was to gather intelligence from gang members. In particular, gang unit officers were expected to stop gang members on the street, document those who were not already documented, and gather intelligence on their gangs. From these stops, they collected information about active disputes and other happenings occurring among neighborhood gangs. Much of the time that officers spent on the street patrolling known gang areas was in pursuit of the *good stop*. The good stop was one that yielded an arrest of a gang member, usually for drug or weapons possession, or on an outstanding warrant. If a stop did not result in an arrest, officers hoped at least to have gathered some new gang-related intelligence.

Although all of the gang units except Inglewood used directed patrol as a general strategy to suppress gang activity, each relied on different tactics. In Albuquerque, officers conducted directed patrols in areas where gang violence had occurred in the past. Patrolling these areas, according to the officers, allowed them to increase police presence in high gang crime neighborhoods and to survey them for potential problems. Directed patrols also increased the probability that officers would come into contact with gang members and make a good stop resulting in an arrest or a newly documented gang member. Directed patrols were officer-initiated; they were performed at times when the officers did not have other priorities.

In Las Vegas, gang unit officers used a much more aggressive strategy that many of them referred to as the *sweep*. The members of each gang enforcement squad worked as a team. The team would split into four pairs, each assigned to its own squad car. At the beginning of the shift, the team would agree on the areas they were going to sweep and the order in which sweeps would be conducted. To begin, generally all four vehicles would rally at a single point outside the specified neighborhood. From there, one pair of officers would patrol down the "hot street" – a street or area where gang members were known to loiter or conduct street-level drug sales. Two other pairs in squad cars would patrol the two streets immediately parallel to the hot street, keeping pace with the lead car. The fourth squad car would remain out of sight at the end of the street, slowly patrolling toward the other three. This tactic involved squeezing gang members toward the center of the targeted area. Then if a suspect fled on foot or in a vehicle, one of the squad cars would be in position to pursue and stop that person.

Las Vegas officers explained that sweeps accomplished several purposes. They were thought to be effective for apprehending individuals engaging in illegal activity, such as drug dealing. Officers also believed that working in teams made their jobs safer. They explained that they often had to deal with groups, and having more officers present helped them to maintain control in difficult situations. The tactic also served as an intentional show of force, sending the message to gang members that the police gang unit controlled the streets, and that if gang members stepped out of line or engaged in illegal behavior, they would be caught. One officer described how he believed the gang managers expected the unit to perform:

Our [managers] want the gang unit to be very proactive. Pick them up for everything, like jaywalking. We want these gangsters to know that we own the streets. [Managers] want us to be aggressive, just short of beating the shit out of them. If they talk back to us, we cuff them, and sit them down and lecture them.

Another officer explained:

We are out here letting gang members know that we are in control of the city. We are proactive, fill out FIs, and use this to prosecute them on gang-related crimes. Mix it up with the gangs. If they run, we chase them. . . . We all work a neighborhood, and we take the neighborhood over. Let them know that we are in charge.

Phoenix took a slightly different approach to patrolling known gang areas. Each enforcement squad was assigned to a specific precinct for the purpose of patrolling and investigating gang crimes. However, even though more than one squad member might be patrolling within a precinct at any given time, the Phoenix officers did not work together as a team to focus on specific locations, as officers in Las Vegas did.

For the past ten years, however, the Phoenix gang unit had been substantially increasing its patrol presence through another kind of strategy – the Operation Safe Streets (OSS) program. During the summer months, officers normally assigned to schools were being reassigned to patrol commanders in order to increase the number of patrol officers on the street. Precinct commanders, in turn, would assign one or two of their patrol officers to the gang unit, where they served as OSS officers. Additionally, every summer, a motor squad comprised of one sergeant and six officers, otherwise responsible for traffic enforcement, would be assigned to the gang unit to participate in the OSS project. These real-locations of personnel resulted in a total of thirteen additional officers assigned during the summer months to work with the gang unit. OSS officers rode with gang unit officers in the areas that the officer normally covered, and they performed all of the typical gang unit officer activities.

As noted in the preceding text, the Inglewood gang unit also patrolled known gang areas, but here they used tactics and strategies that were dif-ferent from those of the other units because their goals were substantially different. According to Inglewood officers, their directed patrols were performed exclusively for the purpose of gathering intelligence. They argued that if they were to conduct arrests of gang members and carry out other traditional enforcement activities, gang members would stop providing them with intelligence. Additionally, they explained, the three gang unit officers did not have the resources to arrest gang members; making arrests would take up substantial time that could otherwise be allocated for intelligence gathering. Inglewood gang unit officers believed that except when the evidence in front of them was overwhelm-ing, and they had no other choice – they did not make arrests.

When Inglewood officers learned of gang violence that was about to occur, or when they witnessed an ongoing criminal act such as street-level drug trafficking, they told us that they contacted the department's ACT, which then performed any necessary enforcement. The officers were firm in their conviction that the gang unit should remain in the good graces of gang members, allowing it to continue to collect gang intelligence, letting ACT officers be the so-called bad guys if an arrest or other enforcement effort was warranted.

Investigation

All of the gang units performed at least some investigative activities (Table 7.1). Albuquerque gang unit officers spent about seventy min-utes a day on investigations, Las Vegas and Phoenix units each spent about fifty-five minutes a day, and Inglewood averaged just over twenty minutes a day. These variations in the amount of time spent, as well as differences in the nature of the units' investigative activities, were consistent with the differences in the gang units' assigned functions. As noted in Chapter 4, three of the gang units (Albuquerque, Las Vegas, and Phoenix) were mandated to conduct activities related to investigations of gang crimes, albeit in different ways. Albuquerque's gang unit was charged with assisting other units and officers with gang-related investigations, but they were not assigned the primary responsibility for investigating gang crimes. On the other hand, Las Vegas and Phoenix's gang units did have primary responsibility for investigating all gang-motivated crimes, with the exception of homicides in Phoenix, and homicides, sexual assaults, and casino robberies in Las Vegas.

Our field observations indicated that Albuquerque's auxiliary investigative role resulted in that gang unit participating in a greater number of investigations than units in the other three cities. Officers and detectives contacted gang unit officers when the investigation of a gang-involved crime required follow-up. Typically, gang unit officers were also called upon for initial consultations, generally to provide detectives with real names to match with street names, recent known addresses, and known associates. As a consequence, Albuquerque gang unit officers spent substantial time discussing cases with officers from other units. Additionally, if the investigation required the questioning of known gang members, gang unit officers assisted in questioning suspects, victims, and witnesses. They believed that previous contacts with gang members gave them an advantage during such interviews, and found that being present during questioning allowed them to collect additional gang intelligence.

In both Las Vegas and Phoenix, although SOPs made the gang units responsible for investigating all gang-motivated crimes (with a few exceptions), typically, their officers investigated only violent crimes. Cases were obtained by gang unit officers in each department in one of two ways. First, during patrol, the officers monitored the radio, and although they were not responsible for responding to calls for service, they did respond when it sounded as if there might be gang involvement. This commonly occurred when a shooting was announced over the radio. In this case, after arriving on location, if gang unit officers determined that the shooting was gang motivated, they took investigative responsibility at the scene and then conducted all of the follow-up work.

In addition, gang unit sergeants could assign cases to their officers for investigation. If an investigating officer elsewhere in the department discovered a gang connection in his case, he could forward it to the gang unit sergeant responsible for the geographic area where the crime occurred. If the sergeant concurred that the crime was gang motivated and that the gang unit should investigate it, he would assign it to a gang unit officer. If the sergeant believed that the crime was not gang motivated, or that it was gang motivated but should not be investigated by his unit for any reason, the sergeant could refuse the case. Our observations and interviews in Las Vegas and Phoenix indicated that the units accepted only cases that were serious in nature or that officers believed would result in good intelligence. As a result, gang unit officers generally had light case loads. Gang unit officers in both Las Vegas and Phoenix noted that they rarely, if ever, had active case loads of more than two cases.

The graffiti detail in Las Vegas was an exception. This detail was responsible for investigating all of the city's gang and tagger group graffiti, a problem that many officers in the department and the gang unit considered to be of minor importance. To report graffiti, citizens were required to call a city office, and then to photograph the damage and submit the photo to the office. (In certain cases, the city might take the photograph.) The crime report and photo were next forwarded to the general investigations or juvenile unit. If the original complainant did not follow up on the investigation by contacting that unit within four days, the unit would usually close the case.

If there were leads or if the offender had signed the graffiti with a moniker (street name), the case was forwarded to the graffiti detail, where all available data, including a scanned copy of the photograph, were entered into the computer system. At this point, investigators in the graffiti detail would attempt to link the evidence to prior offenders or to identify a suspect through leads. According to the officers, cases were typically solved because the unit had intelligence on monikers that could be tied to the graffiti artist's signature. In most cases, the officers explained, apprehended offenders were charged with a felony because of the high cost associated with cleaning up graffiti. Unfortunately, however, we were unable to substantiate their claims because the detail did not keep records of its clearance rate.

Officers in the graffiti detail expressed a great deal of frustration with their jobs. Citizens were expressing concern about graffiti in their neighborhoods because of the public perception that graffiti was associated with gang violence. On the other hand, the graffiti detail's status was low within the department, and within the gang unit, because of the nature of the crime. Graffiti officers frequently noted that they were responsible for all of the city's graffiti, gang-related or not, largely because no one else in the department viewed it as an issue worth addressing.

Inglewood's gang unit was the only one not mandated to perform investigative activities. Our observations of the work of the Inglewood officers indicated, however, that they occasionally did participate in both gang and nongang investigations. Their involvement most often started with individual curiosity rather than with a formal assignment. When a homicide occurred while officers were on duty, they often would arrive at the scene just to find out what had happened. Under those circumstances, their role might simply be that of an observer, or they might assist with keeping the public away from the crime scene. Once in a while, when gang unit officers were on the scene when detectives needed assistance tracking down individuals who might have information about the crime, gang unit officers would be used as auxiliary personnel.

Intelligence

As we discussed in the preceding chapters, having primary responsibility for collecting, processing, and disseminating gang intelligence for the police department was a defining characteristic of the gang units that we studied. Accordingly, each of the units served, at least in part, as the central information broker of gang intelligence for its department.

We observed that gang intelligence originated from a number of sources, and presented itself through a variety of formal and informal media. Regardless of its source or the medium through which it was received, each gang unit was responsible for processing intelligence and disseminating it to others both inside and outside the agency. Because our study focused on gang unit officers and the strategies that they used to collect, process, and disseminate gang intelligence, we discuss these issues as they related to our observations of the gang unit.

Table 7.1 shows that although all four of the gang units were responsible for intelligence functions, the time that they devoted to intelligence activities varied significantly. In Inglewood, gang unit personnel averaged about 3.5 hours a day on intelligence activities, compared with 1.35 hours in Albuquerque, 1.15 hours in Phoenix, and 0.2 hours in Las Vegas. In the sections that follow, we discuss how the gang units performed this function, focusing on three primary tasks: collecting, processing, and distributing gang intelligence.

Collecting Intelligence During Field Interviews. The method for collecting most gang intelligence in all four departments was the FI card. FI cards were used by patrol officers, detectives, and gang unit officers to record basic information about suspected gang members who had been interviewed either during a field stop or in the course of another police-related encounter. Although all of the units used the *suspicion stop* to gather intelligence, each unit was stylistically and strategically unique in its tactics, varying from overtly friendly to blatantly aggressive.

Inglewood gang unit officers were polite and friendly. They all commented that they did not stop suspected gang members in order to make an arrest or to hassle them, but rather the stops were intended to be friendly, fostering relationships and resulting in quality intelligence. This was referred to by the officers as the *friendly stop*. The following excerpts from our field notes represent typical contacts that we observed Inglewood gang unit officers making with gang members:

The officer stopped a black male in his mid-20s wearing all black. He was a member of the Bounty Hunters. The officer asked where he worked, lived, and asked the name of the guy who he had just walked by. After the discussion the officer informed me that he knew that he had lied to him about where he lived and worked because he did not want the officer to know where he was at. However, I noticed that the interaction was positive; both were smiling at one another.

We stopped and talked to three Hispanic males who were all in Inglewood 13. One pretended to run away, clowning around as he did it. The officer knew the three of them by their street names. He asked the kid if he expected him to be "Pacman" and run after him. Another positive encounter. All four of them were laughing.

None of the stops that we observed in Inglewood resulted in an arrest, as we will discuss later in this chapter. The gang unit officers were interested in maintaining positive relationships with gang members. In fact, it became apparent to us that Inglewood officers in the field were choosing not to speak to individuals dealing drugs on the street. They frequently pointed out such individuals, but they never made contact. When asked about this, the officers emphasized that they did not have the resources to engage in enforcement activities, and that their primary responsibility was to gather intelligence. They were concerned that if they did make arrests, gang members would no longer provide them with timely and accurate information, and that they would lose time to processing the arrest. As a consequence, they explained, they called upon other units in the department for follow-up enforcement.

During Inglewood field contacts, however, if an officer determined that an individual met any of the criteria required to be documented as a gang member, and if that person was cooperative and willing, the officer would fill out an FI card. The FI card allowed the officer to collect information such as the individual's name, date of birth, social security number, race, sex, height, weight, hair and eye color, driver's license number, street name, name of business or school, identifying marks, and vehicle information. The cards had predetermined categories for the officer to use in recording criteria for gang membership that the individual had met, and the name of his or her gang. Following the interview, gang unit officers, with permission, would photograph the gang member and any physical evidence of gang membership – a tattoo, a belt buckle, or the individual displaying a gang sign. When an officer gathered intelligence on a person already known to be a gang member, he would record the information on an FI card out of sight of the gang member. This information would then be used to update the gang member's computer record.

In Albuquerque, gang unit officers used two tactics in the field to gather gang intelligence. The first, as in Inglewood, was the friendly stop. Officers would identify an individual or group, and make the stop in the field. This type of stop was consensual, and the officer conducted himself in a good-natured way. For example, the officer would ask how they were doing, what they were up to, and other general questions. In doing so, the officer would ask about gang affiliation and about other people in the neighborhood. If the officer identified an individual as a gang member through self-admission or other visual cues, he would ask further questions about where that person lived and worked, who he dated, and the names of friends. Field notes from our observations provided examples of how such stops were conducted:

We stopped three Hispanic male juveniles.... All had shaved heads, baggy pants, and no visible tattoos. He asked them where they lived... who they knew in the neighborhood. They said they were not in a gang. The officer was very nice to the boys. [He] talked about their dogs. [It was evident that the officer] knew a number of the guys in the neighborhood.

We stopped three Hispanic male adults who were walking by... [a] consensual stop. The officer just... [talked] about neighborhood stuff, who is warring with who, who has been sent to prison, etc. All three were self-admitted gang members... shaved heads, baggy shirts and pants. [The officer] asked where [they] worked, lived, [and who they] dated. He said he would update the card so [the police] knew where [they] worked. One was a victim of a drive-by.

Not all stops made by gang unit officers in Albuquerque were consensual. Gang unit officers occasionally used legal justifications, such as traffic violations, to make stops. However, officers pointed out, they did not invoke minor legal infractions, such as jaywalking or walking on the wrong side of the street, as justification for stops. They argued that such tactics would result in gang members losing respect for the unit, which in the long run, they believed, would result in gathering less intelligence.

Officers in Albuquerque used suspicion stops as a tactic only when they observed illegal activity or when they had a strong suspicion that illegal activity was taking place, and they conducted these professionally and without creating conflict. Regardless of the situation, officers typically remained focused on the goal of gathering gang-related intelligence. Officers would work the stop as if it were for a traffic violation, asking for the driver's license, registration, and insurance information. If passengers were in the car, officers would request identification from them as well. The officer would then check for criminal histories and outstanding warrants. As the information was being run by the central office, the officer would interview the driver and passengers about their involvement in gangs. If someone was a self-identified gang member, the officer would question that person about gang conflict in the neighborhood.

All gang-related information was recorded on a special gang card used by the APD. Albuquerque officers, however, were particular about not recording information on a gang card in the presence of the gang member. They explained that if gang members saw the card being used, they would not provide the information and would deny gang membership. As a result, officers adopted the use of a regular notebook, and then transferred the information onto a gang card after concluding the stop.

In Phoenix, gang unit officers were also professional, respectful, and direct during their contacts, but they were more interpersonally remote than officers in Inglewood, for example. In Phoenix, the primary goal of such stops was an arrest or to gather intelligence from a gang member. Phoenix officers used municipal ordinances and county laws as pretexts for making stops. Typically, with a little patience, actual traffic violations were commonly observed when following a suspected gang member, but occasionally officers became more inventive. As one officer explained, "You have to be creative with the law, then you can work them over to learn stuff and get intelligence." He further explained that officers "liked to use the little piddly stuff to talk to them... because [if] he breaks the law, then they are required to have I.D. [and if they don't], then you can arrest them for that."

Other officers decided on a reason for the stop after it had already taken place. For instance, on one occasion, an officer stopped a Bronco with two Hispanic juvenile males inside. After the officer pulled the vehicle over, but before he got out of the squad car, he had the following conversation with his partner and the field observer:

Partner: Is this a shit stop?
Driver: . . . loud music?
Partner: I didn't hear anything.
Driver: [Observer], did you hear any music?
Observer: I didn't hear anything, but I wasn't paying attention.

The officers then simultaneously exited the squad car and approached the suspect without discussing the matter further.

Gang unit officers in Phoenix primarily worked in the dark at night, making visual identification of likely gang members more difficult. After seeing a suspect up close, officers would have to decide quickly whether he was, in fact, a likely gang member. On a number of occasions, we observed as officers pulled over individuals who from a distance looked like gang members (i.e., they were young, male, and minority) and who were driving substantially over the speed limit. Then on closer inspection, the officer would see that the driver had children in the back seat, or the driver or passenger was an elderly man or woman; the officer would give the driver a quick warning and let him go. Often with such stops, it would have been within the officer's purview to issue a citation or make an arrest for the traffic violation, but if the individual was not a gang member, officers did not believe that they should take time to process the incident.

This, however, did not mean that those stopped by the gang unit were not upset at the police for detaining them unnecessarily. On a number of occasions we observed gang unit officers stop the same (non–gang member) driver more than once in a week, resulting in the driver becoming visibly upset and frustrated. These drivers would make comments such as "You guys do this to me every week, can't you give me a break." Or "I know what you guys are looking for, but I am just sick of this." During each of these occurrences, gang unit officers apologized for the inconvenience and permitted the driver to leave without incident.

When an individual who had been stopped did fit the profile for gang membership, the officer would assess whether he or she was actually involved in gangs. First, officers would order the suspect out of the car and ask for a driver's license, vehicle registration, and insurance documents. Meanwhile, the officers were scanning the suspect's arms, hands, and ankles for gang tattoos, and examining their clothing, belt buckle, shoes, and hair style for indications of involvement in the gang lifestyle. Officers also examined personal property such as school books or bags for gang graffiti, and interviewed the suspect about gang affiliation. The officer would ask the suspect questions: Where are you going? Who are you down with? Who do you hang out with? Were you ever down with a gang? All of this would take place while the officer's partner was running the individual's name for possible warrants. If the officer determined that the individual was a gang member or met the criteria for gang membership, he completed an FI card and took a Polaroid picture of the person. He would also ask permission to search the vehicle. Even though typically no reason was given for searches, all suspects whom we observed permitted the officers to search their vehicles. If the individual had no warrants for arrest and if there was no incriminating evidence, he or she would be released.

Las Vegas also used FI cards to document gang members. Officers in Las Vegas were the most aggressive in tactics and demeanor of the units we studied. As noted in the preceding text, Las Vegas gang enforcement squads moved through neighborhoods in an orchestrated fashion, and officers rarely used any pretext for making suspicion stops. If an individual was thought to be a gang member, or if there was a small crowd of young minority males in a known gang neighborhood, the squad targeted them. Our field data showed that almost all individuals stopped by the gang unit during our observations were minority residents. When we asked one sergeant how the unit dealt with the profiling issue, he explained:

> You have to walk a fine line, because we do target particular kids. While there are white, Asian, etcetera, gang members, we just do not run into them. We primarily deal with blacks and Hispanics. You have to have an administration that backs you up and our department does. It is a very tough issue.... If you have 15 black kids hanging out on a corner and 15 white kids also hanging out on a corner, the blacks are more likely to be questioned.

In Las Vegas, once a vehicle, individual, or group had been targeted by the squad, three or four squad cars moved in harmony toward the target. This strategy startled or frightened most of the individuals contacted by the gang unit. Once the squad car stopped, officers would quickly leave their cars, hands on their guns, requesting the targeted individual to get out of the vehicle (if they were in one). They would place the person(s) in a prone position, either on the ground or against the hood of the squad car, and hand pat him for weapons or other contraband. They would request identification, check for a criminal history, and conduct an interview about the person's activities and gang involvement. This strategy had been used so often by the gang unit that they had developed boilerplate language for documenting stops and searches – namely, all stops and searches, for report purposes, were consensual. During our observations, one new gang unit officer was unsure how the process worked, and asked his partner how he should write up the stop-and-search. Our field notes recorded this interchange:

[Officer A] asked [Officer B] why they originally stopped [the suspects], so he could write up the report. [Officer B] said, "You know how it goes (smiling). If you see a group, you search them in this area." [Officer A] said, "Well I know that, but how should I write it up?" He told [Officer A] to write it up as consensual for the report. I asked [Officer B] further about it and he said you [write them up] as consensual until [you find something] and then it becomes probable cause.

The Las Vegas officers explained that at every opportunity, they would ticket gang members for any infraction or offense, serious or non-serious. If a gang member was driving without insurance, they would write a ticket. If a gang member was seen jaywalking, they would write a ticket. If a gang member was riding a bicycle on the sidewalk, they would write a ticket. They argued that most gang members would not take the time or have the money to pay the fine. Then the next time an officer stopped that gang member, if he or she was disrespectful or did not give the officer information as requested, the officer could arrest the gang member for failure to pay the fine.

Las Vegas officers also used tickets to punish and reward gang members for their attitudes and behavior during suspicion stops. Those who were disrespectful would receive tickets, while those who were cooperative and provided the information requested would not. One observer's field notes described the following two incidents:

We stopped a Hispanic male, 28 years old. He was walking down the street and the officers pulled over and asked him to step over to the car. He ignored them and started to walk away. They said they were the police and he said, "no kidding."...The officers then laid him up on the car because he was being a smart-ass. They said because he lied, they were going to give him a ticket for not using the sidewalk. They asked if he was a gang member. He said he was not and had no tattoos. Just one tattoo that indicated that he was "100% Mexican." They gave him a ticket and told him not to lie again. They said if he would have been cool, they would not have done anything. They seemed to have used more force than was necessary, but he was very non-responsive. Perhaps he was drunk or mentally ill....

The officer stopped a white male, 27 years old with a white T-shirt, baggy pants, and a shaved head, for a jaywalking violation. He admitted to being in a gang in LA. He said he moved to get away from all of that shit. The officers filled out an FI card [asking] questions about his criminal history and gang membership. The gang member commented how everyone else is jaywalking. [The] officer said "We are in the gang unit and primarily interested in gang members." [The suspect said that] he was 16 when he was jumped in. The gang member was shot by a .38 between the eyes and through the neck from a drive by. They took his picture. The officer told him he was not going to give him a ticket because he was being cooperative.

Las Vegas gang unit officers used aggressive tactics to obtain intelligence from suspected gang members as well. For example, officers frequently would demand that suspects pull up their shirts, lift up pant legs, and turn around while an officer physically inspected their bodies for gang tattoos. During our observations, suspects rarely refused the officers' demands, but many appeared embarrassed, and some were visibly offended. On occasion, officers in Las Vegas were observed to use other high-pressure tactics to elicit intelligence from those they stopped. In particular, they would threaten their targets with arrest or citations if they were not provided with intelligence or when they thought that an individual was not being honest about gang membership. The following excerpt from our field notes describes one such occasion:

Went on a fishing trip – pulling over everyone (with cause) who was leaving a fashion show [with] all black attendees. Many were wearing red. We pulled over 2 black male...[adults]. Their car was speeding....One had been arrested for drugs in the past....[One] claimed that he used to be a Piru Blood. But he is 30 now, and said he has not been in a gang for 13–14 years. The [other] was getting an attitude. He was upset that he was pulled over for nothing. The officer continually asked him who he was down with and he said no one. When the officer asked to take the older brother's picture, he asked if that was legal. The cop said absolutely. (They then took the picture.) When they tried to get the younger brother's picture, he (the younger brother) said no, you already have one. The officers became very upset and said they were going to arrest him if he did not cooperate. [An officer] then went over to the (older) brother and asked him who the younger brother was down with. He said no one.

Collecting Intelligence Intradepartmentally. Many of the gang units used intradepartmental intelligence-gathering tactics. All units permitted other officers to document gang members by filling out a FI card. In Inglewood, Albuquerque, and Las Vegas, FI cards had a box for officers to check when the interviewee was a suspected gang member, and a place to indicate the criteria that were met that suggested gang membership.

When an FI card showed that the subject was a likely gang member, a copy of the card would be forwarded to the local gang unit.

However, it was unclear how often outside officers furnished this kind of intelligence to the gang units. Many officers in the units we studied believed that the majority of gang intelligence came from interviews that they conducted themselves, although no one was able to substantiate this assertion. When we inquired why other officers in the departments did not document gang members or provide gang intelligence more often, many stated that patrol officers were too busy and did not want to take the time to process the paperwork. Others believed that patrol officers simply felt that gathering gang intelligence was the gang units' responsibility, not theirs.

Some police departments tried to build and facilitate relationships among those in the field to encourage their assistance with collecting gang intelligence. In Albuquerque, for example, patrol officers and detectives were asked to radio the gang unit whenever they had contact with a gang member. Once notified, the gang unit would arrive at the scene to determine whether in fact the person was a gang member; if so, they would document and interview him for gang intelligence. The gang unit felt that this simple procedure was a relatively easy thing to ask of other officers. It cost them little effort because most of the work was done by the gang unit. The strategy appeared to be somewhat successful. On several occasions, we observed patrol officers and investigators requesting the service. Gang unit officers did note that often when other officers contacted them, the individual who had been stopped turned out not to be a gang member. However, they believed that in order to continue to receive the calls from other officers, they needed to be appreciative and to respond to as many requests as possible.

The Phoenix gang unit formalized this approach by creating a gang liaison program designed to increase communication among patrol and investigative officers and the gang unit. The goal was to increase the amount of intelligence forwarded from other officers to the gang unit. All gang liaison officers received sixteen hours of training, with about four hours spent learning about the department's gang data base system (SIDS) and twelve hours spent discussing issues related to local gangs and gang unit policies and procedures. A civilian in the gang unit was responsible for processing and disseminating the unit's intelligence; that person was also responsible for coordinating the gang liaison program. Although many officers volunteered to become gang liaisons, their interest did not usually last long. Only a modest number remained full participants in the program after training. From the inception of the program in March 1998, through January 4, 2000, according to an informal list given to us by the gang unit (January 4, 2000), 228 officers received gang liaison training (20 detectives and 208 patrol officers). Only about 60 percent ($n = 14$) of the detectives and 32 percent of the patrol officers ($n = 67$) continued with the program after they were trained.

Another internal intelligence-gathering technique used both in Phoenix and in Inglewood was the review of arrest reports. In Phoenix, the civilian in charge of processing and disseminating gang intelligence reviewed the previous day's arrest reports and documented the number of gang-motivated incidents, to monitor the level of local gang crime. Due to the substantial number of arrest reports generated each day, only reports of homicides, drive-by shootings, aggravated assaults, threats, and endangerments were reviewed. Those determined to be gang motivated – that is, criminal acts committed for the purpose of promoting gang status or personal status in the gang – were recorded as gang crimes.

In Inglewood, gang unit officers also reviewed arrest reports, but here, they tracked a wider array of crimes: homicides, felony assaults, rapes, robberies, burglaries, street terrorism act violations, and shootings into dwellings (drive-by shootings). If an offense was determined to be gang related, the information from the report was placed in the gang member's record.

While reviewing the report, if an officer determined that an offense was gang motivated (not merely gang related), he would search the report for additional gang intelligence. Officers stated that on occasion, they would first learn about violent acts having occurred through the daily reports. In this way, they were able to identify trends in disputes between gangs. The information was used either to suppress future gang violence by notifying gang members that the gang unit was aware of their activity, or to give detectives intelligence on crimes already under investigation. If an offender was still in custody, a gang unit officer would attempt to gain an interview. He would focus the interview on the nature of the gang-motivated event, and would try to gather additional intelligence that would assist detectives with their investigations and might help prevent further gang-related activity.

In Albuquerque, this approach was not used because the gang unit supervisor believed that his officers did not have enough time to review crime reports. More important, he and the police chief disagreed on the criteria for gang crime. The chief believed a gang motive was needed for a crime to be counted as a gang crime, while the sergeant believed that if either the offender or victim was a documented gang member, the offense should be recorded as a gang crime. Both the chief and the sergeant informed us that they had discussed this issue on numerous occasions, without resolving their differences.

Las Vegas's gang unit used several practical, undemanding strategies for collecting gang crime data. First, all crime reports included a check-off box that officers were to mark for gang-motivated offenses. The report would then be forwarded to the gang unit for inclusion in the gang crime count. Second, a civilian staff member, a retired police officer, read the newspaper every day searching for homicides that might be gang related. He checked all victims' names against the unit's gang list. If a homicide victim was a gang member, that victim was included in the unit's count of killed gang members. Third, at the end of each year, officers from the gang intelligence squad worked with the department's crime analyst to obtain a count of shootings at occupied structures, or drive-by shootings. From these reports, gang unit officers determined whether the shootings had claimed victims; if so, these were included in the count. The supervisor of the gang intelligence squad mentioned that these strategies for collecting gang crime data was perhaps not as thorough as that of many other agencies, but it was efficient and protected his officers' time for working on other more important issues.

Of special significance is our finding that none of the gang units collected intelligence on gangs per se. Identification of a particular gang's members always preceded documentation of the gang. Only after an individual had claimed membership or had met the criteria for being documented as a gang member could his or her gang be documented. Even then, gang unit officers who were careful about the criteria used for documenting individual gang members did not have to verify that each *gang* documented matched the official definition. In Phoenix and Inglewood, gang units required that for a gang to be counted, it needed at least three documented members. We found it interesting, however, that a gang member could be documented, whether or not his gang had enough documented members to be formally acknowledged by the unit. The bottom line is that, with the exception of Phoenix, none of the gang units that we studied gathered intelligence directly and proactively on gangs as groups.

In Phoenix, the gang unit would occasionally perform a syndicate investigation on a targeted gang. In these instances, gang unit officers would gather previously collected intelligence on members of the targeted gang, attempting to link their activities and associations with one another. This strategy allowed the prosecutor to enact statutes designed to enhance the sentences of convicted individuals belonging to a criminal syndicate. The gang unit officers believed this strategy to be effective, although they pointed out that it was only possible with the more organized gangs.

Collecting Intelligence Extradepartmentally. Three of the four police departments used extradepartmental intelligence-gathering tactics. Albuquerque gang unit officers collected intelligence from New Mexico State Correctional Facility officials and from their prison's gang unit files. During intake procedures, when a prisoner self-admitted membership in an Albuquerque street gang, that information could be used to document him. Gang unit officers also interviewed prison officials about gang activity within the prison and how that activity might influence street gang activity.

Inglewood's gang unit also received intelligence from their state prison system. The unit received faxed bulletins when local gang members were released from the state's correctional facilities. The Inglewood officers, however, did not believe that they needed to collect other intelligence from other agencies on a regular basis. Their gang intelligence computer program, CALGANG, was Internet-based, and participating agencies could enter new data directly and view the records of any gang members who had been documented by any participating agency.

Interestingly, Las Vegas's gang unit intelligence squad was monitoring a few popular Internet chat rooms frequented by gang members. Officers explained that although they rarely found intelligence online to be directly applicable to their issues, the sites occasionally would inform police of an upcoming party or social event. This intelligence, the police believed, led them to people of interest from whom they could then obtain more useful intelligence. During our observations, enforcement squad officers did follow up some leads from the Internet, but none proved to be of use.

In Las Vegas, another source of intelligence was that provided by agents of the district probation and parole office. Some of these agents eagerly described how they participated in documenting gang members by filling out FI cards and forwarding them to the Las Vegas gang unit. However, we were unable to determine how frequently this activity took place or the volume of intellegnce/docuementation that these officers provided.

Processing Gang Intelligence. In all of the departments, once an officer completed an FI card nominating an individual to be documented as a gang member, that card would be forwarded to the gang unit. That unit's procedures would be followed to review, process, and enter data into the gang information database. Each of the gang units we studied used a particular software application to store gang intelligence: Inglewood used CALGANG; Albuquerque used the Gang Reporting, Evaluation and Tracking (GREAT) system; Phoenix used the SIDS; and Las Vegas used the Gang/Narcotics Relational Intelligence Program (GRIP). Although all of the units used computerized systems to store intelligence, their oversight of data processing, input, and maintenance varied.

In Albuquerque and Phoenix, all information nominating individuals to become documented gang members (e.g., FI cards, gang cards, photographs) was administratively reviewed, regardless of which officer or unit had provided it. In Albuquerque, before any individual could be placed in the system and before other paperwork was processed, the sergeant in charge of the gang unit had to approve the action. Likewise, in Phoenix, all nominating materials were forwarded to the daytime investigation squad, whose officers reviewed the materials to assure that the nominee met their formal criteria for becoming a documented gang member. If so, the officer completed and stamped a Gang Member Identification Card (GMIC). The sergeant in Albuquerque and the Phoenix investigative squad officers explained that individuals nominated as gang members by officers were virtually always documented, but the review process provided them with the opportunity to oversee nominations in order to clarify missing, unclear, or contradictory intelligence. This, they argued, would be helpful if the information was ever to be used in court.

In Inglewood, all FI cards and associated intelligence produced by officers outside the gang unit were forwarded to the unit. The gang unit officers then reviewed the materials to assure that the individual met the criteria for documentation, and that all required information had been collected. FI cards and other intelligence produced by gang unit officers, however, were not reviewed by anyone else. In Las Vegas, all FI cards completed by officers, regardless of their units, were forwarded to the gang unit secretarial staff, where they were prepared for processing. No one else reviewed or approved paperwork associated with documenting an individual as a gang member in Las Vegas.

In Albuquerque, Las Vegas, and Phoenix, civilian staff in the gang units were responsible for intelligence data entry and processing; in

Inglewood, gang unit officers assumed this responsibility. In all locations, once an individual had been accepted for documentation, his or her file was forwarded to the appropriate data-processing person in the gang unit. That person would take the necessary steps to compile all available information, and would then create the documented gang member's record in the gang intelligence database. The gang member's criminal, vehicle, and FI records, along with photos, if any, were pulled, and all of the information available was entered into gang intelligence system. A typical record, in all of the units, would include the gang member's name, moniker(s), date of birth, gender, age, ethnicity, criteria for documentation, known address, place of work or school, name of gang, known associates (per FI card data), physical characteristics including scars and tattoos, a reference to the number of photos on file, arrest record, FI record, probation, parole and correctional records, and vehicle information. In Inglewood, Phoenix, and Las Vegas, photographs could be scanned into the system, for ready access.

In Phoenix and Las Vegas, after information was entered into the gang database, the unit would update its departmental criminal history system as well. This would alert officers in other units if an individual they were checking on was a safety risk as a gang member. It also signaled officers to collect gang intelligence, whenever appropriate and possible, and to forward an FI card to the gang unit for processing.

In most of the units, the period between completion of a new FI card and documentation and entry of the data into the gang intelligence system was relatively short, typically around one week. In Las Vegas, however, civilian staff stated that they were about four months behind in processing gang intelligence and entering data into the system. They cited the large number of FI cards generated by the gang unit and the amount of time that it took to process individual files as reasons for the delay.

Once an individual was documented as a gang member, that person's record would remain in the gang intelligence database for a specified time. In Albuquerque and Inglewood, gang member records were purged from the system after five years. In Las Vegas, gang members were considered in active status for two years, dating from the most recent police contact connecting them with a gang. Their records were scheduled for purging after two years of inactivity. In Phoenix, records of associate gang members were purged after one year, and records of gang members were purged after five years.

Three units (Inglewood, Phoenix, and Las Vegas) used automated systems to generate periodic lists of documented gang members who had been in the system for the specified period. They checked the listed names against police records, searching for any further police contacts that included evidence of continuing gang membership, involvement with a gang or gang members, or gang activity. If such evidence was found, that individual's record would be updated and replaced in the gang information system for another one to five years, depending upon the unit.

Each department handled this process differently. In Phoenix, the civilian in charge of the gang information system printed all prior gang intelligence on the individual and forwarded it to the gang officer assigned to the area where the gang member lived. The officer was then responsible for reviewing the record and determining whether the person had been involved in further gang activity since last having been documented. This was typically accomplished by reviewing FI cards and criminal history records. If the officer determined that the individual had been neither involved in further gang activity nor identified in the presence of other documented gang members, the record was approved to be purged from the system.

In Las Vegas and Inglewood, the gang information system automatically generated this list on a monthly basis. Las Vegas and Inglewood then followed the same procedures as Phoenix, except that in Las Vegas, the work was performed exclusively by secretarial staff, and in Inglewood, it was performed by gang unit officers. In Las Vegas and Inglewood, record purging was not supervised or coordinated by a specific person in the unit.[2]

Only Albuquerque's gang intelligence system could not automatically generate these reports. Instead, the gang unit supervisor was responsible for coordinating system purges. He explained that although his gang unit had only recently been created, it had inherited all the information collected by the prior gang unit. He had assigned a civilian volunteer to handle the purging of all gang member records that had been in the system for more than five years, as long as the gang member had had no further contact with police. This action reduced the number of documented gang members from roughly 8,000 to about 7,000. He further explained that in the future, the gang unit would purge the

---

[2] We observed this purging practice in Inglewood, Las Vegas, and Phoenix.

system every five years. In other words, records would not be reviewed individually; instead, periodically all records in the information system would be reviewed simultaneously for possible purging.

In Albuquerque and Las Vegas, all purged records were archived on the chance that police would have a future need for the information. Officers from both units explained that federal guidelines required them to purge the system every five years if they were interested in sharing the information with other agencies or using it in court. As a consequence, the units had two filing systems. One contained the records of current documented gang members, about whom intelligence could be shared with other agencies; the other contained archived, purged records of gang members, about whom information could be shared only for internal police purposes.

Disseminating Gang Intelligence. We observed gang unit officers using four distinct tactics for disseminating gang intelligence: processing requests, participating in gang intelligence forums, distributing aggregate data on gang trends, and distributing intelligence on specific gang activity.

The most basic method of disseminating gang intelligence, used by all four gang units, was processing informal requests for information. Officers within the department or personnel from other agencies would contact the gang unit to request information on a particular individual whom they believed to be a gang member. Because they maintained the gang databases, each unit had a relatively large body of intelligence on individuals believed to be involved in criminal activity. Furthermore, the gang unit's intelligence was usually more up-to-date than that of other police units. As a result, when detectives or others needed to contact a gang member or wanted to link street names of suspects with given names, they often turned to the gang units for help.

Each gang unit processed information requests differently. In Inglewood and Albuquerque, gang unit officers processed all requests themselves. Typically, an officer or member of another agency would telephone the gang unit to request information, and an officer would return the call when he could. In Phoenix and Las Vegas, requests for gang intelligence were usually processed, one way or another, by the units' civilian staff. In Las Vegas, for example, most callers knew to call unit secretarial staff directly for information. If someone called a gang intelligence officer, the officer would simply request the information from the secretarial staff. Although gang intelligence squad officers were responsible for disseminating intelligence, most appeared to be incapable of accessing the computerized gang information systems. Officers explained that many of them had never learned to use a computer; they were concentrating their efforts elsewhere, on what they viewed as real police work. When we asked a supervisor about the officers' reluctance to use the gang information data system, he explained:

They [secretarial staff] enter all gang FIs in GRIPS. If people need things from GRIPS, you get one of the girls to get it, because we don't know computers. I want to use my officers to put bad guys away.

When we asked one of the officers about the use of computers in his unit, he explained that officers used them for public presentations, and that "right now, [we] are working hard on learning... how to use the computers." Our field notes further illustrate this skill deficit:

It [is] apparent that none of the officers are computer literate. They spent an hour the other day trying to save a file from the C to the A drive, and then from the A to the C drive. They have no understanding of paths.... [A supervisor] said they are crime fighters not computer geeks ... that's why [they] have the girls.

In Phoenix, gang intelligence was disseminated by the civilian in charge of data processing. According to our observations, again, most gang unit officers were unable to use the gang information system because they lacked experience with the program. On several occasions, some civilian staff complained about always having to retrieve this information for the officers, explaining that they had repeatedly shown the officers how to use the system, but the officers were either disinterested or incapable of learning to use a computer. As a consequence, most requests for gang intelligence ended up going directly to civilian staff, without going through gang unit officers.

In an effort to decentralize gang intelligence dissemination and to increase the availability of data to officers throughout the department, the Phoenix gang unit placed computers equipped with the gang information system at each substation. The strategy did not work as well as had been hoped. Officers frequently failed to learn to use the program or forgot their passwords. For example, we observed as one gang unit officer entered a substation to access the database and asked the patrol officer inside how to use the system. The patrol officer replied, "You can't, because no one knows the password." "What good is the stuff if we can't get the info?" the gang unit officer responded.

Some units formed or participated in gang intelligence–sharing forums or groups in an attempt to formalize a process for collecting and disseminating gang intelligence. Officers in all four departments recognized that the gangs in their areas did not operate in a vacuum, and that interaction with other gang units in surrounding jurisdictions would enhance their chances of receiving up-to-date intelligence on gangs, gang members, and gang activity.

Officers in both Las Vegas and Phoenix had facilitated or attended multijurisdictional gang intelligence meetings. In Las Vegas, every Wednesday at 3 p.m., while all shifts and teams were on duty, the gang unit facilitated what it called the Rock Pile. The Rock Pile was conceived by a former gang unit lieutenant who was interested in criminal justice agencies coming together to "beat big rocks – the gang problem in the county – into little rocks." The informal meetings, lasting only about twenty minutes, were attended by all gang unit officers, as well as by local probation, parole, and other law enforcement officers, and some federal agents. We observed that about half a dozen non–gang unit criminal justice officials consistently attended Rock Pile meetings, including two probation and two parole officers who consistently attended. During the meetings, each attending officer would share intelligence with the group, requesting assistance when appropriate. An officer might, for example, present information about a dispute between two gangs, a wanted person, or a recently identified trend in criminal activity. Although the meetings appeared to be useful and interesting to those outside the gang unit, they seemed to be of even greater value to the gang unit officers themselves, as a means of sharing information between shifts and teams.

Phoenix's gang unit participated in two gang intelligence forums. The East Valley gang meeting, facilitated by the Mesa, Arizona, Police Department gang unit, was held every month, and attended by about thirty officers and gang crime analysts from criminal justice agencies on the east side of the metropolitan area. The meetings served three general functions: training, intelligence sharing, and networking. Generally, they began with a brief training session. For example, we observed attendees watching a video on a "white power" group that had ties to prison and street gangs. After the training activity, each agency would have an opportunity to share and disseminate intelligence.

Similarly, in the summer during the OSS program, the gang unit would facilitate a gang intelligence meeting for gang intelligence specialists from twenty-three agencies that frequently worked with the Phoenix

Police Department. Officials from the county jail, juvenile and adult probation and correction departments, and representatives from various task forces attended. The meetings typically lasted about an hour, during which individual agencies would each share information about recent events, requesting assistance in locating wanted individuals.

Distributing Aggregate Gang Trend Data. All of the gang units except Albuquerque produced gang activity reports for their respective stakeholders. Each report examined different data, and covered different time periods. In Inglewood, the monthly gang activity report described trends in the amount of gang crimes committed, of gang member arrests by age, and of offenses involving guns or narcotics. They distributed the report to department administrators and the Los Angeles Sheriff's Department Safe Streets Bureau, which was responsible for tracking countywide gang crime.

Phoenix's criminal intelligence analyst produced a similar report monthly, including a current count of documented gang members by ethnicity, age, and gender. The unit also distributed an annual report of the numbers of gang homicides, drive-by shootings, and aggravated assaults for the year. The reports were distributed to gang unit officers and police managers, and the data were presented annually to the city council.

The Las Vegas gang unit produced perhaps the most sophisticated and thorough report, an annual accounting highlighting trends in gang membership and gang activity. Gang crime data were analyzed by month, year, and time of day, and gang membership trends were reported by age and ethnicity. The report discussed the gang unit's strategies for responding to gangs, and any special trends that the unit wanted to emphasize. This report was distributed annually to administrators and newspapers; the public also had access at the department Internet site. Many Las Vegas gang unit managers and officers noted that the data were used internally, as well, for making shift scheduling decisions and to assess the scope and nature of the gang problem in Las Vegas.

Disseminating Intelligence on Selected Gang Activity. The Inglewood and Phoenix gang units used internal unit and departmental bulletins to disseminate selected gang intelligence for strategic purposes. A typical bulletin might include a brief description of recent gang activity for the purpose of locating a particular person or for directing patrol officers to particular areas. For example, the Inglewood gang unit placed the following statement in the April 1999, Inglewood Crime Analysis Bulletin (10 [17]: 1):

Gang Activity on W. Olive. Unidentified gangsters are disrupting the neighborhood around –, –, and – W. Olive. They are harassing the neighbors with reckless driving, underage drinking, and other gang activity. They threaten anyone daring to confront them. Please provide extra patrol.

Education and Prevention

While observing gang unit officers at work, we saw little activity in any of the four units that could be classified as gang education or prevention. As shown in Table 7.1, the only unit that we observed engaging in prevention was Las Vegas, where the unit averaged about four minutes a day on activities related to this function.

In fact, the majority of that time was attributable to a single case, in which Las Vegas gang unit officers (from the intelligence squad) had responded to a request for family counseling from a parent concerned that her son had joined a gang. In this case, with the parent's permission, officers had searched the youth's room for evidence of gang membership. When they had talked with the young man about gang involvement, they learned that he had not been able to find a job, and therefore had too much time on his hands. The officers had contacted a prominent casino on the Las Vegas strip on his behalf, and the casino subsequently hired him.

The officers explained to us that the casino had approached the unit years before with a hiring program for underprivileged youth. They offered to hire gang members, under certain circumstances. In order to qualify, applicants could not have been arrested for serious violent offenses, although less serious charges, including drug trafficking, would not necessarily be held against them. Over time, the gang unit had developed a relationship with casino personnel that had allowed them to direct gang members toward the legitimate employment opportunities.

Our interviews with gang unit officers in all four study sites suggested that they occasionally presented gang training sessions to other law enforcement agencies and educational talks to public groups. We did not directly observe these kinds of activities, but we reviewed the units' training and education materials. Officers told us that they had offered training primarily to other officers from smaller agencies just outside their jurisdictions and to other criminal justice officials such as probation, parole, and social workers.

Training presented by gang unit officers was usually basic, supplemented with stories from the field. Instructional materials tended to convey simple information such as gang colors; how, as part of gang culture, gang members must be "jumped" into the gang; and reasons that children might join gangs, such as not getting attention at home, being from single-parent families, and needing protection from other gangs. Training materials also reviewed basic policies adopted by the gang units as part of their gang control efforts, but rarely explored alternative gang-control strategies in any depth.

Gang unit officers did note that they sometimes gave presentations to public groups. They described these as similar to their presentations for criminal justice professionals, but without the discussion of departmental policies or confidential information. The officers would present lectures on actions that citizens could take to prevent gang crime in their neighborhoods or that parents could take to dissuade their children from joining gangs. These were filled with conventional advice, for example, develop good communication with your children; occupy your children's free time; set limits; and start a neighborhood block watch program. Records indicated that from July 1, 1998, through June 30, 1999, the Las Vegas gang unit had conducted twenty-four public presentations.

Interviews with Phoenix gang unit officers suggested that they had done the same. Also, in an effort to educate the public and criminal justice officials about street gangs, the Phoenix gang unit had developed several handbooks. Some outlined how various organizations could respond to gangs, offering tips on recognizing gang members and early warning indicators, and giving gang prevention suggestions specific to various kinds of organizations. Others informed residents about city and police resources that could help community members combat gang problems. Another handbook addressed issues of interest to criminal justice officials and officers in other units of the Phoenix Police Department. This one provided background information on gangs, gang culture, and the gang environment in Phoenix, and included chapters on identifying gang members, officer safety, and how to interview and interrogate gang members.

Administrative, En Route, and Non-Police-Related Time

We found significant differences among the four gang units in the time officers spent for administrative tasks, driving from one location to another, and non-police-related activities (Table 7.1). The data showed that those units that spent more of their time on enforcement activities also spent more time on administrative tasks. This, we found, was largely due to the amount of paperwork required for processing arrests and evidence, and for testifying in court as a consequence of enforcement activity. Gang unit officers in Inglewood spent little time on enforcement, and consequently, they spent only a small proportion of their time on administrative tasks.

We also found differences in the amount of time that officers spent en route from one location to the next, not including patrol time. Again, this was dependent upon the types of activities conducted by the gang units. Compared with the other units, Albuquerque averaged almost two to three times as much time traveling from one location to the next, largely because of their auxiliary investigative function. It was not unusual for Albuquerque gang unit officers to spend a substantial part of their shifts trying to locate a suspect, traveling to several possible locations. Conversely, because Inglewood's primary function was carried out in the office, they had few work-related reasons to be driving from one location to another.

As with any job, gang unit officers spent a portion of their time engaging in non-police-related activities, such as eating meals and snacks, running personal errands, and relaxing. During our observations, Albuquerque officers averaged about 60 minutes per eight-hour shift on non-police-related activity, compared with 81 minutes in Phoenix, 103 minutes in Inglewood, and 136 minutes in Las Vegas. The Las Vegas unit attributed the relatively high amount of non-police-related activity (about 28 percent of their time in an eight-hour shift) to the hours that they were assigned to work and the temperature during summer months, when it was not uncommon for the temperature to be well over 100 degrees until sunset. As a result, officers explained, there was little street activity during the day. This led the officers to take the time between 3 p.m. and 5 p.m., at the beginning of their shifts, to catch up on office gossip, get dressed for the shift, and relax. From 5 p.m. to 6 p.m., officers ate dinner, after which they started working. In Phoenix, a city with a summer climate at least as hot and uncomfortable as Las Vegas, gang unit officers spent far less time engaging in non-police-related activities.

When compared with Albuquerque and Phoenix, Inglewood also spent more time on non-police-related activity, probably due to the substantial amount of time officers spent collecting and processing intelligence. Inglewood officers spent long periods sifting through volumes of paper reports and entering data into the gang information system.

Although they occasionally took breaks from this activity to patrol neighborhoods and to attempt to gather intelligence on the street, they also took breaks to talk with other officers throughout the department as a way to relax.

GANG UNIT OFFICER CONTACTS

As we observed gang unit officers at work, we documented their contacts with others outside the gang unit. For purposes of this study, our defini-tion of a contact was similar to the definition of a Full Encounter (Parks et al. 1999, 505). Specifically, any verbal or physical contact involving police business that lasted longer than approximately one minute and/or that included a *meaningful* verbal or physical exchange was designated as a contact. The term *meaningful* here is intended to reflect the sig-nificance of the exchange from the point of view either of the officer or the person having contact with the officer. For example, if a person were to call a gang unit officer and the telephone conversation lasted less than one minute, but significant information was shared by either party, we would count it as a meaningful contact. If an officer stopped a suspected gang member, then upon closer inspection decided that the person was not a gang member and released him, the exchange would be considered meaningful because the officer exercised his authority to detain or release that person – no doubt a meaningful exchange from the perspective of the other person.

In the following sections, we discuss the frequency of officer contacts with others, typical ways in which contacts were initiated, and the iden-tities of the persons contacted. In addition, because it was the method used for a significant number of the units' contacts with gang members, we discuss the use of *suspicion stops*.

Mobilization of Gang Unit Officers

Inglewood gang unit officers were mobilized significantly more often than officers in any other unit (Table 7.2).[3] During an average eight-hour shift, Inglewood officers altogether were mobilized about thirteen times, compared with about four or five times per shift for gang unit officers in Albuquerque, Las Vegas, and Phoenix. We found few differ-ences among the four units in whether mobilizations were initiated by

[3] The term *mobilize* refers to the gang unit officer being initiated into action, put into movement, or being activated in some matter.

TABLE 7.2. *Average Number of Mobilizations per Eight-Hour Shift, by Medium*

Source of Mobilization	Inglewood	Las Vegas	Albuquerque	Phoenix
Telephone	6.08	0.78	1.05	1.28
Walk-in	3.16	0.10	0.38	0.06
Gang unit officer – initiated	3.29	3.12	2.11	2.82
Radio	0.00	0.10	0.57	0.25
Other	0.12	0.26	0.00	0.43
TOTAL	12.65	4.37	4.13	4.85

officers, radio calls, or other sources. However, the units did differ in the frequency with which officers were mobilized by telephone calls or walk-ins. In Inglewood, where the gang unit office was colocated with other units in the department, other officers routinely visited to request intelligence, and gang unit officers often received telephone requests for gang intelligence from other criminal justice agencies.

Individuals Contacted by Gang Unit Officers

We examined the types of persons with whom gang unit officers had contact and how much time officers spent on these contacts. The number of contacts that gang unit officers had with gang members and the average length of these encounters were perhaps our most interesting findings.

As seen in Table 7.3, Las Vegas gang unit officers had the most frequent contact with gang members, with about three contacts per eight hours. Similarly, the contacts that Las Vegas gang unit officers had with gang members lasted longest, averaging about forty-one minutes per contact. Our observations of the gang units suggested that this finding reflected Las Vegas's aggressive gang enforcement strategy.

Inglewood had the next highest number of contacts with gang members, but the duration of their contacts was the shortest of the four gang units – most likely a reflection of the type of contacts that the Inglewood gang unit officers had with gang members. The officers made only friendly stops to collect intelligence, and did not contact gang members for enforcement purposes.

Phoenix and Albuquerque each averaged about one contact with gang members per eight hours, encounters averaging twenty and thirty-two minutes in length, respectively.

TABLE 7.3. *Gang Unit Contacts: Averages per Eight-Hour Shift*

	Inglewood		Las Vegas		Albuquerque		Phoenix	
	Number	Length	Number	Length	Number	Length	Number	Length
Internal stakeholder	4.68	46.17	0.57	8.18	2.20	26.99	1.22	24.83
External stakeholder	4.55	42.37	0.52	2.03	0.96	14.21	0.67	6.50
Gang member	2.15	12.02	3.07	41.34	1.24	32.56	1.22	20.30
Victim	0.25	3.79	0.52	7.09	0.09	1.73	0.18	4.35
Witness/third party	0.25	3.16	0.78	11.68	0.76	7.59	0.49	10.06
Other suspect	1.39	3.16	1.72	12.93	1.44	13.45	2.57	42.19
Citizen	0.25	5.06	0.26	1.25	0.00	0.00	0.36	3.80
TOTAL	15.06	115.73	6.93	84.50	6.14	96.53	6.99	112.03

With regard to investigative contacts (i.e., with victims, witnesses, other suspects), Las Vegas and Phoenix had the highest numbers; each had roughly three investigative contacts per eight working hours. During our observations in Phoenix, investigative encounters consumed roughly one out of eight working hours, while in Las Vegas, the time spent on investigative contacts averaged just over thirty minutes per eight working hours. This was largely a result of these units being responsible for investigating gang crime. Albuquerque's gang unit, where officers were responsible only for assisting other units with gang-related investigations, had slightly fewer investigative-related contacts ($n = 2.29$) and spent slightly less time on these contacts than officers in Las Vegas and Phoenix. Inglewood's gang unit had the fewest investigative contacts ($n = 1.89$) and spent less time with them (10.11 minutes) over an eight-hour period, largely because the unit did not have investigative responsibilities.

With the exception of Inglewood, gang unit officers in all of the departments rarely had contact with internal stakeholders (other police officers inside their department) or external stakeholders (criminal justice officials outside the department). Gang unit officers in Las Vegas had contact with an internal stakeholder or with an external stakeholder only once every other eight-hour shift, on average. Likewise, the length of their encounters with stakeholders was extremely short – eight minutes with internal stakeholders and two minutes with external stakeholders. Similarly, Phoenix gang unit officers had contact with

TABLE 7.4. *Phoenix Intelligence Requests*

	Requests (#)	Time Spent (hr.: min.)
April 1999	113	13: 40
May 1999	80	07: 35
August 1999	94	06: 30
December 1999	61	10: 00
January 2000	70	10: 40
March 2000	105	07: 25
May 2000	71	07: 10

internal stakeholders only once per eight hours and had contact with external stakeholders only once every other shift. These findings reflected the lack of officer-disseminated intelligence in Las Vegas and Phoenix; when these units disseminated intelligence, civilians handled the task. A civilian employee in Phoenix's gang unit had tracked the number of requests per month that he processed and the amount of time required to process the requests. Although not all records were available, those we examined indicated that he had been processing 61 to 113 requests per month (Table 7.4), and he was spending 6.5 to 13.66 hours every month on this activity – or about forty-one minutes per eight hours in his busiest month.

Albuquerque's gang unit officers had substantially more contact with internal and external stakeholders, spending more time with these stakeholders than officers in Las Vegas and Phoenix. This was largely a consequence of the added time that Albuquerque officers spent on intelligence, compared with Las Vegas and Phoenix officers.

On the other hand, when compared with the other units, Inglewood gang unit officers had substantially more contact with internal and external stakeholders. In an average eight-hour shift, gang unit officers averaged contact with just over four internal stakeholders and more than four external stakeholders, totaling about nine stakeholder contacts per eight-hour shift. These contacts were lengthy, as well, averaging forty-two to forty-six minutes each. Inglewood gang unit officers explained that this many internal stakeholders were contacting them because of the unit's reputation for giving quality gang intelligence. Asked why others turned to the gang unit for information, one of the gang unit officers explained:

Probably the knowledge of knowing almost everybody on the street, because our job is to contact and talk and become personally involved in these gangsters' lives, their family lives, their mothers, their school lives, so we get to know the people.

We don't know them all, I mean, there is just too many of them to know, but we know most of them, the ones that are the most active, and we know a lot about them, and they talk to us, and we know a lot of what is going on in the street. And so we are kind of like an encyclopedia here of what is going on in the city, and everybody comes to us because of it. . . .

Another officer felt that the unit was counted on to have answers:

As a resource. They know that we know the gangsters. They hear of a particular problem and they come to us with it, and if they know of a subject that is running from them or something like that and they can identify them, nine times out of ten, a basic description from a gang member that we are familiar with, we can drop out of the top of our head, "that is so-and-so from whatever gang," so we start writing up warrants. They use us a lot as a resource.

Our observations suggested that criminal justice officials outside the police department did, in fact, rely heavily on the unit for gang intelligence. Some surrounding police departments, including the LAPD, contacted Inglewood's gang unit for intelligence almost daily. When we asked the officers about this, they gave a few different reasons why other agencies contacted them so frequently. One officer's explanation focused on the inability of the LAPD to collect its own gang intelligence:

LAPD CRASH can not get fuck for intelligence. All they do is enforcement. They bust heads, so nobody will talk to them. . . . We go out there and make friendly contacts. We get to know the guys.

Another officer stated that other agencies contacted Inglewood's gang unit because of the mobility of gang members from Inglewood:

These people call because the Inglewood gang members do shit in other cities, so the police departments come to us for information because they do not know who they [gang members] are.

Last, the data showed that none of the gang units had much contact with citizens who were not suspects, victims, witnesses, gang members, or criminal justice officials. These findings were consistent with our finding that gang unit officers did not participate in community policing activities, as we will discuss in Chapter 8.

Suspicion (Field) Stops

As we discussed in the preceding text, gang unit officers spent substantial time conducting suspicion stops for the purpose of arresting or

TABLE 7.5. *Suspicion (field) Stops by City*

	Inglewood	Las Vegas	Albuquerque	Phoenix
Field stops (#)	1.77	2.29	1.05	2.14
Average length of field stop (min.)	12.90	40.92	24.97	31.27
Males (%)	89	88	92	87
Minorities (%)	92	98	92	95
Under thirty years old (%)	96	88	92	79

gathering intelligence from gang members. About 88 to 92 percent of those stopped by gang unit officers from all four units were male, 92 to 98 percent were minorities, and 79 to 96 percent were under thirty years old (Table 7.5). Although the profiles of individuals contacted and interviewed in the field were fairly similar among the units, the number, duration, and nature of the contacts varied substantially. For example, in Albuquerque, gang unit officers averaged 1.05 suspicion stops per eight hours, compared with Inglewood officers, who made about 1.8 stops per eight hours, and Phoenix and Las Vegas officers who made just over two stops per eight hours. Likewise, in Inglewood, field stops tended to last ten to fifteen minutes, whereas in Albuquerque they lasted about twenty-five minutes, in Phoenix they lasted about thirty minutes, and in Las Vegas they lasted about forty minutes.

We examined the results of suspicion stops made by gang unit officers. Analysis showed that some units were more effective at making stops that actually resulted in contact with or an arrest of a gang member (Table 7.6). In Las Vegas, Albuquerque, and Inglewood, 60 to 67 percent of all suspicion (field) stops resulted in contact with a gang member, whether self-admitted or documented by the officer.

In Phoenix, only 29 percent of suspicion stops resulted in contact with a gang member. When we asked the Phoenix officers why relatively little contact with gang members resulted from their suspicion stops,

TABLE 7.6. *Results of Gang Unit Suspicion (field) Stops by City*

	Inglewood	Las Vegas	Albuquerque	Phoenix
Gang member contacted (%)	60	67	64	29
Gang member arrested (%)	na	30	55	11

almost all explained that gang activity had declined substantially, and they were simply seeing fewer gang members on the streets as of late. This explanation was confirmed by an examination of gang crime trends in the city (Chapter 4).

Albuquerque had the highest proportion of stops resulting in arrests, at 55 percent. Next was Las Vegas with 30 percent, Phoenix with 11 percent, and Inglewood with none. These patterns reflected not only the cities' respective levels of gang unit activity, but also the gang units' enforcement patterns. In Albuquerque, gang unit officers were selective in their stops, making a point of stopping only those whom they believed to be acting suspiciously or engaging in criminal activity. Las Vegas had higher arrest rates per stop because they arrested and booked gang members for the most minor offenses (e.g., jaywalking, driving without a license). In Inglewood, gang unit officers stated that they would not make an arrest unless they had no choice. In Phoenix, officers had fewer contacts with gang members, and thus presumably fewer opportunities for making an arrest.

In two of the communities, we had a few opportunities to talk with gang members out of the presence of the officers, and we asked them about the gang unit and gang unit officer behavior. This anecdotal data suggested that gang members perceived a difference in the tactics and strategies employed by the gang unit and those employed by other units in the department. In particular, gang members stated that gang unit officers talked to them or asked questions more often than other officers. The following is one such conversation between an observer and a Las Vegas gang member:

Observer:	What do you think about the gang unit?
Gang Member:	I don't think about them, man.
Observer:	What about the guys you hang out with?
Gang Member:	No, man, no one gives a shit. They don't mean nothing, man. No one thinks about them.
Observer:	Do they influence how you act?
Gang Member:	No, man, I told you. I don't even think about them.
Observer:	What do you think about the police here in Las Vegas?
Gang Member:	They're assholes, man. They jack you up.
Observer:	Has it happened to you?
Gang Member:	Yeah, they beat the hell out of me a couple of times.
Observer:	Why?

Gang Member: I was talking shit to them. They have taken a couple of friends of mine out to the desert and done things to them there.

Observer: Has the gang unit done this to you or anyone you know?

Gang Member: No, man, they just talk, talk, talk, talk. They just talk your ear off.

Observer: What do you think about the gang unit documenting [you]?

Gang Member: I don't give a shit. It don't mean nothing.

Observer: What do you mean? You just don't care?

Gang Member: No, man, I don't care. All they'll do is fine me. Who cares?

Interviews with two gang members in Albuquerque yielded similar results. Our field notes indicated:

I talked to the female [gang member] and the male [gang member] about how the officers treated them. They said it depended on the cop, but if they (the police) think you are a gang member you get treated worse. They said there was not much difference in how gang unit officers and patrol officers treated them [except that] gang unit officers asked a lot more questions. Both of them [said that they] had been pulled over by gang unit officers twice before.

At one suspicion stop in Albuquerque, we had the opportunity to interview a police-described gang leader while the officers were gathering intelligence from other gang members. This excerpt is from the observer's field notes on that interview:

...talked to ____ , a major gang [leader] in the city. He said he is harassed by officers all of the time. I asked him how, and he said he gets harassed. He said that they stop him and all of the gang members all the time. I asked how the gang unit treated him, [whether it was] different than patrol officers. He said he knew most of the gang unit officers and they were cool because they knew how to talk to gang members and understand [them]. I asked if that makes a difference in how he communicates with gang unit officers and he said no. He said that some cops are cool and some are pussies. "The pussies, even if you are straight with them, they give you shit." He said that other than gang officers being able to communicate more effectively and understanding the gang culture better, he did not think that there was any difference between gang unit officers and patrol officers.

SUMMARY

One way of examining the functions of an organization is to examine the activities its people perform and the relative emphasis placed on each activity. With this in mind, we analyzed how gang unit officers in four police departments spent their work time, the different strategies and tactics they employed, the types of individuals that gang unit officers came into contact with during their work, and how those contacts were initiated.

A principal finding was that although considerable organizational and cultural emphasis was placed on the enforcement function, in reality, the gang units all engaged in a wide variety of other activities, relegating enforcement to a relatively modest role. This was surprising, given that our interviews with gang unit officers suggested that they prized enforcement over any other function, and little in their SOPs would have prevented them from spending more time on enforcement activities. We had also found that the gang units generally had little supervision, and they were more or less free to set their own priorities. Although we did not query internal or external stakeholders about their perceptions of the use of time by their gang units, we suspect that they would be surprised to learn that their gang units averaged only about two hours per shift on enforcement actions, and that one unit spent over one-fourth of their time on non-police-related activity.

Although intelligence was an official function of all of the gang units, the emphasis placed on it varied widely among them. The Inglewood unit spent a substantial amount of time on intelligence; Albuquerque and Phoenix spent a more modest amount; and Las Vegas spent minimal time on intelligence. The gang unit placing the most emphasis on intelligence gathered information using the friendly stop, in which officers went out of their way to build rapport with gang members. Our interviews with Inglewood internal stakeholders indicated that from their perspective, the rapport-building, friendly stop strategy employed by their unit produced quality intelligence used in investigations. Gang units placing less emphasis on intelligence tended to be more aggressive during their contacts with gang members. Consequently, anecdotal evidence suggested that the more enforcement-oriented the unit, the less intelligence they were able to gather, and that the intelligence that was gathered was less useful.

A number of internal and external strategies were used by the gang units to collect intelligence on gangs, gang members, and gang crime. All of the gang units permitted other officers in their police departments to nominate individuals to document as gang members. Some cultivated intelligence by creating formal and informal partnerships within their

police departments and with persons working for other criminal justice
agencies. Others examined departmental arrest data, newspaper clip-
pings, and information obtained by interviewing arrestees who were
gang members. All of the units used special computer database applications to process and store gang intelligence, but the amount of oversight
for the collection, processing, and documentation of this data varied
substantially among the units.

All of the gang units that we studied disseminated gang intelligence.
Most of it was distributed as requests for information coming from outside the units. In Inglewood and Albuquerque, requests were processed
by officers; in Phoenix and Las Vegas, they were typically processed
by civilian unit staff. In Phoenix and Las Vegas, the two units most
heavily invested in gang enforcement, we found that many officers had
not learned to operate their computerized gang intelligence systems, and
even those that did know how to use the system believed that officer time
should be spent on "more important" activities such as enforcement.

Some units initiated and participated in gang intelligence exchange
forums, where they met with other police officers and criminal justice
officials to exchange tactical intelligence. A few units used bulletins to
alert their agencies' officers to timely intelligence about specific gang
members, gangs, or patterns of gang crime. Three units distributed
aggregate data on trends and gang intelligence about the number of
gangs, gang members, and gang crime in the city. Most of this information was extremely cursory and broad in nature. One gang unit (Las
Vegas) published a more thorough document analyzing the state of the
gang problem in the city and describing the strategies and tactics that
the unit was using to respond to the city's problem.

We found the gang units to be engaging in few activities that could
be construed as gang education or prevention. With regard to prevention, some of the officers in one department were observed counseling gang members and their parents about issues related to gangs; and
were observed helping gang-involved youth find jobs. None of the gang
units engaged in educational activities during our observations. However, they provided us with materials that supported the contention that
their officers did train other officers from smaller agencies and outside criminal justice officials on gang-related issues, make educational
presentations to community groups, and produce handbooks and pam-
phlets on the prevention of gang membership for other agencies and
members of the community.

Additionally, data in this chapter documented the number and types of contacts that gang unit officers had with individuals outside the gang unit. In particular, we found that gang unit officers had less contact with gang members than many might expect. Most gang member contacts resulted from suspicion stops made for the purpose of trying to make an arrest or gather intelligence. Furthermore, analysis showed that some units were more effective than others in their use of suspicion stops.

Related, we observed a pattern of gang unit officers using their traffic enforcement powers, as well as their status as a gang unit officer, to harass individuals in gang neighborhoods. Specifically, our data showed parallels with the national problem of racial profiling. Gang unit officers were repeatedly observed stopping and detaining individuals because of their profile – young minority males in gang neighborhoods – and not because they were observed engaging in criminal activity that otherwise would have resulted in a stop had they not fit the profile. In fact, we found that many of the core operational strategies used by the study gang units were not only based on such principles, but these tactics and strategies were promoted by supervisors who instructed new gang unit officers how to circumvent legal barriers by falsifying official records. For example, on several occasions while conducting observations we saw and heard gang unit officers discussing the fabrication of pretext and probable cause information to be included in official police documents in order to provide what appeared to be a legal rationale for stops and searches. This occurred with sufficient frequency in at least two of the study cities to make it appear as if it were a Standerd Operating Procedure.

Once detained, gang unit officers in at least one of the study sites further harassed gang members by issuing citations for jaywalking and other minor infractions. It was widely recognized that the individuals could not afford to pay fines, and that they would be jailed at a later date due to the issuance of a bench warrant. They also used their police authority inappropriately by threatening gang members with citations and jail if they did not provide the police with the intelligence (e.g., self-admitting gang membership) they believed the person possessed.

Our findings were also supportive of Klein's (1995a) assertions that directed patrol or selective street enforcement by the police most likely have little influence on gang behavior, and in fact may be counterproductive. Klein argues such tactics are intended to send a "deterrence message to present and potential gang members" (163), but in fact typically results in few gang members being apprehended and even fewer being arrested or incarcerated for any serious offense. This, he maintains, results in gang members believing that the police are out to "hassle" them, which generates greater conflict between the police and gang members, and eventually leads to increased gang cohesion and possibly more gang crime.

Our findings are supportive of Klein's assertions in the fact that we observed very few gang members being arrested on serious charges during the course of directed patrol. Instead, we found that most of the contacts between the police and gang members resulted in intelligence gathering, but few resulted in an arrest for a felony charge. Of those arrested, most were for bench warrants for unpaid fines or for a misdemeanor offense. Very few gang members were arrested on felony charges or for offenses that had the potential for a lengthy prison sentence. These findings suggest that the police might want to reassess the value of directed patrol as a tool for generating gang arrests and deterring gang activity.

Additionally, we found wide variations in the amount of contact that gang unit officers had with stakeholders and community members. Our data showed that the more decoupled the gang unit was from its parent department the fewer contacts its officers had with stakeholders. First, the more the unit was structurally decoupled from the core organization because of office location or enhanced security measures, the less contact the gang unit had with those outside the unit. Second, the more the unit was operationally decoupled from the core technologies of the department the less contact the gang unit had with those outside of the unit. These factors combined necessarily resulted in less intelligence being exchanged between the gang unit and stakeholders. These observations were confirmed through our interviews with stakeholders (see Chapters 5 and 6).

Last, we found that all four of the study gang units had little, if any, contact with community members. Due to each gang unit's emphasis on intelligence, these findings were somewhat surprising. Providing forums for the community to express their concerns about neighborhood problems has been an increasing operational strategy used by the police for identifying problems (i.e., intelligence gathering) and responding to them (Greene 2000). Of further interest was the fact that, as discussed in Chapter 5, gang unit officers have a great deal of discretion in which activity they perform, and from our analysis it appears that when given the choice gang unit officers isolate themselves not only from the rest of their police department, but also from the general community.

Furthermore, the time use and contact data illustrated that gang unit officers, when left on their own, chose to engage in the most traditional forms of policing, and that many of the reforms related to community policing over the past decade have not taken root in gang units. This will be discussed in greater detail in the next Chapter.

8

Policing Gangs in a Time of Community Policing

> Community policing is thought to break down the barriers separating the police from the public while inculcating police officers with a broader set of community service ideals. Organizationally, community policing is thought to shift police policymaking from a traditional bureaucracy to one emphasizing greater organizational-environmental interaction. Simultaneously, the shift to community policing is said to be accompanied by flattening of the police hierarchy and the development of coordinated service delivery with any number of public and private agencies that affect neighborhood safety. These are indeed profound changes should they continue to be implemented and shape the institution of policing.
>
> – Jack Greene, Community Policing in America, in *Policies, Processes, and Decisions of the Criminal Justice System*, Julie Horney, ed., 2000, 301

The rise and growth of police gang units parallels another important development in American law enforcement, the shift or attempted shift toward community policing. For much of the twentieth century police organizations in the United States were characterized as being highly legalistic, bureaucratic, and centralized (Kelling and Moore 1988). As a consequence, a technocratic culture spread throughout agencies, and police departments became much more functionally complex and specialized (Reiss 1992). As of late, however, police reformers have attempted to reverse the trend toward organizational complexity and have suggested that police agencies make fundamental changes to their organizational structure so that they are better able to incorporate many of the new demands being imposed on the police as part of community policing (i.e., greater citizen interaction, enhanced problem solving). In particular, reformers argue that for the police to fully implement community policing they must decentralize, deformalize, and despecialize, thereby transforming the police organization into one that has fewer rules and regulations, is territorially and administratively dispersed, and makes use of police generalists (Maguire 1997).

Community policing has changed much about how the police and policy makers think about how police work should be organized and performed. However, this dialog has primarily been focused on the core function of police work – patrol – and has rarely focused on how these broader organizational changes in policing have impacted other specialized police functions, such as gang control efforts. In this chapter we consider how gang control efforts have been integrated with community policing and whether or not the use of police gang units is compatible with the achievement of community policing.

As such, we do not reiterate the many structural and operational issues that have been discussed in prior chapters. Instead, we pay particular attention to the perceptions and beliefs held by gang unit officers, managers, and stakeholders toward policing gangs in a time of community policing. The first section of this chapter focuses on the impact of community policing on the police response to gangs. Here, we were interested in how the principles of community policing may have been incorporated into the functioning of the gang unit. The second section examines the scope and nature of each gang unit's involvement in community-policing activities, from the perspective of the gang unit officer, and assesses stakeholder perceptions of community-policing activities practiced by the gang unit. The last section focuses on the impact of community policing on each community's gang problem. In other words, we were interested in whether police officials thought that community policing was a successful strategy for combating gangs.

THE IMPACT OF COMMUNITY POLICING ON THE POLICE RESPONSE TO GANGS

Many gang unit officers in each of the sites made it clear that they believed that community policing, regardless of their agency's emphasis on community policing, had little if any impact on the operational strategies used by their gang unit. For example, a number of officers in Albuquerque referenced that community-policing principles and practices had been adopted by the rest of the department, but that it was not practiced by the gang unit.

Outside of the gang unit, [community policing is practiced] quite a bit. Within the gang unit, because we're so specialized and because we have higher priorities right now, I don't think we're able to. I would like to go out to our community center and talk to people about the gang problem, but a lot of times you see that – and I'll give you a quick instance – last night we were walking around – one of the few times you'll see us walking around wearing our gang unit jackets – and a lot of people actually stopped us at the mall and asked us, "I didn't realize we had a gang unit. Do we have a gang problem?" I'm not sure whose problem that is. But for people not to realize that we do have a gang problem kind of blows my mind.

Another gang unit officer gave the following response:

I don't know if it is practiced that much. I mean, we say that we are doing it, but I don't even know to what extent, or what we are doing. I have no idea. Because when you work SID [Special Investigations Division] like I worked, there is not much community-oriented policing done here. It is usually done out there with the patrol officers out on the street. But here, we are talking hard-core.

One gang unit officer in Albuquerque went as far to blame the implementation of community policing for the *demise* of the gang unit: "Well, this chief's community policing wiped out a 20-man gang unit. It devastated it, actually. It really did, and now we are playing catch-up."

Many gang unit officers in Las Vegas also believed that that department's implementation of community policing had had very little impact on the operation of the gang unit. Some officers simply responded by making brief responses, such as an officer who stated simply, "I am not aware of any." Other officers, however, stated that community policing had had almost no impact on the police response to gangs because the community had been unwilling to participate. For instance, one officer responded, "I'd say very little [impact], and the only reason is apathy amongst the citizens."

Likewise, in Phoenix some gang unit officers indicated that community policing had not had an impact on the gang unit, while others were uncertain, or believed that its impact had been minimal, such as one who said: "I don't think it has [had an impact], I think it's a whole different concept." Some officers thought that it would be difficult for the gang unit to be involved in community-policing activities. The comments of this officer were representative of those made by others:

. . . from my squad and the area I'm working, I'd say it's pretty minimal. The guys who work North Side, you know, they're the ones going on those marches and stuff, and stuff that those marches are getting, or they're going on spurts where they'll send a whole bunch of them all at once, and they'll kind of die out for a while, so they go to those, and that affects them more as far as that's concerned. You know, we work such – you know, the whole city really, I mean we're assigned a precinct, but we really work the whole city, so it's kind of hard for us to get into a community, if you will.

Some gang unit officers, however, believed that their department's implementation of community policing had had an impact on their response to gangs. Gang unit officers in Inglewood were the most consistent in their views that community policing had impacted the police response to gangs. This was curious given that the Inglewood Police Department had placed the least amount of emphasis on community policing when compared to the other three study sites (see Chapter 2, pp. 26 – 28)

Specifically, Inglewood gang unit officers were quick to point out that the implementation of community policing helped the gang unit become more effective by focusing on long-term solutions to the gang problem and by increasing the amount of information originating from the community. Many of the Inglewood gang unit officers made comments similar to the following:

Better understanding and faster response.... Because we are realizing our community policing style, we have a better understanding of what the citizens are actually talking about.... You know we always get five or six gang members ... utilizing the community style policing, that certain address where our community affairs officers go out there to get that information. Say [xxx] is where they hang out, but when the police get there, they run to the back yard, they go in the garage, they do this, they do that. Now we have a better understanding when we get that call at [xxx] West Queen, they say Bloods are hanging out, and we get there and they are not there, it is not a bogus call ... they have seen us, so the next time we come, we are not going to come this way, or we may just go back. It gives us more of an impact on how we handle calls.

Similarly, most of the gang unit officers in Albuquerque believed that department's implementation of community policing had had a positive impact on the unit's response to gangs. Many of them focused on the fact that community policing led to improvements in communication and interaction with the community.

I think we deal with the public a lot more, a lot better than we used to. I think a lot of them feel free to call up and get information. Just help on problems that they're having and letting us know directly, when before, they were kind of going through the field officers that they saw in the field and they would say, "Hey, we're having problems." They wouldn't even deal with us. Or they'd say, "Can you contact somebody who can help us out?" And they left it up to the field officer who's busy doing something else. And he wouldn't call us.

You can tell. I think the bottom line in my opinion of community policing is communication. Between the citizens, which have the problem – the gangs – and address that with us so that we can address them . . . oftentimes before, they would talk to the cops. It's just that communication is the biggest thing.

Some gang unit officers in Phoenix and Las Vegas also believed that the community had had a beneficial impact on the police response to gangs. While some indicated that it resulted in more intelligence coming into the unit, others believed that it had resulted in a closer relationship between the gang unit and the community and other city agencies. For example, some gang unit officers in Las Vegas gave responses similar to the following:

I think [community policing] actually has had a very good effect . . . for instance, in our briefing right now, we were told that there are certain members of the community that have come forward and said that we don't want this element living in our housing projects. And for that, we have gotten consent from a couple of these neighborhoods to be able to transport off the property people that are committing crimes. Selling dope, possession of guns, things like that. And we also have a close relationship with HUD. We have that relationship with a lot of the agencies in this town and that helps us quite a bit.

Gang unit officers in Phoenix made comments such as:

I'd say it's had an impact. These neighborhoods, we feel more responsible for the gangs that are in these neighborhoods. When these community groups or neighborhood block groups put the pressure on the police department because of gang problems in their neighborhood, then the police department will put the pressure on the gang unit to go solve those. So in kind of an indirect way, we're solving the problem that the community is bringing to us.

I think it has had a major impact, because we're getting into the community and we're finding out what the problems are. By doing that, we're breaking down some of those barriers and improving some of those trust levels, and people can come and contact us and talk to us. And now we can find out who is doing what as opposed to we know it's happening, but we don't know who's involved and nobody will tell us, we're breaking those barriers down a little bit, and people are starting to trust us a little bit more. With that trust, we get information and intelligence, and that goes right back to when we have something happen, we need to be able to draw from that intelligence pool.

To further understand the affect of implementing community policing on the police response to gangs, we asked police managers about their perceptions of the compatibility between their department's approach to community policing and their specialized police gang unit. Only one police manager commented on the inconsistency he saw in using a geographically centralized unit (the gang unit) when community policing emphasizes geographic decentralization. Instead, managers in all of the departments did not believe that that the organizational structure or operational strategies of their gang unit was incompatible with their department's approach to community policing. However, while most managers did not believe that there was any inherent conflict between the two, none of the managers provided an explanation of how the two were necessarily related to one another; or how COP principles guided the response to gangs or how the operational strategies of the gang unit fit into their department's community-policing strategy.

Instead, some police managers focused on the gang unit's "auxiliary role" in community policing. For instance, one Inglewood manager described the gang unit as "on the periphery" of their community-policing approach, and explained that information provided by the gang unit to other police units was instrumental in addressing gang problems in the neighborhoods. Managers in all of the departments described how the gang unit was a resource for community groups, such as block watch, to talk to about their gang problem, exemplifying the compatibility of community policing and gang unit activities. A Las Vegas manager's response was similar to many:

Community policing is where you find out what are the community's concerns. Because as you know, what we feel is a real concern isn't the community's concern. And the community has consistently over the years said that gangs are a concern. So the gang unit really is – its whole existence is in response to the community. So the whole unit is a giant community-policing thing. Because it's a high concern for the community, so this is how we are responding to it.

Additionally, many managers attempted to make inferences about the compatibility between community policing and their gang unit by providing perfunctory examples of the gang unit's contact with the community. For example, one Phoenix manager told of the gang unit's involvement with a neighborhood activist group:

...we do neighborhood marches with NAIL'EM, which is...she's a neighborhood activist, and I don't know what exactly the acronym stands for, but they go out and they get the neighborhood association groups from around the city when neighborhoods are having gang problems or drug problems, they'll go out, you know, 50 or 100 strong, and they'll march the neighborhood with megaphones and yelling, or not yelling but just saying, "Hey, listen, gangster," and "It's time to leave...the neighborhood is fed up with it," or drug dealers. "Get out here," and

"We know who you are...." We go out and march with them, basically to show our support for them, but also to provide security for them...they get rocked and bottled in some of the neighborhoods that they're going to that are scary. I wouldn't want to go in without a gun, you know....

SCOPE AND NATURE OF GANG UNIT INVOLVEMENT IN COMMUNITY POLICING

We were also interested in understanding how each gang unit employed the use of community-policing practices in their response to gangs. In doing so, we focused on two core principles of community policing: problem solving and community partnerships. In the following sections we detail our findings pertaining to each gang unit's use of formalized problem solving and their perceptions of the role of the community in responding to gangs and gang problems. We then use stakeholder data to further understand how the gang unit enacted community policing through their principal programs and activities, as observed by those outside the gang unit.

Problem Solving

The defining feature of problem solving is that it requires the police to identify the underlying causes of problems rather than simply respond to the problem itself. Problem solving can be enacted in a number of ways. For example, it can involve the police mobilizing and consulting with neighborhood residents to analyze the root causes of problems or it can involve the police identifying root causes of problems through thorough and sophisticated forms of crime analysis (Walker and Katz 2005: 321). None of the gang units that we studied engaged in formal problem solving.

For instance, when we asked Inglewood gang unit officers whether they engaged in formal problem solving, they responded only in general terms. They viewed their routine daily activities as problem solving, but did not suggest that they were using formalized problem-solving strategies or techniques.

Every day [we engage in problem solving]. We are an intelligence unit. Our job is to go out there and be amongst the gang members, and so we are part of the community. Like I said, they know us, they don't even see us and they know our cars, just by seeing the car. They see us coming a mile away, "here comes __." So we are an intelligence unit, gang intelligence unit, we are a big part of it.

A fellow gang unit officer shared this view:

> [We are] just more into intelligence information and, you know, getting more people involved, getting more resources, gang members are hanging out at a certain apartment complex, we get the owner involved. Even if it is so small as getting a key to the gate, you know to the secure doors, we get the owners involved, we get the managers involved, we get some of the residents involved.

Likewise, gang unit officers in Albuquerque could not detail the process used or provide examples of how problem solving was implemented in their unit. One officer thought that they would be using the SARA model in the future: "... since we've been assigned to our individual area commands, we're all going to be writing up our own different types of tact plans and [we'll] use the SARA model to address that." Another officer indicated that the unit had to use problem solving because they were "so specialized." His colleague, however, stated: "I don't think we ever used the SARA model, just because when we got down-sized, there were just four of us. Then one left and so we went for 7 or 8 months with just the three of us. We didn't have enough manpower to do anything."

In Las Vegas most of the gang unit officers indicated that they personally used problem solving, some indicating that they used it "quite a bit," "a fair amount of time," or even "daily." However, when we pursued the question, we found that most appeared to be using the term generically to refer to enforcement activities in response to incidents, or even to patterns of incidents, but without the benefit of formal scanning or analysis. In other words, they tended to see traditional law enforcement as a problem-solving activity and police officers as inherently being problem solvers.

> Yeah, I think we do problem solving all the time, if we know a particular gang is engaging in criminal activity in a certain area, or if they are on the uprise because of a friend that has been killed, or so on and so forth. We saturate that area; we hit that area hard. So I think we are problem solving all the time. We get information on areas that need to be hit, then we work that area. That way they know that we're out there in force, and we know they're up to something.

> I think we use it quite a bit. I mean, we wouldn't know ... until somebody comes to us and says hey ... like Saturday, we're on a car stop, and an officer says we're taking rocks and bottles every time we come into this complex. People are throwing them at us. There's a problem and we try to solve it. We come in from different angles in the middle of the night trying to find gang members out there and take them to jail, and find their dope and find their guns. In our job we try to be proactive, but a lot of it is reactive.

One officer contended that the investigative process was equivalent to the SARA problem-solving model:

I don't think they know the full SARA-type model and stuff like that, because they are probably using it already like an investigative tool. So when you do your investigation, you already have . . . you've scanned it, you already know what the problem was, you don't really do the analysis much. Your response is going to be the investigation, evidence. And your assessment is going to be basically how well you did the report. Guys don't understand that SARA is just a simple model tool that people have put an acronym on, that is done on a daily basis.

So I *think* they do it, but I don't *know* if they do it . . . like Eric and I are starting a program right now with our Students Academy Alumni. And we're going to have them do retail store checks throughout Clark County for locking up paint. And if they are locking up paint, then they get an "atta boy" slip and a nice certificate. If they are not locking it up, we're giving them the code violation and telling them we are going to be back in 6 weeks to check. But we go back the next week, and if they don't have it locked up, they get cited. Again, that's a POP project.

We're working it from our end, and we're using Citizens' Academy people to do something for us. I guess we're using it, but it just depends how well you know how to use it.

Phoenix gang unit officers as a group were barely familiar with formalized problem solving in the department, or with the SARA problem-solving model. Some asked interviewers to describe the model to them; others simply admitted that they knew nothing about formal problem solving or SARA. A few indicated that formal problem solving occurred at higher levels, such as the "chief's level," while others knew of problem-solving efforts carried out at the precinct level:

In the gang unit, [problem solving] really isn't up here, because it's more an investigative detail, there's a certain way things have to be done. But when you go to the precincts, their net squads, their bike squads, they use it a lot, all the time. In fact, I don't think you're going to find a guy on one of the bike squads that's been there any amount of time that hasn't had a lieutenant or sergeant come to them and say, "Hey, you need to come up with some kind of model, some kind of action plan to take care of this problem."

That's a big thing . . . SARA model . . . Weed and Seed programs are designed to target specific troubled neighborhoods. And doing that, you clean out a neighborhood, now obviously you're going to push people to a different neighborhood, and you've got to continuously attack it that way. And I think the only way to attack it in a progressive and a proactive manner is through these problem-solving techniques.

Although a few Phoenix gang unit officers indicated that they used problem solving to address the gang problem, they generally provided descriptions of something other than formal problem-solving strategies:

> I think we use that on a regular basis. If we hear or see a gang problem, like at a house, we'll do our standard workup on the house. Who lives there, what have they been arrested for, if anything, who lives down the street from them, are there friendlies to that gang house. If we're going to go sit up on that house, we know who's behind us, that kind of thing. I would say we use that type of approach on almost everything.

> We actually use it a lot, you know, if we have two rival gangs shooting it up between each other, or there's been a homicide or what not, you know, we spend more time in that neighborhood, just by going down there and making an arrest, gathering, using informants, just a show of force could bring our presence down in a community more often... could dismantle the gang for a little bit and move them to a different location.

Community Partnerships

At the core of community policing is the assertion that one of the most effective ways of reducing neighborhood crime and disorder is through a collaborative relationship between the police and the community. Community-policing advocates argue that cooperation between the police and the public will result in the police having greater access to information about neighborhood problems, which in turn will lead to the police being more responsive and directed to crime and disorder. As such, a central principle of community policing is that the police become more integrated and in tune with their community and the community becomes more involved in local crime control efforts (Walker and Katz 2005: 314).

Bayley (1995) in his seminal book *The Police for the Future*, points out that two elements are necessary to ensure that the police and public become coproducers in crime control: consultation and mobilization. Consultation, according to Bayley, involves the implementation of formal forums where the public feels free to express their problems and needs and where the police can educate the public about their efforts and their successes. Mobilization involves community capacity building with the ultimate goal of increasing community cohesion and formal and informal social control.

Accordingly, we were interested in exploring the role that the community played in responding to gangs in each of the study cities. We began by focusing on the kind of relationship that the gang unit officers thought that the unit *should* have with their community. Most officers, regardless of the unit, stated that it was important for the unit to have a close relationship with the community. For example, in Albuquerque all of the gang unit officers recognized the importance of having a good relationship with the community; in fact, they used words such as "good," "open," "close," and "working" to describe the ideal relationship. One officer summed up their perspectives this way:

I think it needs to be a good relationship. We need to go to the neighborhood meetings and things like that. The problem comes in with some of the neighborhoods where it is multi-jurisdictional, and they feel that we are just picking on the young kids. They feel that it is their right to be a gang member. You know, it's just a way of life for them. So it depends. The people that are trying to clean up the neighborhoods and be a part of the solution, yeah. But the people that are part of the problem, we have to build relationships with them. When you're in the business of law enforcement, that's what we need to do.

Likewise in Inglewood, when asked about the kind of relationship that should exist between the gang unit and the community, one officer responded, "I think it should be an open line of communication where the community can express their concerns, their ongoing problems, with different gang members." A fellow officer emphasized this communication model, and described the existing relationship:

I like the relationship that we have now. It's pretty close. We do have citizens that call on a regular basis. Sometimes it can be a nuisance, but we can't shut them off because a lot of times, they are a resource. So I like the way it is now. They feel comfortable calling us on a day-to-day basis. We just have to utilize our patience, and something might not even deal with gangs. Sometimes they call us and we try to help them out, so it is a real close-knit relationship.

Still another officer mentioned communication, with even greater emphasis on the role of the community in communicating with the gang unit:

I would say that the community has to share the problems. They have to let us know, because they are our ears, our eyes; they know what is going on in the community. They know a lot better than we do. They have to tell us what is going on, we can't always guess and know just by talking to the gang members. They have to tell us what is going on over here. And they do.

Many of the Las Vegas gang unit officers had difficulty expressing the type of relationship that should exist between the gang unit and the community and instead focused on the fact that the unit currently had a problematic relationship with the community. Some Las Vegas gang unit

officers described it as a conflict between gang unit enforcement practices and the community's expectations. The officers knew that community policing promoted and cultivated openness with the public, but
at the same time, they felt compelled to maintain secrecy about intelligence functions and certain enforcement activities. One officer gave
this rather negative assessment of the unit's current relationship with
the community it served:

I wish it were better. But a lot of times we need to be secretive, and we can't
disseminate all of our information. There are some things we need to share. But
I don't think the community is receptive as a whole...the community itself. I'm
not talking about our leaders; I'm talking about the public. Not very receptive;
they don't feel we have a problem. They don't want to acknowledge it.

Another officer described the current situation, one in which business
as usual meant keeping enforcement tactics out of the public eye, but he
also pointed out the need for increased public support and participation:

I have some mixed thoughts in that, only because the community itself wants to
stop the gang activity, suppress it, don't let it happen to my kid. And there are
certain things we need to do, to do that. You don't violate their civil rights or
anything like that. We go out there with a heavy hand and zero tolerance on these
things. The community wants to know, why are you picking on my kid. So I think
if they realized what we are doing, they might not like it, and maybe they'll take
a softer approach. "Well, we don't want you to do it that way." But at the same
time, that's the way it has been for so many years, and the police department has
to say, "I know what's best for this community, so we are going to do it that way."
It can't be that way anymore. We have to have the support and the participation
from the community, because if we don't, we're going to fall apart. So that's where
I think the department needs to improve it better.

Another officer painted a pessimistic picture of gang unit–community
relations. He expressed frustration with public criticism of gang unit
tactics emanating, in his opinion, from the community's lack of understanding of their activities. When asked how they might address such
problems, however, this officer did not suggest better communication
as a potential solution.

My biggest pet peeve with people who criticize the police department is they don't
know what we do, and how we do it, and why we do it. There are so many times
that we stop people on the streets and we get, "You're harassing them." And it
bugs the heck out of me, because they don't know why we do what we do. Then
they go tell somebody else, so they make it known that we're harassing them.
Then somebody else says, "Oh, yeah, they're harassing them." They don't even
know why.

Most of the time we're out there, we do consensual stops and say, "Hey, what's going on?" We get their information and take their pictures. If we have a normal citizen that sees us do that, they have a real problem with that. The unfortunate thing is they don't [know] why we do it. On the flip side of the coin is, there are things that they don't need to know, that they shouldn't know how we do our intelligence, why we do the things that we do. We're not out violating people's civil rights, we're not out slamming people on the hood, 'cause I could tell you at least five times in a shift, somebody will come up and say, "Do you see me slamming into the hood, do you see him in handcuffs, do you see him this or that?" And they still have a problem with that. If somebody needs to be in handcuffs or needs to be under arrest, then we have to do what we have to do. But we don't go out there looking for people to hurt, we don't go out there looking for people to put in handcuffs, or make an example of.

But, my point is, people don't understand why we do what we do, and until you walk a mile in my shoes, don't criticize me or what I do. And I think the public is not educated enough on why we do what we do, and I don't think they ever will be. And I think we're going to have to battle with a lot of people in the public on what is happening. I mean it is getting worse.

However, while many of the gang unit officers pointed out that the relationship between the police and community was poor, several gang unit officers also expressed the view that the relationship between the unit and the community should be more open. They believed that they derived benefits from an open relationship, and one officer said that working toward this end was resulting in increased information and resources.

I think it should be an open, good relationship. I mean, there again, if those doors are opened up to people, other than receiving a traffic ticket from a policeman and having to call 911. Then they will be more apt to give us information when there's a crime. They will be more apt to donate equipment when a fund thing erupts through the voters, they will be more apt to give us these fund increases.

Most of the gang unit officers in Phoenix indicated a need for good working relationships and communication between the unit and the community, especially when communication facilitated investigations:

[We need] [a] good one! The same as them reporting regular criminal activity, they can report any gang activity or gang graffiti to us because, obviously, activity and graffiti are intelligence for us that lets us know again what's going on in the neighborhood. If we know what's going on in a neighborhood between graffiti itself, if there's fresh graffiti and its been crossed out, and another gang has put their name on top of it, we know that in the near future that there might not only be a fight, but a shooting between these two groups, because they are trying to control one area and sooner or later, somebody is going to control it, which means either the other gang is going to step aside, which doesn't happen, or they're going to take over the other gang, and obviously that's something we need to know about.

Additionally, several officers described the relationship with the community as important in order for the community to better understand and support the gang unit:

I mean, I think there's got to be a relationship, you know, maybe a better understanding of how we work or what we do, but I mean I know I don't want to ride around with somebody and, you know, I mean there's definitely times when it's to our benefit to do that, or it's necessary for us to do that, but I don't want a ride-along every night. I mean it would be stupid for me now, but when I worked nights, you know, we'd just go out and do it, you know, and a lot of times that that happened, whoever called – whoever wanted to ride, rode, and it's like, okay.

I would like to see a relationship where we can go into a neighborhood, and they are aware that we are actually there to help them. We're not there to harass a particular minority group, we're not there to arrest their babies, and thump on them and do what they think we do, which that's what the majority of the people think. I would like to be called by the community and given information so that I can make their community better. I mean it may sound kind of hokey, but I do this job because I want to make it better.

Although communication was a strong theme in the officers' responses, we did note that few of the officers, with the exception of officers in Phoenix, referred to a two-way exchange; rather, they idealized communication flowing from the community to the gang unit. None of the officers in Albuquerque, Inglewood, or Las Vegas desired a partnership with the community, nor did they express the fact that the gang unit had an obligation to proactively mobilize the community or to have formalized relationships with the community to identify gang problems. The closest was the Phoenix gang unit officers, who tended to describe the most desirable relationship with the community as one that generated more communication and useful information coming from community members into the unit, and as one that allowed the community to better understand and support the gang unit.

After inquiring about what police officials believed the relationship between the gang unit and community ought to be, we asked police managers about the actual involvement of the community in the response to gangs. In all four study sites, police managers indicated that the community played a very minor role in responding to their community's gang problem. Of those managers that did believe that the community played a role in responding to gangs, it was limited to reporting neighborhood gang activity or attending neighborhood meetings and providing intelligence to the police.

For example, police managers in Albuquerque explained that the community was playing some role in addressing the gang problem. However, the managers did not attach much importance to the public's contribution. They tended to characterize the community as most concerned with graffiti, and as often misperceiving crime. One manager described community input as follows:

Yeah, I think they, you know – we get a significant amount of input just based on the amount of community meetings that we have had. You know, we have some groups that are more active than others and give us more input than others. But yeah, I think they have had a voice in it. I wouldn't say that it has been significant. Most of the public outcry is for the graffiti, than for the gang violence. Graffiti is more of an immediate recognition of a problem.

A second manager also implied that community input was suspect, often arising from misperceptions:

We just did a survey city-wide and asked them what their major concerns were. Crime was one of the main concerns in Albuquerque. Later on, we asked them what was the crime problem in their neighborhood, and that was one of their least concerns. So, the perception of the crime city-wide is bad, but when it comes to their neighborhoods, no, they don't have a crime problem. Not a serious crime problem. Which tells you that the perceptions are different than what the reality is. And I think that is similar to involvement in the gang activity. They know we have gang activity, and so often in the news, "...well, sources in the police department believe that it is gang related," or "sources in the police department think that this is narcotics related." And all of that is, in some degree, true. But I think people in the community get that, in some areas, that it is all gang infested. Well, maybe it is or maybe it isn't.

Inglewood police managers also gave mixed responses when asked about the community's role in addressing the gang problem. Some pointed to block watch and volunteer groups as examples of community involvement. However, others believed that the community was less of a factor: "Not really; they have trusted us to come up with a strategy."

One Las Vegas manager described a positive impact, not in terms of gang abatement, but of improved relations with the community:

When we go into a community, especially into a minority community or public housing, the interaction, aside from what we are doing at the activity, the interaction before, during, and after with other people, because we are trying to do the positive dialogue, I think that does have an impact. So we drive into a small community, we are not normally greeted with rocks and bottles and things like that. I think that is indicative of the relationship developed as a result of trying to apply community policing philosophies.

Some Las Vegas managers were unclear whether the local community was playing a significant role in addressing the gang problem. At least one manager responded, "I really don't have a handle on that, I'm not sure." Another indicated that the community was involved, but only to the extent that they were informing the department of their problems: "To a degree, when they communicate problems in their neighborhoods, we listen carefully, and based on their concerns and their statements, we try to respond with police resources to address those concerns and handle those problems that they are telling us."

Not all Las Vegas managers were this noncommittal about community contributions. One individual gave a local neighborhood positive recognition for its efforts:

There's our predominantly black culture that lives in what we call the West Las Vegas area. Some people refer to it as the Westside. They are very active in getting involved in the gangs. All the... pastors of all of the churches over there are proactively going out in the neighborhoods, and talking to these kids about the violence and how stupid it is. It all helps.

Phoenix police managers saw the role of the community in addressing gangs as embedded in public support for the Phoenix Police Department as a whole:

They always have a big role, because we – our job is to listen to what the citizens say... a citizen advisory group to the city council, I think, has made a major impact on how we do business... these different functions we attend... I think people like us here, I think the good people like us, and that has made it a lot easier to deal with here, compared to Los Angeles... they have such a lousy reputation with the public, they'll never get new equipment... where we feel confident, you know, coming about an election... you know people will vote for us and get new equipment... we have the citizens' police academy where 30 to 40 citizens go through a little academy... we give a dog and pony show, and that opens some eyes on how we do things. I think its positive for the department.

Stakeholder Perceptions of Gang Unit Involvement in Community Policing

In addition to interviewing gang unit officers and their managers about the gang unit's involvement in community policing, we asked the gang units' internal and external stakeholders whether their gang unit practiced community policing, and if they did, to provide us with some specific examples. Stakeholders from the four study sites either indicated that their gang unit had not implemented strategies reflective of community policing, or stated that their gang units participated in community policing, but could not provide any substantial examples of community policing.

For instance, when we asked Albuquerque's stakeholders whether the gang unit practiced community policing and to give specific examples several responded with short statements such as "I would think so," "I think it does," "I'm not sure," or more directly, "I don't know;" sometimes adding that they had little knowledge of the inner workings of the gang unit. Other stakeholders gave ambiguous answers, such as the one provided by a sheriff's deputy: "I know the patrol officers do work beats. I don't know if they have a COPS unit like our department does. I'm not too sure."

An internal stakeholder, a commander, observed that from his point of view, the gang unit did not practice community policing:

Well, I think that because the unit itself is insulated from community policing in the Special Investigations Division, I don't believe it participates in community policing to a very large degree. I think that's problematic. I just think they're insulated from it. They have in the past gone to meetings, but they're not involved with that process. And to be real involved with community-based policing, you need to interact with community, and they're not doing that.

However, a School Resource Officer had a different perspective:

The gang unit works through different units in the police department, and that's the way that they interact with different facets of the community. And that's really basically what the gang unit is comprised of. It's trying to gather all this information about individuals who are involved in gang activity. And because your average gangster, the ones called *veteranos*, as I would call them, all started in elementary and up to middle school. And sometimes their whole families were gangsters. The gang unit interacts with different facets of school detectives and SROs, and that to me would be involved in community policing.

Somewhat differently, while most Las Vegas stakeholders stated that their gang unit engaged in community policing, none of them provided current examples of the gang unit's involvement in community policing. Instead, when asked for specific details, nearly all of the stakeholders referenced examples from the past, when the gang unit had apparently exacerbated tensions between the police department and the community.

The description provided by a patrol lieutenant of his involvement in gang sweeps provided insight into this source of tension between the police department and the community:

We did Operation Colors when I was leaving the gang unit, which is our first-ever major operation where we went after gang members from a racketeering point of view.... Some community people questioned why there's a big proportion of African American people affected by the search warrants. But, you know, fortunately no one was hurt in an execution of multiple warrants. And you know, they were big operations!

The same lieutenant described other gang unit and police joint activities that proved problematic in terms of community relations:

We used to do reverse sting operations in the neighborhoods where street narcotics were sold openly. And the interesting thing about that is that we would take over and have officers posing as gang members and selling the drugs. What I did not like about it was that we would have officers, white officers, put black paint on their faces to be – to pretend they were black. That was justified in their minds due to the fact that we didn't have any [African American] officers at the time in the gang unit, which led me to say, "Well, we need more [African American] officers in the gang unit."

So I was able to recruit more on my team. And then we would work those operations with them. Because to me, in the early '90s, to think that we would have white officers be black-faced... and I was quite offended by that. We've come a long ways.

A lieutenant working on the west side of the city offered some strong opinions about the nature of the gang unit's orientation to the community, as well as about their performance in his command area:

You know, I'm in the neighborhood. I know people in the neighborhood, you know, and it pisses me off when I hear a white officer, a lieutenant say, telling me what's best for those good people in West Last Vegas. Well, you don't know about anything. Who have you talked to in West Las Vegas? Who have you talked to? Who?

This lieutenant went on to describe in detail how he had helped organize the community in an effort to prevent disruption when the second Rodney King verdict came down. He made the point that he was able to rely on his knowledge and relationships within the community, which he believed that the gang unit was unable to do.

An area commander described a gang unit operation that increased tensions among the residents in his command area. He had been in the midst of working with a particular segment of the community on problem-solving activities, when without his knowledge, the gang unit conducted a sweep in that neighborhood. He first learned of the operation when he began receiving citizen calls complaining about the operation. He attributed the incident to a lack of communication between the gang unit and patrol, but he also said that communication between the two units had been improving.

Stakeholders in Phoenix generally saw the gang unit's response to gangs as being consistent with community policing, and provided a few examples of the community-policing activities engaged in by the gang unit. First, stakeholders pointed out that the gang unit was focusing on a problem – that is, gangs – that the community wanted something done about, which necessarily meant that the unit was practicing community policing. One Neighborhood Enforcement Team (NET) officer made the following comment:

...the majority of the community wants the gang problem quashed, and a lot of the stuff we deal with are community complaints. Again, I don't really know their bureau. I don't know their manuals and their policing plan, but the way I see things being done, I think [their response reflects community policing].... We let [gang members] know we're watching them, and when they commit a crime, they usually get the most sentencing we can give them as far as their prosecution goes, because they're documented and things like that. I think that we're on the right page.

Likewise, an assistant prosecutor offered this opinion, similar to that of several other stakeholders:

I think it does [reflect community policing], because the gang problems really affect not the community at large, but primarily the neighborhood where that activity is going on, when you get the citizenry saying, "I can't walk outside my front door, I can't stand in my front yard and talk to my neighbors, because I'm afraid of X." And I think that's where the police department has done a good job of getting out there, making the public and getting the citizens to assist them to at least start an investigation, and follow up on them.

On the other hand, other stakeholders articulated that the gang unit incorporated community-policing principles into its organizational structure and operational strategy by being responsive to line-level officers within precincts. One detective working the graffiti detail explained:

I think it does [reflect community policing goals and objectives] now more so than it used to at its inception, in that they actively work with precincts on a precinct-by-precinct basis, and then the precinct in turn is working with given neighborhoods in a mile-by-mile square. So the gang unit tends to be more of an assistance that the precinct can call on, to use as the precinct is doing the hands-on, neighborhood community policing thing, and then they're able to bring in this outside force to help deal with that community policing issue.

Interestingly, this same detective pointed out that until three or four years ago, others in the department used to refer to the gang unit as the "goon squad" instead of the "gang squad." He said that "given the tactics used by the squad, no one thought their cases would hold up in court, but they did, since the gangster didn't know anything about the law."

Similarly, a lieutenant serving as an area manager in the same precinct had a different perspective on the unit's incorporation of community-policing principles into their response to gangs:

Yes and no – yes, from a standpoint that there is liaison and they are dealing with the internal customers, mainly patrol officers, yes. No, from the standpoint that they are not solving problems long term, they are solving them short term ... the short-term reactionary issues ... now, I don't totally put this black cloud over them, because when they do RICO cases, they are good at it, and those RICO cases may go 3 or 4 months with a lot of arrests being made, that part I still say is a success. Long term, though, changing the complexion of a neighborhood so they don't have to come back next year and do it again, that's the mark they're missing.

A contrary perspective was offered by at least one stakeholder from a neighboring police department who deplored what he called the "enforcement only" approach used by the gang unit. He also complained about how difficult it was to communicate with the gang unit. He offered the following, representing the views of several other stakeholders:

If we are talking about the gang unit, I would say no. . . . When you call the Phoenix P.D. right now and you're going to call their gang unit, you'll get a secretary or somebody, but you may not find any of the guys. You say, "Well, if I wanted someone to come and give me a prevention talk on gangs, who would I contact?" And they give you another number. I don't think that's being very open to community policing.

Inglewood's internal and external stakeholders both tended to see the gang unit as engaging in community-policing activities, and some were able to point to particular community-policing activities and programs. Many stakeholders focused on the function or role of the gang unit and how it supported department-wide community-policing efforts. For example, some detectives indicated that the intelligence and information provided by the gang unit was invaluable in support of other police operations that included community policing:

The gang unit as a service provider is where we have shined over the years. We have cracked a lot of cases using information from the gang unit. They provide good intel. They're a great source of information. They know about crime.

However, other stakeholders gave rather weak examples of community-policing activities conducted by the gang unit. For example, one detective thought that because "gang intelligence could be used to address problems of physical and social disorder, it could be viewed as a community policing activity." A detective in the anticrime unit pointed to the gang unit spending time talking to gang members and "being out there" as examples of community policing. One external stakeholder commented, the police department had a vested interest in working with the community to solve the gang problem – insinuating that merely having a gang unit demonstrated commitment to community policing. Another external stakeholder involved in graffiti abatement complained, however, that a communication problem between the police department and his department had hindered his ability to do his job.

It should be mentioned, however, that in Inglewood, some stakeholders provided specific examples of their gang unit's involvement in community policing. For instance, "early childhood development" and "midnight basketball" programs were identified by some detectives as community-policing activities engaged in by the gang unit. Of interest here was that while Inglewood was the only department that had not implemented community policing, their gang unit was perhaps the most organizationally committed toward implementing the key principles of community policing through roles, responsibilities, and programming.

IMPACT OF COMMUNITY POLICING ON THE GANG PROBLEM

Last, to further examine the role of community policing in the response to gangs, we interviewed managers about their perceptions of the impact of community policing on the gang problem. We were interested in understanding how police managers viewed the success of community-policing principles and practices on their city's gang problem to better assess the fit between community policing and specialized police gang units. Our analysis indicated that police managers largely gave mixed and vague assessments of the impact of community-policing practices on the gang problem, and that police managers were generally not convinced that community policing had any significant impact on their city's gang problem.

For example, in Albuquerque most managers dismissed the idea that community policing might be having an impact on the gang problem, responding, "Not really," or "To some degree, but not a great degree." However, at least one manager offered a different perspective:

Community policing is basically officers talking with the community and working together and being honest and each doing their part. Yeah, I think that helps in the gang problem, but it also helps whether it is burglaries or the prostitution problem. It is something that we have spent a long time on in this department, and the process came out and we became more formalized on how we account for the community policing efforts. I think this department has done it for a long time, but did not call it community policing.

Inglewood police managers gave more mixed assessments of the impact of community-policing practices on the gang problem. While some managers gave responses such as "I haven't seen it," or "I would like to hope so, but I don't have any information on that," other managers were slightly more positive, pointing out that because community policing had had a favorable impact on the crime problem in general, it followed that it had similarly affected the gang problem, in particular. Only one manager felt that community policing was helping to deter gang activity:

I think that putting the community policing presence in the community, that the gang members know also . . . we would not have any impact on it if the gangs or the people involved in that activity didn't have a perception that the citizens were also involved. So I think there is an integral tie to community policing, citizen involvement as partners, and the impact on the crime problem.

Although certain that the gang unit was practicing community policing, some police managers in Las Vegas were less convinced that community policing was having an impact on the gang problem. One manager's uncertainty focused on problems with measuring potential impacts:

That's hard to measure – very, very hard to measure. I know, because of our relationship with most of the gang members of this community, we can get information, and they know who we are and what we do. We know who they are and what they do, and we communicate with them. But we're not going to change them . . . they basically say that they are a bad guy and you have got to catch me.

Other managers had a more modest impression of the impact of community policing. One individual related the following success story:

You know, it probably has [had an impact], because in some areas we worked closely with patrol stations. We identified gang problems, we worked with the management of several apartments and, if nothing else, at least displaced that, at least out of a couple of the apartment tracts for a while. So I think it has had an effect; it made it harder for them to operate in that area for a while.

When asked to assess the impact of community policing on the area's gang problem, Phoenix police managers' responses were vague. As an example of a positive impact, some emphasized that closer contact with the community increased their acquisition of information. The following two responses reflect the managers' perceptions of the community as an information source:

They're an excellent source of information for us, because they lived in the neighborhood, they have been around these kids for years and years, and they know them, they know where they live and what's going on, so if we can get the community to give us information . . . I mean we can work with it and do a lot more. The problem is, you have kids in the neighborhoods and the people who live there are intimidated by them, so they don't want to give the information freely as they normally would.

I think it has, I think what it does is give ownership back to the citizens . . . we can't be the eyes and ears always, you know, we need their help 'cause we're getting a lot of calls . . . we got a gang hotline, people call up and say, "Hey, I got this gangster lives at this house and his name is this . . . I have information he may be involved in a homicide or drive-by," or "You know he pulled into his yard yesterday and his back window was all shot out, he's out there fixing it right now, you may want to check it out," you know, something like that . . . it's giving them the opportunity to help us . . . they feel more comfortable with us and they feel more comfortable with the knowledge they get, and they feel comfortable with the way they are relating to us, and they feel stupid . . . making a big something out of nothing.

Additionally, Phoenix police managers pointed out that the community was playing a legitimate role in addressing gangs, but they had some qualifications:

Yes, I think so, and in areas where they have neighborhood associations, you're going to get more contact with them, and you're going to get phone calls, and you're going to get more information than the normal neighborhood where one neighbor might call sometime this year, and another neighbor might call sometime the next year, but nobody really pulls together, and they don't voice all their opinions about it, they just kind of keep to themselves and kind of just live with that.

SUMMARY

One of the purposes of this study was to assess the fit of community policing with the police response to gangs, or gang units. We started by examining the impact of community policing on the police response to gangs, followed by the scope and nature of gang unit involvement in community policing, and the perceived impact of community policing on the gang problem.

We found similarities across agencies in terms of perceptions of how community policing had affected their department's response to gangs. Specifically, regardless of the agency, while some gang unit officers indicated that community policing had little or no impact on the police response to gangs, most believed that community policing had had a positive impact on their partnership with the community. For the most part, those who believed that community policing had not had an impact on their unit's response to gangs acknowledged that community policing had been implemented in their department (with the exception of Inglewood), but that the gang unit had been immune from the organizational changes. Those who believed that community policing had had an impact on the response to gangs typically pointed to the department's broader implementation of community policing, and how department-wide community-policing efforts had benefited the gang unit through a stronger relationship with the community. Gang unit officers frequently expressed satisfaction with the fact that community policing led to the community being more likely to contact the gang unit and inform them about gang problems. However, none of the gang unit officer's acknowledged that community-policing principles or activities had been implemented in the gang unit as a result of implementing community policing at the departmental level.

Many police officials attempted to make gang unit tactics appear as if they were part of the gang unit's community-oriented approach to policing. Many managers explicitly stated that any contact with the community outside of normal enforcement activity was considered community policing. None of the police managers in our study sites mentioned how the agencies implementation of community policing actually impacted the structure or day-to-day operations of the unit. For example, they did not explain that due to the implementation of department-wide community-policing efforts the gang unit began to use SARA, or any other problem-solving strategy, nor did they establish formal community partnerships with neighborhood groups such as Mothers Against Gangs, nor did they restructure their unit to become more integrated with the technical core of policing. Put plainly, very few of those interviewed mentioned any processes that were implemented as part of the agency's community-policing approach. Instead, if respondents did believe that the unit practiced community policing they tended to focus on broadly defined outcomes, such as increased intelligence capability or increased political capital.

Although respondents reported that problem solving was practiced in their departments, they most often described it in conventional terms, such as solving a particular enforcement problem in traditional ways, rather than in contemporary professional terms. Few officers appeared familiar with formal police problem-solving methodologies, such as the SARA model, and there was no evidence that formal problem-solving strategies were used in any of the gang units. Instead, we found that officers in these units placed high value on traditional police strategies and tactics (see Chapter 6) and devalued prevention-oriented strategies and activities that otherwise might be labeled as community-oriented policing.

Likewise, we found that our study gang units had not established formal partnerships with the community. While almost all of those interviewed agreed that the gang unit *should* have a close working relationship with the community, none reported that the gang unit worked with the community on a regular basis, and few reported that the community played even a modest role in the unit's gang control efforts. Instead, we found that our study police gang units were very traditional in their relationship with their community. Many gang unit officers and managers expected the community to provide the police with timely intelligence, which was to be used in a fashion that was thought best by the police. Conversely, gang unit officers did not believe that they were necessarily responsible for providing the community with information on the gang problem, providing the community with feedback on the police department's efforts to combat gangs, nor did they necessarily feel compelled to be responsive to community requests for service. Some officers went as far to note that much of the intelligence and information offered by the community was not valuable. As such, we found that the relationship between our study gang units and their community's was restricted to individual citizens reporting gang behavior to the police, and the police responding to that problem through enforcement activities if they believed it was necessary.

Respondents appeared almost guarded in their assessments of the impact of community policing on local gang problems; few thought that it had had any major impact. Some indicated that they would view increased engagement with and input from the community as beneficial in addressing the gang problem, and they associated this kind of community interaction with community-policing practice. Specifically, they noted as a primary benefit the potential increase in community-generated information on gangs and gang activity, information that could be put to use for enforcement. Other respondents reported, or hoped for, an indirect benefit from community policing: An engaged and informed community could become a source of political support, passing local bond issues for the acquisition of equipment and other resources. However, some stakeholders, both internal and external, did report that certain gang unit enforcement activities had actually put a strain on police–community relations.

As such, our findings are contrary to others that have found police gang units engage in community policing. Specifically, Weisel and O'Connor (2004) reported that in their study of two gang units that, "There is little evidence that specialized gang units conflict with community policing in principle or practice, indeed, gang units, can complement community policing by providing resources to focus on specific problems related to gangs" (i). Conversely, we found strong and consistent evidence that police gang units did not engage in community or problem-oriented policing. In fact, many gang unit officers were unclear about exactly what those terms meant. Gang unit officers did not to enter into partnerships with their communities, and they were not proactive in seeking citizen input. None had used formal problem-solving strategies to plan their approaches to gang-related problems. Accordingly, it should not be surprising that gang managers did not believe that community policing had had an impact on their city's gang problem. In Chapter 9, we discuss why today's gang units are structurally, operationally, and culturally incompatible with contemporary community-policing principles and practices.

9

Conclusion and Implications

The purpose of this book has been to provide a detailed account of the realities and experiences of the police gang unit, and those who are in them. Furthermore, it was to understand the assumptions, issues, and problems that shape the police gang unit's response to the gang problem. The objective of the book, however, was not to denounce the police gang units under study for their inadequacies, but, to understand how they respond to their community's gang problem, and the factors that might influence their response, with particular emphasis on the problems that may result from the performance of their duties.

This final chapter summarizes and discusses the results from the study. In the first section of the chapter, we discuss the five principal findings of our research and their implications for policy makers. In the second section, we present our final thoughts and make recommendations for what we believe a more effective gang unit might look like.

POLICE GANG UNITS AS AN INDIRECT RESPONSE TO AN OBJECTIVE PROBLEM

All four cities had documentable gang problems at the time that their police departments decided to establish gang units. However, that decision in each police department occurred in response to political, public, and media pressure, and not to the objective reality of the gang problem. In other words, the creation of the gang units was an indirect rather than a direct response to local gang problems. In our assessment, a strict constructionist interpretation of the formation of gang units misses the mark, at least for our study sites.

Most earlier researchers examining the creation of police gang units have argued that gang units have not been established in response to an objective threat, but rather to *moral panics* and *social threats* (Archbold and Meyer 1999; McCorkle and Miethe 1998; Zatz 1987). Researchers have also argued that police officials, along with the media, have socially constructed local gang problems, demonizing minority and other marginalized youth, in order to support campaigns for additional resources (McCorkle and Miethe 1998; Zatz 1987). We have no doubt that each of the cities that we studied had very real gang problems with their attendant crime and violence, and none of those gang problems were constructions of the police department for any purpose. We also found no evidence that any of the police departments had created gang units in order to control marginalized populations perceived as threatening; rather, we found evidence to the contrary.

Much of our data suggested that minority communities were playing a major role in shaping the nature of the police organizations' responses to the gang problem. In almost all of the communities studied, we found evidence that as gang violence became a local reality, community members, especially those in minority communities, began publicly criticizing police for lack of action. In a number of cases, widespread rallies, meetings, and protests took place, as the public demanded that police "do something" about the gang problem. Their demands typically motivated local policy makers to inquire into the problem, which in turn resulted in the media focusing more intensely on gangs and gang incidents, public outcry, and policy makers' actions.

Although in each community a local gang problem had preceded the creation of its police gang unit, in no case was the gang unit a direct response to the problem. In fact, the police departments' responses, at least initially, had little to do with enhancing operational efficiency and effectiveness. Instead, the specialized units were created in response to the institutional environment, in which public pressure to act was being applied. The fact that the specialized gang units were created in response to political-institutional considerations, rather than to purely rational needs, eventually resulted in problems for some of the departments.

In all of the cities, we encountered what appeared to be a growing lack of consensus about the magnitude and nature of the local gang problem, largely with respect to their nature and declining scope. Interestingly, *internal* stakeholders tended to see the problem as diminishing, whereas *external* stakeholders and at least some gang unit officers claimed that the problem continued to be serious. This split was complicated by the fact that little thoughtful analysis had been conducted to clarify the issue.

The statistical assessment of local gang problems typically consisted of little more than counting the numbers of gangs and gang members. The absence of detailed analysis was surprising, given recent advances in information technology, crime analysis, GIS mapping, and the current emphasis on formal problem solving in policing with models, such as SARA, that emphasize analysis. As a result, the study participants whom we interviewed could provide only subjective evaluations of the local gang problem, which in turn made it difficult for us to objectively assess the goodness of fit of local responses to local problems. More often than not, study participants seemed to have based their appraisals of the situation on dated media accounts of the local gang problem, official reports from years past, and their own gang unit's cultural lore.

We concluded that the police agencies were often not well-positioned to respond efficiently or effectively to their gang problems with their gang units. Once the gang units had been created, abundantly staffed, and given ample resources, their autonomous organizational structures and operational strategies rapidly became entrenched within the agencies. None of the structures or strategies allowed for rational organizational adaptation, should the community's gang problem, albeit still in existence, become less serious.

ABSENCE OF DIRECTION, CONTROLS, AND ACCOUNTABILITY

Our examination of the gang units, and of their parent police departments, found few formal mechanisms in place for directing and controlling gang units or for holding the units and their officers accountable. Many units lacked governing policies, procedures, and rules. Most of the departments did not adequately train officers to perform the specialized tasks and activities necessary to fulfill the functions of their gang units. None of them used formal performance measures to examine the effectiveness of their gang units or to hold them accountable for carrying out designated responsibilities.

First, with the exception of Las Vegas, the gang units either did not have special policies, procedures, and rules guiding officer behavior, or those they did have were overly modest in nature and scope. The fact that some units had not so much as a mission statement spoke to the minimal direction that the parent organizations were providing. As a result, unit functions and activities were largely driven by either the unit supervisor or an officer who had been with the unit for a long period of time. The chief of one police department admitted that he did not know exactly what the gang unit did or how they did it. The unit had been around for a long time, he explained, and he was confident that his officers were doing whatever they were supposed to be doing.

Although we had no reason to think that any individual officer was acting inappropriately in any way, we did believe in general that the lack of formal direction given to the units (and to their supervisors) hampered the departments' effectiveness in developing coherent and well-articulated plans for controlling community gang problems. Since the 1960s, police agencies across the country have sought to control the discretionary behavior of officers.

The gang units that we studied were decoupled, both organizationally and strategically, from the rest of their departments. Given the autonomous nature of their work, decoupling made control and accountability even more elusive, and more critical. Departmental policies, procedures, and rules not only would have helped to guide the activities conducted by gang unit officers, but also would have established behavioral boundaries, so that officers could be held accountable by a clear standard. Instead, the gang unit officers were a force unto themselves, free to engage in whatever activities they wished, with little input from supervisors or administrators.

To be sure, in accord with recently established principles of community and problem-oriented policing, agencies have been encouraged to limit the number of policies and procedures that interfere with the good judgment and discretion of officers. But this recent paradigm shift calls for more educated and better trained officers, with the capacity to move beyond responding to calls for service to solving long-standing problems within the community. The gang unit officers whom we studied were, for the most part, poorly trained by their departments on gang-related matters. Although all of the officers received the generally mandated trainings, most were not required to be trained for their specific positions within the gang unit – at least not beyond such basic elements as an introduction to gang culture, how to document gang members, and how to use the gang information system. As a consequence, officers learned primarily by on-the-job training, a method that was found to have its own problems.

Accountability was further complicated by the fact that officers in three of the gang units were expected to engage in investigative functions. Yet most had never performed any police function other than patrol before they were assigned to the unit. Although expected to investigate serious crimes, these officers had received no formal training in how to properly conduct such investigations. Gang unit officers were also responsible for disseminating gang intelligence. Officers in the two largest gang units, however, did not know how to operate their computerized intelligence applications. The officers acknowledged that they had received some training on the system, but with little prior computer experience, they still were not comfortable or proficient with the technology. This left the majority of gang unit officers unable to engage in this part of the very activity for which they were responsible.

Compounding the problem, the gang unit officers were widely recognized by policy makers, the public, and even other police and criminal justice officials as experts on gangs, gang members, and gang activity. Accordingly, they often were called upon to serve as advisors and educators by other community agencies and law enforcement officers, elected officials, and the public. They served as experts and consultants on the gang problem – a problem about which they had not been adequately trained or educated. Serving in these capacities, the officers shared information based on their own deeply held cultural beliefs, not on objective data that had been subjected to rigorous analysis. Important decisions were being based on such information, both within and outside the department.

This problem was even further extirpated with regard to the influence gang unit officers had in the courtroom. Gang unit officers were often times the only "gang experts" that judges and juries had at their disposal for understanding gang-related incidents and responses to those incidents. Once again, gang unit officers were found to not be adequately trained to be considered gang experts. Furthermore, the fact that we found that gang unit officers frequently engaged in prohibited street enforcement tactics and regularly falsified official reports further lends evidence to the fact that gang unit officer testimony in court is often not only based on lack of formal training and gang unit culture, but may also be based on purposefully misleading information.

Finally, the gang units that we studied lacked adequate performance measures. Measuring police gang unit performance is important for several reasons. First, and perhaps most obvious, evaluation is vital for assessing the fundamental success of the unit. Performance evaluations provide critical feedback to police managers about their organizations' gang control efforts, informing managers about strengths and weaknesses in their organizational structures and operational activities. The information from performance evaluations is used to guide decisions about disbursements of limited resources, and to support individual and organizational accountability for specific problems (Bureau of Justice Assistance 1997).

Gang units should be evaluated for other important reasons as well. Without performance measures, managers are unable to make effective administrative decisions relating to training, officer evaluations, and promotions. Performance measures allow managers to provide feedback and guidance to unit personnel, so they can continue to grow in productivity and effectiveness. Systematic evaluation of the unit and its personnel provides information to managers concerning the means that the unit uses to address gang-related problems. It keeps management up-to-date on the support (i.e., personnel and other resources) needed to address the gang problem (Mastrofski and Wadman 1991; Oettmeier and Wycoff 1998).

Performance evaluations provide a means of formally socializing gang unit officers and holding them accountable. The measures convey agency expectations and inform unit officers, in an official and formal way, about the mission, goals, and priorities of the unit. Performance measures are essentially a detailed list of expectations regarding the types and numbers of activities that are to be performed and their quality. Performance evaluations also socialize officers informally, communicating acceptable styles of policing, and they help to create a shared vision of what constitutes successful gang control. Finally, performance measures facilitate professional development among officers in the unit (Oettmeier and Wycoff 1998).

Not only did we find that these four police departments rarely conducted evaluations of or within their gang units, but also even when evaluations did take place, performance and effectiveness were typically judged using global, subjective measures. Many participants in this study were hard-pressed to offer specific *evidence* of gang unit effectiveness, even though they assessed the local gang problem as substantial, and had given us generally positive assessments of their gang units. Interestingly, when we asked stakeholders and police managers about the units' utility, they frequently mentioned the value of gang intelligence, but they seldom addressed the units' impact on the amelioration of the local gang problem. Without objective performance measurements, management decisions about the configuration of the gang unit, or even about whether or not to continue having one, were necessarily premised on something other than hard evidence.

INFORMATION AS THE PRINCIPAL GANG UNIT COMMODITY

Although the gang units placed organizational and cultural emphasis on enforcement activities, one of our principal findings was that they were engaging in a wide variety of activities, with enforcement playing a relatively modest role. Clearly, gang unit officers and some internal stakeholders valued suppression-oriented enforcement activity. Internal stakeholders of the gang units that did not spend much time on enforcement were quick to point that out as a failing. Many gang unit officers argued that enforcement activities gave the gang unit legitimacy. They also argued that prevention activities had no place in a gang unit and should be the responsibility of community relations or another unit. At the same time, however, few internal or external stakeholders commented upon the *value* or *effectiveness* of their gang units' enforcement efforts (e.g., directed patrols, crackdowns, investigations) in reducing the community gang problem or in supporting outside units' or agencies' efforts. Stakeholders seemed to view enforcement as something that gang units ought to do, but almost no one suggested that the gang units' enforcement or suppression strategies were proving effective.

In part, this might have been a recognition of the limited contact that occurred between gang unit officers and gang members. We found that gang unit officers averaged only one to three gang-member contacts per eight-hour shift, depending on the unit. Of those contacts, most resulted in intelligence gathering, not an arrest. As such, stakeholders may have not considered gang unit enforcement activities effective because gang unit officers were not arresting and confining large numbers of gang members, at least not enough of them to have a substantial effect on gang crime. This seems consistent with evidence (see Chapter 7, Table 7.3) that indicates that the "dosage" of gang enforcement is relatively low, and it may not be realistic to expect much of an impact on gang crime.

Actors in the gang units' environments received the most benefit when the units produced and disseminated of gang intelligence. Internal stakeholders frequently commented on the usefulness of such information in solving crimes. External stakeholders often made reference to the importance of intelligence to their agencies' gang suppression, intervention, and prevention efforts. However, few resources in the departments or in the gang units were actually dedicated to producing and disseminating intelligence (with Inglewood being the exception), but from the perspectives of the stakeholders, this was clearly the gang units' most important contribution.

Incorporating the intelligence function helped the gang units establish and maintain partnerships with other organizations that had a high degree of legitimacy. Intelligence-related activities were often conducted in coordination and cooperation with established institutions such as criminal justice agencies, schools, and formal community groups that could lend organizational support to the gang unit. By associating and aligning themselves with organizations that had achieved high levels of legitimacy, and by making themselves useful to these organizations, the gang units were able to gain and sustain legitimacy from the organizations, as well as from those organizations' constituents and other supporters. As a consequence, although some of the gang units emphasized the enforcement function internally, the intelligence function permitted them to survive because of the technical efficacy that it brought to the unit.

We noted that gang units that prioritized gang intelligence conducted street activities differently than those that did not. In Inglewood, for example, gang unit officers acknowledged that in order to maintain productive relationships with gang members, they could not make arrests unless they had no other choice. Instead, when they observed crimes, they referred them to the department's crime suppression unit. The officers believed that arresting gang members would create mistrust between the gang unit and gang members, hampering intelligence gathering. Similarly, in Albuquerque, gang unit officers placed great importance on treating gang members respectfully, making contacts only when they were certain that an offense had occurred or when they had a strong possibility of gathering useful intelligence. Albuquerque gang unit officers explained that "bogus" stops and disrespectful treatment of gang members could cost the unit the trust of gang members and future opportunities to gather intelligence.

The Las Vegas and Phoenix gang units, which placed more emphasis on enforcement, were less concerned about gang members' perceptions of the unit. For instance, the gang unit officers in Las Vegas often cited the youths for walking the wrong direction down the street, jaywalking, and driving infractions. We observed them frequently stop, frisk, and question youths for no legal reason. In Phoenix, although not as aggressive as in Las Vegas, gang unit officers did frequently stop individuals for minor traffic offenses, hoping to gather intelligence. In both communities, such actions not only caused gang members to share far less intelligence with gang unit officers, but it also resulted in community dissatisfaction with police conduct, because ordinary citizens in their own neighborhoods frequently were stopped when gang unit officers mistook them for gang members.

STRATEGIC AND STRUCTURAL DECOUPLING OF GANG UNITS

All of the police departments studied had decoupled their gang control units in one or more ways from the parent police organization. Decoupling stands in contrast to the normative theoretical position that structural patterns within an organization should be tightly coupled with activities, so that the structures conform to a consistent and clearly articulated set of expectations (Donaldson and Preston 1995). In contrast, institutional theorists maintain that some organizations function better if structure and activities are decoupled, enabling the organization to carry out core activities while at the same time engaging in activities substantially different from those core activities (Meyer and Rowen 1977).

The gang units' activities occurred well apart from the parent organizations' operational practices and activities. They were not well-integrated or connected with departmental structural patterns or activities. As prescribed by the loose-coupling perspective, we found the gang units we studied to be strategically and structurally decoupled from the larger police organization. In accord with the decoupling, gang unit officers were not held responsible for performing core policing activities. Instead, the gang units that we observed allowed their officers to engage in buffet-style policing, picking and choosing what to do and when to do it.

Gang unit officers were generally not responsible, for example, for responding to calls for service or performing other tasks associated with routine patrol activity. The gang unit officers only responded to calls that interested them. For example, if an officer believed that a call for service broadcast over the radio might be gang related, he might back up the dispatched patrol officer. Efforts like this typically were made when an officer suspected that valuable intelligence might come from the contact. Supervisors and officers strongly emphasized that the unit was not required to handle calls for service, however, and that they considered responding to them a distraction from the unit's core missions.

Similarly, in most of the gang units that we studied, officers were highly selective when accepting cases for investigation. Gang unit officers were typically only interested in investigating (whether in a primary or auxiliary capacity) gang-involved cases with a high probability of giving up valuable intelligence and in high-profile cases. As a result, gang unit officers most often investigated crimes such as homicide, drive-by shootings, and aggravated assaults. Even when they were clearly gang related, the gang unit officers did not normally handle less serious crimes.

In most of the gang units, such strategic decisions were not dictated by a superior nor did they emerge from a well-articulated vision of what the gang unit ought to be doing toward achieving its goals. Rather, operational activities in most units tended to arise from the unique work-group subculture that existed within the gang units, reflecting the officers' shared beliefs about the nature of the gang problem and the appropriate response to that problem.

The gang units in Las Vegas, Albuquerque, and Phoenix reflected the pattern of structural decoupling by police organizations in their response to gangs. All of the gang units that we observed exhibited high degrees of autonomy, with several factors contributing to this. Physical location was among the most important, and these three units were all operating from off-site, "secret" facilities. Nearly all other police officers and criminal justice stakeholders were kept in the dark about their locations. Even those select few who may have been told where to find them could not enter unescorted; the facilities were secured, and only gang unit officers had keys and access codes.

Various rationales were offered to justify the secret locations. The principal one was to offer protection from gang retaliation for officers who felt safer working in the secure, off-site facilities. Protection was an issue for the officers; some took further precautions, traveling varied routes from work to avoid being followed home. In a few instances, we thought that the espoused need for secrecy had become cloaked with a cold war, spylike quality, some gang officers asserting that their regular precinct stations or police headquarters had become subject to penetration by gang members, rendering intelligence files vulnerable to destruction or manipulation.

When the police departments that we studied decided to centralize the responsibility for responding to local gang problems in a specialized unit, that decision meant that the gang units would almost certainly become decoupled from their parent organizations. Police departments have two alternatives for disbursing resources allocated to responding to community problems. Traditionally, police departments have administratively and geographically centralized these resources. More recently, however, with the advent of community-oriented policing, departments have begun to administratively and geographically decentralize, realigning resources more closely with the neighborhoods and communities they serve and the problems they address. As they configured their responses to gangs, the four departments we studied had to decide whether to disburse their gang-response resources and conduct related activities at the precinct or neighborhood level (decentralization), or to consolidate resources and activities at one location (centralization). Nationwide, gang units had come to represent a form of organizational centralization; true to form, none of the units that we studied were decentralized.

Centralization and autonomy are not necessarily identical, but in these units, it appeared that they went hand-in-hand. The gang unit supervisors and officers we interviewed believed that consolidation and centralization would permit their officers, through training and experience, to develop more highly developed technical skills than otherwise would be possible. Additionally, they pointed out, administratively and geographically centralizing resources allowed more orderly distribution of gang-related work and enabled police departments to coordinate their responses to community gang problems.

Whatever its potential advantages, centralization and the structural decoupling of the gang units had created several problems for their parent departments. First, we found that decoupling had isolated the gang unit officers from the rest of their police organizations. Because the gang units were strategically and structurally removed, gang unit officers interacted infrequently with patrol officers and investigators. They also tended to isolate themselves from the community. Gang units and gang unit officers were found to pick those with whom they would interact. That is, most interactions with outsiders were initiated by the officers for their own purposes, instead of in response to requests for assistance from patrol officers, detectives, or even citizens.

We also found that being decoupled from the larger police organization reduced the gang units' capacity to receive and provide information especially to and from units engaged in core policing activities within the departments, particularly such as patrol and investigations. We noted previously that gang unit stakeholders within police departments considered the information contained in gang intelligence databases to be the most valuable commodity controlled by the gang unit. These stakeholders' overall assessments of their gang units often were directly related to their perceptions of the local unit's performance in developing and providing intelligence. Stakeholders tended to view the gang units most positively when they perceived the units as proactive in developing and freely disseminating intelligence, and as appreciating the gang-related intelligence contributed by others in the police organization.

Internal stakeholders in the Inglewood police department (the most tightly coupled unit of those we observed) tended to give positive evaluations to their gang unit, largely because they could easily access gang intelligence to use in criminal investigations. On the other hand, in Albuquerque, Phoenix, and Las Vegas – departments more loosely coupled then Inglewood – department stakeholders complained that their gang units failed to provide intelligence and that the officers seemed disinterested in cooperating to generate new intelligence. Stakeholders' overall assessments of the gang units' performance reflected their dissatisfaction in this area. For example, in Las Vegas some supervisors noted that you had to have personal contacts in the gang unit to get information readily, and patrol commanders bemoaned the fact that the gang unit did not take advantage of patrol, the "eyes and ears of the street," an important source of intelligence. The potential for gang units to fail to produce products valued by other police units is a problem often associated with loose coupling, one that affects the support received by gang units from other parts of the organization. When internal stakeholders perceived their gang units not to be taking care of business, they were less likely to view those units as legitimate, and that, in turn, threatened the units' institutional viability.

Centralization that included off-site and secretive locations (and other organizational characteristics that promoted autonomy) had consequences for both the gang unit and the parent police department. Not only are centralized units more likely to become autonomous, but so are their officers. Both formal, direct line supervision and informal supervision (e.g., officers being observed by supervisors in other units) was often minimal in the gang units that we studied. Autonomy makes it difficult for departments to maintain oversight and hold gang units and their officers accountable for their actions and results. In fact, we found that the police departments that we studied had left the organizational character of the gang unit by default largely to the subculture of the gang units.

A still greater problem with loosely coupled gang units, and related to the preceding, is the potential for them to develop unique internal subcultures that can become at odds with the mission of the parent department, or even with the law. This problem is exemplified by findings from the investigation of corruption in the LAPD's Rampart Command Area.

That investigation included LAPD's own investigation of the Rampart Areas CRASH unit, the department's version of a gang unit. Investigators concluded that the decoupled gang unit had developed a culture that contributed to the corruption scandal that, among other things, involved gang unit officers framing gang members.

> The "Rampart Way" mentality was particularly strong with Rampart CRASH. The inquiry uncovered ample evidence that Rampart CRASH had developed its own culture and operated as an entity unto itself. It routinely made up its own rules and, and for all intents and purposes, was left to function with little or no oversight. This certainly perpetuated a feeling of cultural elitism and was a significant factor in this corruption incident.
>
> (Los Angeles Police Department 2000, 61)

Interestingly, the LAPD Rampart CRASH unit demonstrated that complete physical isolation is not necessary for decoupling to occur, because the CRASH unit shared facilities with patrol prior to moving into separate quarters. The separation conducive to decoupling was found to be in part social-psychological, and not entirely physical. The following excerpts from the LAPD report illustrate this point:

> The CRASH unit developed into an entity unto itself. It maintained its own booking bench and only CRASH supervisors provided booking approval and signed arrest reports. At one point CRASH had it own kit room, separate from the patrol kit room. This became problematic when a watch commander attempted to identify officers involved in a complaint, but could not find a worksheet for the CRASH vehicles.

Separate roll calls from the patrol division, a unique patch and jackets, an emphasis on narcotics enforcement, and an outward appearance of elitism were common CRASH traits that Rampart shared with other CRASH and specialized units. The supervisor who took over Rampart CRASH in 1992 had prioritized making every CRASH officer into a narcotics expert. Although CRASH's primary function was gang intelligence, the supervisor justified the narcotics enforcement emphasis by pointing out the correlation between gangs and narcotics.

A wide chasm developed between patrol supervisors and Rampart CRASH officers. Several supervisors recalled the CRASH practice of specifically requesting a CRASH supervisor at the scene of a crime. If a patrol supervisor showed up instead, CRASH officers would tell him that he was no longer needed, or that a CRASH supervisor was on the way. Similarly, CRASH would often specifically request a CRASH unit when backup was needed. These practices fostered a sense of exclusion that resulted in other officers and supervisors avoiding CRASH incidents (Los Angeles Police Department 2000, 69).

The Los Angeles Police Department's own findings in this case illustrated some of the consequences of decoupling gang units that we have mentioned in the preceding text. For example, LAPD identified weak supervision as part of the problem: "The apparent lack of supervisory and management control over the CRASH unit was a significant factor identified during this inquiry" (Los Angeles Police Department 2000, 61). The chasm between Rampart CRASH and patrol reflected the decoupling consequence of autonomous units not being responsive to others. The emphasis on narcotics in CRASH, while the principal and formally assigned function of the unit was gang intelligence, reflected the loosely coupled unit's characteristic lack of goal consensus. In addition, throughout the report, evidence demonstrated the lack of information sharing between CRASH and other units involved in the technical core of policing, such as patrol.

GANG UNITS AND COMMUNITY POLICING

In recent decades, police departments across the country have responded to local gang problems by establishing specialized police gang units, coinciding with the nationwide emergence of community-oriented policing. Community-oriented policing emphasizes geographic decentralization and despecialization, but the inherent nature of gang units seems to promote the opposite. The conflict raises several questions that we sought to answer in this report: Do police gang units support and facilitate community-oriented policing? Is the character of police gang units compatible with community-oriented policing philosophy and practice, or conversely, do the units constrain or even undermine development of community-oriented policing within the department? Are the organizational and structural characteristics and practices of gang units consistent with community-oriented policing principles and practice?

In both scholarly and practitioner literature, a good deal of attention has recently been paid to the key features and principles of community-oriented policing (Cordner 1999; Dunworth and Abt Assoc. Inc. et al. 2000; Greene 2000). Police scholars and practitioners have not reached complete consensus on all of the defining characteristics of community policing, but they are in general agreement about the core features that distinguish it from traditional "reactive" policing: citizen input, geographic focus, emphasis on prevention, partnerships, formal problem solving, and management (Dunworth and Abt Assoc. Inc. 2000).

Citizen Input

Community policing seeks direct input from citizens. It then uses that input to identify and prioritize community problems, and to formulate responses. The gang units that we observed had generally made little or no systematic effort to obtain or use direct citizen input, even though the initial formation of the gang units was in response to community pressure to do something about a local gang problem.

Although the gang units rarely sought citizen input, we did observe some exceptions. For example, in Albuquerque, the gang unit was working closely with a neighborhood organization to reduce local gang-related crime. Likewise, in Phoenix, at the request of several neighborhood associations, the police department had allocated additional personnel to the gang unit to devote more attention to the north side of the city. Overall, however, we found little evidence of regular dialogue between citizens and gang units, and even less evidence of gang units systematically pursuing citizen input to identify and solve neighborhood problems. The lack of communication between citizens and the gang unit became particularly problematic when the unit attempted to carry out enforcement operations. We found that enforcement operations conducted without prior citizen input or awareness – not to mention without the input and awareness of other police units – were creating serious community-relations problems. For example, during one unannounced gang unit action in a Las Vegas neighborhood, a district commander recalled getting calls from the neighborhood's residents describing an invasion of officers in ninjalike uniforms. Not only were the residents upset, but the area commander was also unhappy as well, that an action had been carried out in his community policing area without prior consultation or warning. Such occurrences distanced the gang unit from the community, and especially from minority communities, because most gang unit operations were conducted in nonwhite neighborhoods.

Geographic Focus

Unlike traditional reactive policing, community policing designates geographic areas, such as neighborhoods and police beats, as the basis for assigning accountability, as well as for assessing performance in managing crime levels and community problems. Police gang units have often had a geographical focus, because in the past gangs were turf-based. The common measure of success, at least from the public's perspective, has usually been areawide reduction in gang-related crime and activity.

Sustaining that geographical focus had become challenging for nearly all the gang units that we observed, however. In their view, local gangs were becoming less territorial. In Las Vegas, gang unit officers maintained that destruction of public housing had displaced and dispersed gang members formerly based in those complexes. As a result, they argued, gangs were no longer associated with specific neighborhoods; members of a given gang were likely to be scattered, living in several different neighborhoods.

The Phoenix gang unit was the exception. Here, gang unit squads were assigned to carry out operations in specific precincts, and individual officers were responsible for particular gangs in their precincts. The Phoenix officers argued that this configuration increased their familiarity with assigned neighborhoods and their knowledge about particular gangs, which in turn had been helpful in investigations of gang-related crimes. Still, we found no evidence that officers or squads were being held accountable for gang control efforts in particular geographic areas.[1]

Prevention

Community policing emphasizes prevention as a key tactic for managing crime and disorder. Officers are to be proactive, addressing potential problems before they materialize. As Klein (1995a) pointed out, however, only about 8 percent of gang units carry out prevention-related activities. Klein's finding proved to be the case for the four gang units that we observed. Officers in all of these units believed their responsibilities did not include addressing underlying problems related to gang crime. They argued that the nature of the job was essentially reactive; they were to respond to real problems, after they occurred. Some officers counted directed patrols in gang areas and investigation of gang crimes as prevention, because the activities deterred future crimes.

Generally, the few activities with prevention potential that were carried out by the gang units took the form of educational presentations at schools, community groups, and other law enforcement agencies. These typically covered topics such as the gang unit's mission, the history of the local gang problem, and typical gang member beliefs and behaviors.

---

[1] With the exception of Phoenix, the gang units that we observed were not held accountable for long-term reductions in gang-related problems. Only process indicators were measured, such as the number of arrests or the number of individuals documented, to assess gang control efforts – not outcome measures.

We found these were not given for the purpose of addressing or reducing underlying gang-related problems, however. Instead, as the officers explained, the presentations were part of a public service campaign to educate audiences about the role of the gang unit and the nature of the local gang problem and were meant to increase public support. In sum, we found few gang unit activities undertaken with prevention in mind.

Partnerships

An important theme in community policing has been that police can form productive problem-solving partnerships when they coordinate and collaborate with community groups, other government agencies, the private sector, and nonprofit agencies that share their objectives. This could apply to gang control activities, but the number of such partnerships varied in our study sample, with some units having formalized partnerships and others lacking partnerships entirely.

We were somewhat surprised to find that the Inglewood gang unit was functioning nearly completely without partnerships. The Inglewood unit's claim that information and intelligence was its primary commodity would lead one to think that formal and informal networks would be developed to gather and distribute that intelligence; this was largely not the case. Similarly, Albuquerque's gang unit was in the midst of an organizational transformation, and it was not formally partnering with others in the community or with other criminal justice agencies.

Las Vegas and Phoenix gang units had established informal partnerships with several criminal justice agencies. For example, Las Vegas engaged in weekly "Rock Pile" intelligence exchange sessions with department officers and probation, parole, and corrections criminal justice officials. The Phoenix gang unit had a similar arrangement, albeit slightly more organized, with criminal justice agencies in its metropolitan area.

Phoenix's gang unit had initiated a gang liaison program, formalizing its partnership with patrol officers with an interest in gangs, to train them to identify and document gang members. The program was intended to strengthen the relationship between the units. Many participants believed that the program's significance was that it put gang unit officers in closer contact with patrol officers, who had more contact with gang members. Gang unit officers believed that the liaison program increased their intelligence capabilities.

A similar program had been established in Albuquerque. However, in that community, specific gang unit officers were assigned as liaisons to each of the area commands. Area command personnel indicated that these officers were spending time at the commands on a regular basis.

The gang units that we studied rarely formed intentional partnerships with community groups, local businesses, or state and other local agencies. When they did, the partnerships typically were with criminal justice personnel for the purpose of exchanging gang-related intelligence. For example, the Inglewood unit liaisoned with a gang intelligence officer at a state prison who advised the unit when gang members were going to be released back into the community. Similarly, the unit liasoned with the manager of operations at a local cemetery who contacted the unit to determine if a burial service involved a gang member. However, these partnerships were few, and we found no evidence of working relationships with community organizations or neighborhood groups. Nowhere did gang unit officers appear to value information from non–criminal justice agencies, and few of them seemed to recognize the potential value in sharing their own information and knowledge with non–criminal justice personnel. Those attitudes clearly made it more difficult for the gang unit to collaborate with the community in their gang control efforts.

Formal Problem Solving

Formal problem solving using a standardized methodology, such as the SARA model, is a defining element of community policing. Typically, formal problem solving begins with a process to identify crime and community problems, working at the level of a specific police beat, neighborhood, or address. To be successful, problem solving relies upon having certain community policing prerequisites already in place. For instance, close connections with the community are needed to assure that the problems addressed are, in fact, relevant and important in the minds of the community members. Both problem analysis and responses developed as part of the problem-solving process require participants with an interest in the problem or in contributing to its solution, from the community, other police units, and other organizational stakeholder groups.

We observed little evidence of police gang units initiating or participating in this kind of formal problem solving. There appeared to be three principal reasons. First, gang units were decoupled from their parent organizations, and connections with community and other key stakeholders that could have facilitated formal problem solving were generally missing. Second, most gang unit officers were untrained or were only vaguely familiar with SARA or other formal problem-solving models. Third, we found that the gang units simply did not routinely consider formal problem solving as a strategy for addressing local gang problems.

Interestingly, we found none of the police departments engaging in any form of analysis to better understand their cities' gang problems. Community gang control activities most often were planned and implemented in accord with popular beliefs about problems, rather than being grounded in thoughtful analysis. It appears, then, that if gang units are to engage in any formal problem-solving efforts, they should begin at this point – collecting and carefully analyzing available data about their particular gang problems.

Management Tactics

Community policing calls upon managers to rely less upon formal rules and policies to guide organizational decision making and employee behavior, and more on intentionally developing an organizational culture and values. This is typically done by creating and communicating mission statements, participatory strategic planning, and coaching and mentoring. The objective is to empower officers to take reasoned risks as they respond to problems, but at the same time, to provide enough organizational direction to ensure that officers work toward common goals (Cordner 1999).

Two of the four gang units studied (Phoenix and Las Vegas) had mission statements, broadly articulating that the units were to engage in gang control and setting out the primary functions of the units (enforcement and intelligence). Two units did not have written mission statements, and were given no other verbal guidance pertaining to their goals and functions. In both Inglewood and Albuquerque, senior gang officers, one a sergeant and the other an officer with twenty-five years of experience, had essentially determined an implied mission and set of functions, simply in the way that they conducted business. In those units, police executives relied heavily upon these officers' expertise and knowledge to focus their units' efforts on "what really mattered."

Only the Phoenix unit had engaged in a formal strategic-planning process. Gang unit supervisors there had worked with the city council to develop a long-term strategic plan to address the community's gang problems. Afterward, they met with city council members each quarter to discuss trends in gang-related activity and gang unit performance (e.g., number of arrests, amount of drugs confiscated, number of guns taken off the street, number of gang members documented). Based on this information, the city council would redistribute resources.

For the most part, gang unit officers worked with little or no supervision. When officers worked the streets, they might go weeks or longer without a sergeant observing them. When asked, officers and supervisors in all gang units agreed that the autonomous nature of gang work was not conducive to field supervision. Only the best officers were selected for the gang unit, they argued, so the independence afforded by the job would be unlikely to lead to problems. In addition, written guidance (e.g., a mission statement, policies and procedures) was unavailable in two of the sites studied, and oral guidance (e.g., supervision, coaching) was lacking or rarely occurred for gang units at all four sites. This accounted for the fact that the practical mission and functions of each gang unit had evolved by the time of this study to reflect the units' subcultures and strong individual interests.

In sum, the police gang units that we studied were generally poorly designed to engage in or support community policing efforts. The units tended to be geographically centralized, while community policing emphasizes decentralization. Frequently, they were geographically isolated from the communities and neighborhoods they served. Community partnerships were largely absent, and when they existed, they tended to be entered into solely for the purpose of increasing the unit's access to information, and not for the coproduction of public safety. Although gang unit members and gang unit stakeholders saw gangs and gang crime as a problem, there was little evidence of the "problem orientation" that characterizes community policing and its variants. The gang units that we studied were barely familiar with community policing problem-solving strategies, much less engaging in them.

We concluded that the gang unit officers in these units were free to undertake any activity that interested them, had few expectations to meet, and had virtually no policies or training to guide their decision making. Gang unit officers were also rarely under the control or supervision of police management. They were physically and operationally isolated from the rest of the police department, and typically had little contact with "regular" police officers, criminal justice officials, the public, or community groups. In short, these gang unit officers were on their own.

FINAL THOUGHTS

Our observations of the workings of police gang units led us to several conclusions and recommendations. The gang units that we observed could be placed in two different categories that have some features in common, but that are really very different. Inglewood's gang unit was in a category of its own, as a single-function intelligence unit tasked with developing information on gangs and gang members and disseminating that information to other units in the police department. The other three gang units (Albuquerque, Las Vegas, and Phoenix) were multifunctional gang units or comprehensive units tasked with various functions – intelligence, enforcement, and prevention.

Our general conclusion is that for Inglewood, in the context of that community and police department, a relatively small gang unit (three sworn officers) focusing entirely on intelligence made sense. The Inglewood Police Department and the city of Inglewood had faced one financial crisis after another, and it was extremely important for the police response to gangs to be as cost-effective as possible. Although we had no hard measure of this, we suspected that the level of Inglewood's financial investment in the small single-function gang unit was appropriate, especially in comparison with the cost of multifunction or comprehensive gang units. As we noted previously, stakeholders in the Inglewood Police Department greatly valued the intelligence function of their gang unit, and were able to provide fairly dramatic examples of its utility in solving crimes.

Interestingly, external stakeholders also valued the Inglewood unit's intelligence function. For example, the director of a large Inglewood cemetery, the largest single industry in Inglewood, pointed to occasions when gang unit intelligence had enabled him to take special precautions in conducting funerals involving the victims of intergang shootings so that conflicts would not flare up at the funeral ceremony.

Inglewood's gang unit was not located off-site, but was in the central police facility in close proximity to the criminal investigation bureau. Colocation facilitated the sharing of information, the gang unit's principal commodity, and generally kept the unit's "customers" satisfied. However, this is not to imply that the gang unit's customers were completely satisfied, or that the unit was completely integrated into the larger police organization. In the view of some internal stakeholders, over time the gang unit had become less proactive in developing new intelligence. They were seen as spending too much time in the office and not enough in the field, where they needed to be if they were to identify new gangs and gang members and track changes in patterns of gang activity.

In contrast to Inglewood, the other gang units that we observed seemed to share common patterns of development that reflected increasing decoupling. They also exhibited similar consequences; as a rule, they were isolated from core policing technology units, lacked supervision and accountability, were inaccessible to the community, lacked strategic vision, and had developed a separate gang unit subculture. The gang units' inability or reluctance to share information with others in their police organizations caused their internal stakeholders to devalue the units. Furthermore, if these units seemed isolated from mainstream policing in their respective departments, they were even more isolated from community policing activities. Occasional exceptions were found, illustrating the potential for gang units to play a stronger role in both traditional and community policing activities.

We also noted that at least two departments were searching for ways to reduce the effects of decoupling and to reconnect their gang units with core policing units. We have concluded that the recoupling of gang units should be a high priority for police departments throughout the country, as they continue to seek more effective responses to local gang problems, and at the same time, to more fully implement community policing. High-profile incidents, such as the Los Angeles CRASH unit's framing of gang members, or more recently in Chicago where gang unit personnel are alleged to have participated in drug trafficking, are dramatic reflections of the consequences of decoupling gang units from the larger police organization. These two examples are the exception, not the rule, but the need to recouple gang units with their parent organizations also stems from needing to find more cost-effective responses to the gang problem, while concurrently implementing community-oriented policing more fully.

Our observations convinced us that police organizations need to reassess the organizational configurations of their responses to gangs, and the investment of resources in those responses. The starting point is a careful and thoughtful assessment of the local gang problem to learn whether or not it is presently of sufficient magnitude to warrant a specialized unit. To be sure, the gang units that we observed had been established in communities with substantial gang problems, and the specialized gang units were a reasonable response. However, we suspect that a substantial number of gang units developed in the last decade were not in response to local gang problems, but were the result of mimetic processes (DiMaggio and Powell 1991).

Mimetic processes are a consequence of organizations modeling themselves after other organizations. DiMaggio and Powell (1991, 67–8) explain that mimetic processes may occur when 1) little consensus exists as to which organizational structures and operational activities are most efficient and effective, 2) organizational goals are unclear, or 3) the "environment creates symbolic uncertainty" (e.g., is there or is there not a gang problem in our community).

The authors argue that organizations mimic others in response to uncertainty. By adopting the same organizational structures and operational activities that are used by organizations considered to be successful, an agency can gain legitimacy. If anything, the authors argue, such a move illustrates to the institutional environment that the organization is acting to improve the (albeit ambiguous) situation.

We suspect that many police departments created gang units for reasons related to institutional legitimacy rather than to actual environmental contingencies. Klein (1995a) alludes to this point in his discussion of Sergeant Wes McBride of the Los Angeles Sheriff's Department (LASD). Many departments across the nation have adopted the structures and strategies recommended by McBride and the LASD because of its national reputation, rather than because the model is necessarily appropriate for their own jurisdiction's gang problem.

We suspect that given the value that internal and external stakeholders place on gang-related intelligence and information, and on information sharing and dissemination, that all police gang units would do well to learn from Inglewood and to place greater emphasis on the intelligence function in support of other core police functions, such as investigation. Additionally, police departments need to develop strategies and tactics to bring their gang units into synch with community policing principles and practices. In large cities gang units are tremendously outnumbered by gangs and gang members and typical suppression strategies have limited potential as the principal police response to gangs. Gang units, like other police units, need to become "smarter," and one way to do this is to emphasize formal problem solving carried out by gang units in collaboration with other core police units, especially patrol.

There is evidence that some police departments are disbanding gang units (Katz, Maguire, and Roncek 2002), but it is unclear whether this is in response to a diminished local gang problem, a growing awareness of problems stemming from decoupled gang units, or other issues. One would hope that these decisions are being made following careful assessment of local gang problems. However, gangs do remain a problem in jurisdictions throughout the country, and therefore they warrant a continued response on the part of police. The challenge becomes one of reassessing present patterns of response and adjusting them to attain the highest possible level of effectiveness.

References

Abt Associates Inc. 1998. *National evaluation of Weed and Seed.* Cambridge, MA.

Abt Associates Inc. 1999. *National evaluation of Weed and Seed.* Cambridge, MA.

Albuquerque Police Department. 1992. *1991 Albuquerque police department annual report.* Albuquerque: Author.

Albuquerque Police Department. 1997. *Citizen satisfaction with police department – 1996.* Albuquerque: Author.

Albuquerque Police Department. 1999. *Gang status report for Albuquerque, NM – 1998.* Albuquerque: APD Gang Unit.

Archbold, Carol and Michael Meyer. 1999. Anatomy of a gang suppression unit: The social construction of an organizational response to gang problems. *Police Quarterly* 2 (2): 201–24.

Arizona Republic. 1980. Teen-age gangs. June 18.

Arizona Republic. 1981. Police chief calls for greater effort to thwart gangs. Oct. 17.

Arizona Republic. 2002. L.A. mayor, police chief go after street gangs. Dec. 12.

Associated Press. 2005. L.A. police settlement to reach $70M. March 31, 2005. http://abcnews.go.com/us/wirestory?id+629514. Accessed on April 7, 2005.

Austin, Marcia. 1989. Police accused of harassing blacks. *Las Vegas Review-Journal,* sec. B. Jan. 18, 1989.

Bardwell, S. K. 1998. Police shoot man 12 times in drug raid. *Houston Chronicle.* July 21, 1998. http://www.november.org/txshooting.html (accessed March 26, 2002).

Bates, Warren. 1987. L.A. street gangs flood Las Vegas. *Las Vegas Review-Journal.* Oct. 11.

Battin-Pearson, Sara, Terence Thornberry, David J. Hawkins, and Marvin Krohn. 1998. *Gang membership, delinquent peers, and delinquent behavior.* Washington, DC: Office of Juvenile Justice and Delinquency Prevention.

Bayley, David and Harold Mendelsohn. 1969. *Minorities and the police.* New York: Free Press.

Bayley, David. 1995. *Policing for the Future.* New York: Oxford University Press.

Beall, Christopher. 1986a. Youth gangs divided down ethnic lines. *Las Vegas Review-Journal*. Apr. 2.

Beall, Christopher. 1986b. Police unit targets increasing gang activity. *Las Vegas Review-Journal*, sec. A. Apr. 4.

Beall, Christopher. 1986c. Community efforts to end gangs emerge. *Las Vegas Review-Journal*. Apr. 6.

Behavior Research Center Inc. 1996. *City of Phoenix community attitude survey*. June 16. Phoenix: Behavior Research Center.

Bittner, Egon. 1967. The police on skid row: A study of peace keeping. *American Sociological Review* 32: 699–715.

Blau, Peter and Marshall Meyer. 1971. *Bureaucracy in modern society*. New York: Random House.

Bogardus, Emory. 1926. *The city boy and his problems: A survey of boy life in Los Angeles*. Los Angeles: Rotary Club.

Bogdan, R. C. and S. K. Biklen, eds. 1992. *Qualitative research for education: An introduction to theory and methods*. Boston: Allyn & Bacon.

Brantley, Alan and Andrew DiRosa. 1994. Gangs: A national perspective. *FBI Law Enforcement Bulletin* May: 1–17.

Brokaw, Tom, Wayne Ewing (producer), and Paul Greenburg. 1989. *Gangs, cops and drugs*. NBC News Productions.

Burbank, Jeff. 1990. Las Vegas gang hot line goes on line. *Las Vegas Sun*. Sept. 1.

Bureau of Justice Assistance. 1997. *Urban street gang enforcement*. Washington, DC: Government Printing Office.

Bureau of Justice Statistics. 1995. *Sourcebook of criminal justice statistics, 1994*. Washington, DC: Government Printing Office.

Bureau of Justice Statistics. 2001. *Law enforcement management and administrative statistics, 1999: Data for individual state and local agencies with 100 or more officers*. Washington, DC: Government Printing Office.

Burns, Edward and Thomas J. Deakin. 1989. A new investigative approach to youth gangs. *FBI Law Enforcement Bulletin* Oct.: 20–4.

Burrell, Susan. 1990. Gang evidence: Issues for criminal defense. *Santa Clara Law Review* 30: 739–90.

Bynum, Tim. 1998. *National evaluation of the youth firearms violence initiative: Inglewood case study*. Cambridge, MA: Abt Associates Inc.

Casey, Richard F. 1995. Police vs. gang. *Phoenix Gazette*, front sec. Mar. 25.

Chemerinsky, Erwin. 2000a. Report of the rampart independent review panel-executive summary. (Unpublished manuscript.) Sept. 11.

Chemerinsky, Erwin. 2000b. An independent analysis of the Los Angeles police department's board of inquiry report on the rampart scandal. (Unpublished manuscript.) Nov. 16.

Chereb, Sandra. 1999. Nevadans willing to spend more on many state programs. *Las Vegas Review-Journal*. Associated Press State, Regional and Local (PM) eds. Jan. 13.

Chesney-Lind, Meda, Anna Rockwell, Nancy Marker, and Howard Reyes. 1994. Gangs and delinquency. *Crime, Law and Social Change* 21: 201–8.

Chicago Tribune. 2005. Chicago murders fall 35% in 2004: After leading U.S. in 2003, city sees 155 fewer slayings. *Chicago Tribune*. Jan. 2.

City of Albuquerque Planning Department. 1993. *Albuquerque citizen satisfaction survey – November 1992*. Albuquerque: Author.

CNN.com. 2000a. Testimony: Alleged corrupt LAPD cops gave each other awards. Feb. 10. http://www.cnn.com/2000/us/02/10/lapd.scandal.

CNN.com. 2000b. Outside probe of LAPD corruption scandal demanded. Feb. 16. http://www.cnn.com/2000/us/02/16/lapd.scandal.

Cogan, David. 1998. The gang's all there. *Los Angeles Magazine* Aug.: 1–2.

Cohen, Roger. 1991. Spreading gang violence threatened western cities. *Houston Chronicle*, sec. A. Oct. 20.

Compiler. 1996 (Fall). *Street gangs and violence*. Chicago: Illinois Criminal Justice Information Authority.

Connell, Rich. 1994. Safety hopes in Inglewood rest on curfew. *Los Angeles Times*, Metro, part A. Apr. 8.

Contreras, Guillermo. 1998. APD shifts some gang unit cops to patrol. *Albuquerque Journal*. Feb. 20.

Cordner, Gary. 1999. Elements of community policing. In *Policing perspectives*, Larry Gaines and Gary Cordner, eds., 451–68. Los Angeles: Roxbury Publishing.

Cornett, Richard. 1983. Police report gang violence on the rise in communities. *Las Vegas Review-Journal*. June 15.

Covey, Herbert, Scott Menard, and Robert Franzese. 1997. *Juvenile gangs*. Springfield, IL: Charles C. Thomas.

Creswell, John. 1994. *Research design: Qualitative and quantitative approaches*. Thousand Oaks, CA: Sage Publications.

Crowder, Carla and Colleen Heild. 1995. Chamber: City needs public-safety tax. *Albuquerque Journal*, final ed. Aug. 30.

Crowder, Carla, Colleen Heild, and Rebecca Roybal. 1995. Gangs' lethal grip. *Albuquerque Journal*, final ed. Dec. 10.

Curry, G. David, Richard A. Ball, Robert J. Fox, and Darryl Stone. 1992. *National assessment of law enforcement anti-gang information resources: Final report*. Washington, DC: National Institute of Justice.

Curry, G. David, Richard A. Ball, and Scott H. Decker. 1996. *Estimating the national scope of gang crime from law enforcement data*. Washington, DC: National Institute of Justice.

Curry, G. David, Richard A. Ball, and Robert J. Fox. 1994. *Gang crime and law enforcement record keeping*. Washington, DC: National Institute of Justice.

Daniels, Bruce. 1998. APD stats show serious crime down. *Albuquerque Journal*, Metro and New Mexico. Jan. 1.

Decker, Scott H. and Barrik Van Winkle. 1994. "Slinging dope": The role of gangs and gang members in drug sales. *Justice Quarterly* 11: 584–604.

Department of Public Safety, Special Investigations Division, Criminal Information and Analysis Bureau. 1995. *Street gang update – 1994*. Albuquerque: Author.

DiMaggio, P. and W. Powell. 1991. Introduction. In *The new institutionalism in organizational analysis*, W. W. Powell and P. J. DiMaggio, eds., 1–38. Chicago: University of Chicago Press.

Domrzalski, Dennis. 1996a. Police move in on gang turf. *Albuquerque Tribune*, Evening ed. Feb. 6.

Domrzalski, Dennis. 1996b. Anti-gang effort nets many arrests. *Albuquerque Tribune*, Midday ed. Feb. 22.

Donaldson, T. and L. E. Preston. 1995. The stakeholder theory of the corporation: Concepts, evidence and implications. *Academy of Management Review* 20: 65–91.

Dunworth, Terrence and Abt Associates Inc. 2000. *Police department information systems technology enhancement project (ISTEP)*. Washington, DC: Department of Justice, Office of Community Oriented Policing Services.

Easley, Michael. 1993. *Inglewood police department 1992 annual report*. Inglewood, CA: Inglewood Police Department.

Easley, Michael. 1995. *Inglewood police department 1994 annual report*. Inglewood, CA: Inglewood Police Department.

Easley, Michael. 1996. *Inglewood police department 1995 annual report*. Inglewood, CA: Inglewood Police Department.

Easley, Michael. 1998. *Inglewood police department 1997 annual report*. Inglewood, CA: Inglewood Police Department.

Fagan, Jeffery. 1989. The social organization of drug use and drug dealing among urban gangs. *Criminology* 27: 633–69.

Fagan, Jeffery. 1996. Gangs, drugs, and neighborhood change. In *Gangs in America*, C. Ronald Huff, ed., 39–74. Thousand Oaks, CA: Sage Publications.

Federal Bureau of Investigation. 2002. Crime in the United States, 2001. Washington, DC: U.S. Government Printing Office.

Fernandez, Luis A. Jr. 1997. *Evaluation of the Phoenix anti-gang initiative*. Phoenix: Morrison Institute for Public Policy, School of Public Affairs, Arizona State University.

Flanagan, Tanya. 1997a. Young death. *Las Vegas Review-Journal*. June 15.

Flanagan, Tanya. 1997b. Laying the blame. *Las Vegas Review-Journal*, sec. A. June 15.

Flannery, Pat. 1989. Guardian angels gain key ally. *Phoenix Gazette*. June 23.

Ford, Andrea. 1991. Brothers are in gang shooting. *Los Angeles Times*, Metro part B. June 16.

Freed, David. 1995. Policing gangs: Case of contrasting styles. In *The modern gang reader*, Malcolm W. Klein, Cheryl L. Maxson, and Jody Miller, eds., 288–91. Los Angeles: Roxbury Publishing.

Glaser, B. G. and A. L. Strauss. 1967. *The discovery of grounded theory*. Chicago: Aldine.

Glover, Cindy. 1996. APD will train to identify outlawed gang recruiters. *Albuquerque Journal*, final ed. Aug. 20.

Grazcyk, Michael. 1998. Officers had no warrant in fatal drug raid. *Dallas Morning News*. Aug. 8.

Greene, Jack. 2000. *Community policing in America: Changing the nature, structure and function of the police*. Washington, DC: National Institute of Justice.

Hagedorn, John H. 1998. Gang violence in the postindustrial era. In *Crime and justice: A review of research*, Michael Tonry, ed. Chicago: University of Chicago Press.

Hagedorn, John H. 1988. *People and folks*. Chicago: Lakeview Press.

Harold, Susan. 1989. Phoenix will add 23 officers to combat gangs. *Phoenix Gazette*. May 17.

Harvey, Andrew. 1999. Guidelines for time use data collection and analysis. In *Time use research in the social sciences*, Wendy Pentland, Andrew Harvey, M. Powell Lawton, and Mary Ann McColl, eds., 19–42. New York: Kluwer Academic.

Heild, Colleen. 1995. Leaders fear crime scares away business. *Albuquerque Journal*, final ed. Sept. 28.

Hermann, William. 1995. Gang fight police for neighborhoods; Lack of support angers officers. *Arizona Republic*, front sec. Mar. 11.

Hill, John. 1996. Crack down on gangs seems to be working. *Albuquerque Tribune*, Evening ed. Feb. 19.

Howell, James and Scott H. Decker. 1999. Youth gang homicides: A literature review. *Crime & Delinquency*, 45 (2): 208–41.

Huff, C. Ronald. 1990. *Gangs in America*. Newbury Park, CA: Sage Publications.

Huff, C. Ronald. 1993. Gangs in the United States. In *The gang intervention handbook*, A. P. Goldstein and C. Ronald Huff, eds., 3–20. Champaign, IL: Research Press.

Huff, C. Ronald and Wesley D. McBride. 1993. Gangs and the police. In *The gang intervention handbook*, A. P. Goldstein and C. Ronald Huff, eds., 401–15. Champaign, IL: Research Press.

Hurtt, Harold L. No date. *The evolution of gangs in Phoenix*. Phoenix: Phoenix Police Department.

Hyman, Harold. 1988. Search on for rink shooting suspects. *Las Vegas Sun*. Feb. 17.

Hynes, Mary. 1997. Drive by shooting probed. *Las Vegas Review-Journal*, sec. A. Jan. 8.

Inglewood Gang Intelligence Unit. 1999. *Monthly report from 02-25-99 to 03-26-99*. Inglewood, CA: Author.

Inglewood Police Department. 1993. *Annual report – 1992*. Inglewood, CA: Author.

Inglewood Police Department. 1995. *Annual report – 1994*. Inglewood, CA: Author.

Inglewood Police Department. 1996. *Annual report – 1995*. Inglewood, CA: Author.

Inglewood Police Department. 1997. *Annual report – 1996*. Inglewood, CA: Author.

Inglewood Police Department. 1998. *Annual report – 1997*. Inglewood, CA: Author.

Inglewood Police Department. 1999a. *Annual report from 1989–1998*. Inglewood, CA: Author.

Inglewood Police Department. 1999b. *Inglewood Crime Analysis Bulletin* 10 (17): 1.

Jackson, Robert K. and Wesley D. McBride. 1996. *Understanding street gangs*. Incline Village, NV: Copperhouse Publishing Company.

Johnson, Claire, Barbara Webster, Edward Connors, and Diana Saenz. 1995. Gang enforcement problems and strategies: National survey findings. *Journal of Gang Research* 3: 1–18.

Jones, Jeff. 1999. Officials target gang blamed for scores of rapes. *Albuquerque Journal*. Feb. 25.

Jones, T. M. 1995. Instrumental stakeholder theory: A synthesis of ethics and economics. *Academy of Management Review* 20: 404–37.

Jorgensen, Danny. 1989. Participant observation. *A methodology for human studies*. Newbury Park, CA: Sage Publications.

Joyce, Mairlee. 1985. Residents urged to unite with police to combat gang violence. *Las Vegas Review-Journal*. Aug. 22.

Juarez, Macario Jr. 1995. Albuquerque homicides on rise. *Albuquerque Journal*, Evening ed. Dec. 22.

Katz, Charles M. 1997. *Police and gangs: A study of a police gang unit*. Ph.D. diss., University of Nebraska at Omaha.

Katz, Charles M. 2001. The establishment of a police gang unit: An examination of organizational and environmental factors. *Criminology* 39 (1): 301–38.

Katz, Charles M. 2003. Issues in the production and dissemination of gang statistics: An ethnographic study of a large midwestern police gang unit. *Crime and Delinquency* 49 (3): 485–516.

Katz, Charles M., Edward Maguire, and Dennis Roncek. 2002. The creation of specialized police gang units: Testing contingency, social threat, and resource-dependency explanations. *Policing: An International Journal of Police Strategies and Management* 25 (3): 472–506.

Katz, Charles M., Vincent Webb, and David Schaefer. 2000. The validity of police gang intelligence lists: Examining differences in delinquency between documented gang members and non-documented delinquent youth. *Police Quarterly* 3 (4): 413–37.

Katz, Jesse. 1990. Officer's folksy tactics pay off in gang domain. *Los Angeles Times*. Nov. 5.

Kelling, George and Mark Moore. 1988. *The evolving strategy of policing*. Perspectives on Policing, #4: Washington DC: National Institute of Justice.

Klein, Malcolm W. 1971. *Street gangs and street workers*. Englewood Cliffs, NJ: Prentice Hall.

Klein, Malcolm W. 1995a. *The American street gang*. New York: Oxford University Press.

Klein, Malcolm W. 1995b. Attempting gang control by suppression: The misuse of deterrence principles. In *The modern gang reader*, Malcolm Klein, Cheryl L. Maxson, and Jody Miller, eds., 304–15. Los Angeles: Roxbury Publishing.

Klein, Malcolm. 2004. Gang cop. Walnut Creek, CA: AltaMira Press.

Klein, Malcolm., Cheryl Maxson, and Jody Miller. 1995. *The modern gang reader*. Los Angeles: Roxbury Publishing.

Klima, Joseph B. 1999. *Anti-gang initiative (1996–1998)*. Phoenix: Phoenix Police Department.

Koch, Ed. 1988. Gangs create worst problem LV has faced in 30 years. *Las Vegas Sun*. Nov. 16.

Koch, Ed. 1989. Metro seeks funds to fight drugs, gangs. *Las Vegas Sun*. Mar. 2.

Kossan, Pat. 1995. Valley police making its own "hit list." *Phoenix Gazette*, Metro. Apr. 6.

Kruger, J. Gutierrez. 1988. Gang war rips San Jose. *Albuquerque Tribune*. June 13.

Kwok, Abraham. 1990. Will my child be safe? 150 protest gangs. *Phoenix Gazette*. Feb. 28.

Kwok, Abraham. 1993. Immediate increase in police proposed: $12 million plan for Phoenix. *Arizona Republic*, sec. A. Oct. 12.

Kwok, Abraham. 1995. Residents left leery by police crackdown. *Arizona Republic*, sec. A. Nov. 18.

Lacey, Marc. 1990a. Drugs, gang violence blamed for 50% jump in Inglewood murders. *Los Angeles Times*, Metro, sec. B. Jan. 14.

Lacey, Marc. 1990b. Violence prompts call for increased security at Inglewood schools. *Los Angeles Times*, Metro, sec. B. Oct. 26.

Las Vegas Metropolitan Police Department. 1995. *Gang unit annual report – 1994*. Las Vegas: Author.

Las Vegas Metropolitan Police Department. 1996. *Gang unit annual report – 1995*. Las Vegas: Author.

Las Vegas Metropolitan Police Department. 1997. *Gang unit annual report – 1996*. Las Vegas: Author.

Las Vegas Metropolitan Police Department. 1998. *Gang unit annual report – 1997: Gang investigations*. Las Vegas: Author.

Las Vegas Metropolitan Police Department. 1999. *Gang unit annual report – 1998*. Las Vegas: Author.

Las Vegas Metropolitan Police Department. 1999. *Gang trends*. Las Vegas: Author.

Las Vegas Metropolitan Police Department Gang Unit. 1999. Gang trends in Las Vegas. (Unpublished document.)

Las Vegas Review-Journal. 1997a. Police veterans deny wider ramifications in drive-by shooting. sec. E. Jan. 19.

Las Vegas Review-Journal. 1997b. The driver. sec. E. Jan. 19.

Las Vegas Review-Journal. 1997c. Fewer incidents of gang violence noted. sec. B. Oct. 9.

Las Vegas Review-Journal. 1998. Murder case takes twist. sec. B. Aug. 25.

Las Vegas Sun. 1984. Teen pleads innocent in gang slaying. July 3.

Las Vegas Sun. 1988a. Metro mobilizes against LV gangs. Mar. 24.

Las Vegas Sun. 1988b. Gang diversion unit called a success. May 3.

Las Vegas Sun. 1989. Mass gang arrests staged. Oct. 19.

Las Vegas Sun. 1990. Hotline on gangs. Aug. 31.

Lightly, Todd and Steve Mills. 2000. *Hillard to split up anti-gang cop unit*. Mar. 15. http://chicagotribune.com/news/nation.html (accessed July 2, 2001).

Lincon, Yvonna S. and Egon G. Guba. 1985. *Naturalistic inquiry*. Beverly Hills, CA: Sage Publications.

Lofland, John and Lynn Lofland. 1995. *Analyzing social settings: A guide to qualitative observation and analysis*. Belmont: Wadsworth Publishing.

Los Angeles City News Service. 1988. Police chief urges declaration of national drug emergency. Apr. 20.

Los Angeles Police Department. 2000. *Rampart area corruption incident*. Public report, Mar. 1. Los Angeles: Author.

Los Angeles Times. 1988. Local news in brief: Churches' anti-gang role. South Bay Digest, Metro. Mar. 20.

Los Angeles Times. 1991. Gang feels the heat of summertime sweep. Metro, part B. June 20.

Los Angeles Times. 1994. 11 youths arrested as Inglewood's tougher curfew goes into effect. Metro, part B. Mar. 20.

Maguire, Edward. 1997. Structural change in large municipal police organizations during the community policing era. *Justice Quarterly* 14 (3): 547–76.

Manning, Peter. 1977. *Police work*. Prospect Heights, IL: Waveland.

Marshall, Catherine and Gretchen Rossman. 1995. *Designing qualitative research*. Newbury Park, CA: Sage Publications.

Martin, Hugo. 1988. Program tracks habitual offenders: Inglewood adopts plan to fight youth crime. *Los Angeles Times*, Westside, sec. 9. Aug. 18.

Mastrofski, Stephen and Roger Parks. 1990. Improving observational studies of police. *Criminology* 28: 475–96.

Mastrofski, Stephen and Robert Wadman. 1991. Personnel and agency performance measurement. In *Local government police management*, William Geller, ed. Washington, DC: International City Management Association.

Maxson, Cheryl L. 1999. Gang homicide. *Homicide: A sourcebook of social science*. Thousand Oaks, CA: Sage Publications.

Maxson, Cheryl L. and Theresa L. Allen. 1997. *An evaluation of the city of Inglewood's youth firearms violence initiative*. Los Angeles: Social Science Research Institute, University of Southern California.

Maxson, Cheryl L., Karen Hennigan, and David Sloane. 2003. For the sake of the neighborhood: Civil gang injunctions as a gang intervention tool in Southern California. In *Policing gangs and youth violence*, S. H. Decker, ed. 239–66, Belmont: Wadsworth.

Mayor's Council on Gangs. No date. *A community design to address gang violence and criminal gang activity*. Albuquerque: City of Albuquerque.

McCabe, George. 1988. Officials get word on gangs. *Las Vegas Sun*. Oct. 13.

McClannahan, Rory. 1997. Grant targets gangs. *Albuquerque Journal*. June 19.

McCorkle, Richard and Terance Miethe. 1998. The political and organizational response to gangs: An examination of a "moral panic" in Nevada. *Justice Quarterly* 15 (1): 41–64.

McCorkle, Richard and Terance Miethe. 2002. *Panic: The social construction of the street gang problem*. Upper Saddle River, NJ: Prentice Hall.

McCort, Michael C. 1994a. *Gangs: The control of violence*. Phoenix: Phoenix Police Department.

McCort, Michael C. 1994b. *Street gangs in Phoenix*. Phoenix: Phoenix Police Department.

McCutcheon, Chuck. 1995. Package to fight gangs. *Albuquerque Journal*, final ed. June 29.

Merriam, Sharan. 1988. *Case study research in education: A qualitative approach*. San Francisco: Jossey Bass.

Meyer, John and Brian Rowan. 1977. Institutionalized organizations: Formal structure as myth and ceremony. *American Journal of Sociology* 83: 340–63.

Meyer, Marshall. 1979. Organizational structure as signaling. *Pacific Sociological Review* 22: 481–500.

Miller, Walter B. 1962. The impact of a total community delinquency control project. *Social Problems* 19: 168–91.

Miller, Walter B. 1982. *Crime by youth gangs and groups in the United States*. National Institute for Juvenile Justice and Delinquency Prevention, Office of Juvenile Justice and Delinquency Prevention, U.S. Department of Justice. Washington, DC: Government Printing Office.

Millican, Anthony. 1992. Reeling from raw violence; Crime: Students in Inglewood and Lennox are at risk of being caught in the cross-fire of feuding Latino gangs. *Los Angeles Times*, Metro, part B. Oct. 4.

Moeser, Chris, Richard Ruelas, Chris Fiscus, and J. W. Brown. 1995. Cops, gangs spar for control of area; police push necessary, leaders say. *Phoenix Gazette*, front sec. Mar. 24.

Montano, Nick. 1979. *Street gangs in Albuquerque*. Albuquerque: Albuquerque Police Department.

Moore, Joan. 1978. *Homeboys*. Philadelphia: Temple University Press.

Moore, Joan. 1985. Isolation and stigmatization in the development of an underclass: The case of Chicano gangs in East Los Angeles. *Social Problems* 33 (1): 1–12.

National Advisory Committee on Criminal Jusitce Standards and Goals. 1976. Report of the Task Force on Juvenile Justice and Delinquency Prevention. Washington, DC: US GPO.

Needle, Jerome and William Vaughan Stapleton. 1983. *Police handling of youth gangs*. Reports of the National Juvenile Justice Assessment Centers. Washington, DC: Government Printing Office.

Office of Juvenile Justice and Delinquency Prevention. 2003. *National youth gang survey trends from 1996 to 2000*. Washington, DC: Government Printing Office.

Office of Juvenile Justice and Delinquency Prevention. 2004. *2002 National youth gang survey*. Washington, DC: Author.

Ottmeier, Timothy and Mary Ann Wycoff. 1998. Personnel performance evaluations in the community policing context. In *Community policing: Contemporary readings*, Geoffrey Alpert and Alex Piquero, eds., 275–305. Prospect Heights, IL: Waveland Press.

Pappa, Erik. 1989. Poll eyes problem. *Las Vegas Sun*. Feb. 14.

Parks, Roger, Stephen Mastrofski, Christina Dejong, and M. Kevin Gray. 1999. How officers spend their time with the community. *Justice Quarterly* 16 (3): 483–517.

Phoenix Police Department. 1998. *Gang enforcement handbook*. Phoenix: Author.

Phoenix Police Department. 2000. *Standard operating procedures*. Phoenix: Author.

Phoenix Police Department. 2002. *Operation safe streets*. Phoenix: Author.

Pillsbury, Samuel H. 1988. Gang sweeps only look good. *Los Angeles Times*, Apr. 17.

Pitzl, Mary Jo and Judi Villa. 1995. Police target area of attack on cops; Mayor promises to "to break backs" of Phoenix gangs. *Arizona Republic*, sec. A. Mar. 24.

President's Commission on Law Enforcement and Administration of Justice. 1967. *The challenge of crime in a free society*. Washington, DC: Government Printing Office.

Puit, Glenn. 1997. Crime wave strikes near UNLV. *Las Vegas Review-Journal*, sec. B. Mar. 30.

Puit, Glenn. 1998. Ganging up on gangs. *Las Vegas Review-Journal*, sec. B. Apr. 6.

Reiss, Albert. 1992. Police organization in the twentieth century. In *Modern policing*, vol 15, Michael Tonry and Norval Morris, eds., 51–98. Chicago: University of Chicago Press.

Research and Polling Inc. 1992. *1992 Albuquerque citizen satisfaction survey*, Nov. Albuquerque: City of Albuquerque.

Richardson, Lisa and Gordon Dillow. 1994. Inglewood posts reward in killing spree by gangs. *Los Angeles Times*, South Bay, part J. Feb. 3.

Rossmiller, David. 1989a. Street gang violence rose sharply in 1988, police report. *Phoenix Gazette*. Mar. 7.

Rossmiller, David. 1989b. Crackdown vowed on gang violence. *Phoenix Gazette*. Apr. 17.

Rossmiller, David. 1993. Curfew missing gangs, critic says. *Phoenix Gazette*, Metro. Apr. 22.

Rotella, Sebastian. 1987. Police drive pulls wheels out from under gang members. *Los Angeles Times*, Metro, part 2. Nov. 24.

Rotella, Sebastian. 1989. 20 new officers in Inglewood; drug raid to help pay for police. *Los Angeles Times*, Metro, part 9. Feb. 16.

Rubel, Arthur. 1965. The Mexican American palomilla. *Anthropological Linguistics* 4: 29–97.

Rush, Jeffery P. 1996. The police role in dealing with gangs. In *Gangs: A criminal justice approach*, J. Mitchell Miller and Jeffrey P. Rush, eds., 85–92. Cincinnati: Anderson Publishing Company.

Sanchez-Jankowski, Martin. 1991. *Islands in the street: Gangs in American life.* Berkeley: University of California Press.

Schafer, Joseph A. 2003. From rhetoric to reality: How police officers view implementation of generalized community policing. *Justice Research and Policy* 5 (1): 1–30.

Schatzman, Leonard and Anselm L. Strauss. 1973. *Field research: Strategies for natural sociology.* Englewood Cliffs, NJ: Prentice-Hall.

Schultz, Ray. 1989. Goddard, Ortega acts to ease dramatic upsurge in crime. *Phoenix Gazette.* May 13.

Schumacher, Geoff. 1988a. Gang fight terrorized little leaguers. *Las Vegas Sun.* Sept. 30.

Schumacher, Geoff. 1988b. LV gangs fire shots near dance. *Las Vegas Sun.* Sept. 4.

Scott, Susanne G. and Vicki R. Lane. 2000. A stakeholder approach to organizational identity. *Academy of Management Review* 25: 43–62.

Scott, W. Richard. 1995. Introduction: Institutional theory and organizations. In *The institutional construction of organizations*, W. R. Scott and S. Christensen, eds., xi-xxiii. London: Sage Publications.

Sherman, Lawrence. 1992. *Policing domestic violence.* New York: Free Press.

Shetterly, Caryn. 1985a. LV street gangs a different breed. *Las Vegas Sun*, sec. A. May 8.

Shetterly, Caryn. 1985b. Special police units probe gangs in Southern Nevada. *Las Vegas Sun*, sec. B. May 9.

Shetterly, Caryn. 1986. Group examines Clark County gang problems. *Las Vegas Sun*, Mar. 13.

Skolnick, Jerome H. 1990. The social structure of street drug dealing. *American Journal of Police* 9: 1–41.

Skolnick, Jerome H. 1994. *Justice without trial*. New York: Macmillan College Publishing Company.

Smith, John L. 1997. Letter to the editor: Young man's cold blooded killing draws chilling responses. *Las Vegas Review-Journal*, sec. B. Jan. 12.

Snow, David and Leon Anderson. 1993. *Down on their luck*. Berkeley: California University Press.

Spergel, Irving A. 1993. The national youth gang survey: A research and development process. In *The gang intervention handbook*, Arnold P. Goldstein and C. Ronald Huff, eds., 359–400, Champaign, IL: Research Press.

Spergel, Irving A. 1995. *The youth gang problem: A community approach*. New York: Oxford University Press.

Spergel, Irving A. and David G. Curry. 1990. *Survey of youth gang problems and programs in 45 cities and 6 sites*. Chicago: The University of Chicago Press.

Spergel, Irving A., Ron Chance, Candice Kane, Ruth Ross, Alba Alexander, Edwina Simmons, and Sandra Oh. 1994. *Gang suppression and intervention: Problem and response*. Washington, DC: Office of Juvenile Justice and Delinquency Prevention.

Steckner, Susie. 1995. Gang crackdown brings 83 arrests. *Phoenix Gazette*, Metro. Mar. 28.

Steckner, Susie and Chris Moeser. 1995. Officials blamed for rise in tension. *Phoenix Gazette*, front sec. Mar. 24.

Suchman, M. C. 1995. Managing legitimacy: Strategic and institutional approaches. *Academy of Management Journal* 20: 571–610.

Taylor, Carl. 1990. Gang imperialism. In *Gangs in America*, C. Ronald Huff, ed. Newbury Park, CA: Sage Publications.

Thornberry, T. P., M. D. Krohn, A. Lizotte, C. Smith, and K. Tobin. 2003. *Gangs and delinquency in developmental perspective*. New York: Cambridge University Press.

Thrasher, Frederic. 1927. *The gang*. Chicago: University of Chicago Press.

Tobin, Alan. 1988. Las Vegas police double anti-gang force. *Las Vegas Review-Journal*. Dec. 13.

Tracy, Paul. 1978. *An analysis of the incidence and seriousness of self-reported delinquency and crime*. Ph.D. diss., University of Pennsylvania.

Turpen, Roy. 1990. *The drug problem in Albuquerque and inequities in the federal drug grant program*. Interoffice correspondence.

United Press International. 1985. Regional News, California. February 20, 1985, Wednesday, AM Cycle.

United States Bureau of the Census. 1990. http://www.census.gov.

United States Bureau of the Census. 2000. http://www.census.gov.

Veloz, Steban V. and Eric R. Spivak. 1993. *Gang experience*. Glendale: Arizona State University.

Venkatesh, S. A. 1997. The social organization of street gang activity in an urban ghetto. *American Journal of Sociology* 103: 82–111.

Vigil, James Diego. 1988. *Barrio gangs: Street life and identity in Southern California*. Austin: University of Texas Press.

Vigil, James Diego. 1990. Cholos and gangs: Culture change and street youth in Los Angeles. In *Gangs in America*, C. Ronald Huff, ed., 116–28. Newbury Park, CA: Sage Publications.

Vigil, James Diego. 1992. *A rainbow of gangs: Street cultures in the mega-city.* Austin: University of Texas Press.

Villa, Judi. 1995. Officer shot in leg; ambush by gang snipers suspected. *Arizona Republic*, Valley and State eds. Mar. 23.

Wagner, Dennis and Pat Kossan. 1995. Stop the violence. *Phoenix Gazette*, final ed. Mar. 24.

Wagner, Dennis and Chris Moeser. 1995a. Residents: Crackdown adds to rage. *Phoenix Gazette*, final ed. Mar. 24.

Wagner, Dennis and Chris Moeser. 1995b. Stop the violence. *Phoenix Gazette*, sec B. Mar. 24.

Walker, Samuel and Charles M. Katz. 1995. Less than meets the eye: Police department bias crime units. *American Journal of Police* 14: 29–48.

Walker, Samuel and Charles M. Katz. 2005. *Police in America.* New York: McGraw Hill Publishing.

Webb, Vincent J. 2000. Some strategic information issues in the development of community policing in the United States. *Police Practice and Research* 1 (3): 323–43.

Webb, Vincent J. and Charles M. Katz. 1997. Citizen ratings of the importance of community policing activities. *Policing: An International Journal of Police Strategy and Management* 20: 7–23.

Weick, Karl E. 1995. *Sense making in organizations.* Thousand Oaks, CA: Sage Publications.

Weick, Karl E. and Karlene H. Roberts. 1993. Collective mind in organizations: Heedful interrelating on flight decks. *Administrative Science Quarterly* 38: 357–81.

Weisel, Debrah and Tara O'Connor. 2004. Specialized gang units; forms and function in community policing. Final Report submitted to the National Institute of Justice. Washington, DC.

Weisel, Deborah and Ellen Painter. 1997. *The police response to gangs: Case studies of five cities.* Washington, DC: Police Executive Research Forum.

Westley, William. 1970. *Violence and the police.* Cambridge, MA: MIT Press.

Whyte, William. 1943. *Street corner society.* Chicago: University of Chicago Press.

Wingard, Laura. 1989. Police say millions needed to fight gangs, drugs. *Las Vegas Review-Journal.* Mar. 7.

Winter, John and Jim Walsh. 1989. Gang trouble rising, county attorney says. *Phoenix Gazette.* Feb. 24.

Winton, Ben. 1993. Gang police miss mark, report says. *The Phoenix Gazette.* Oct. 16.

Wood, Richard and Mariah Davis. 2002. Rethinking organizational change in policing. Final Report to the National Insitute of Justice: Washington, DC.

Youth Resource and Analysis Center. 1994. *Evaluation of the Albuquerque gang prevention/intervention program: Interim report.* Albuquerque: University of New Mexico.

Zatz, Marjorie S. 1987. Chicano youth gangs and crime: The creation of a moral panic. *Contemporary Crises* 11: 29–158.

Zhao, Jihong "Solomon," Matthew C. Scheider, and Quint Thurman. 2002. Funding community policing to reduce crime: Have COPS grants made a difference? *Criminology and Public Policy* 2 (1): 7–32.

Index